LET HIM HAVE JUSTICE

The True Story of Derek Bentley,
Hanged for a Crime He Did Not Commit

LET HIM HAVE JUSTICE

The True Story of Derek Bentley,
Hanged for a Crime
He Did Not Commit

IRIS BENTLEY

WITH

PENELOPE DENING

SIDWICK & JACKSON

First published 1995 by Sidgwick & Jackson

an imprint of Macmillan General Books
Cavaye Place London SW10 9PG
and Basingstoke

Associated companies throughout the world

ISBN 0 283 06228 2

Copyright © Iris Bentley 1995

The right of Iris Bentley to be identified as the
author of this work has been asserted by her in accordance
with the Copyright, Designs and Patents Act 1988.

1 3 5 7 9 8 6 4 2

A CIP catalogue record for this book is available from
the British Library

Typeset by CentraCet Limited, Cambridge
Printed by Mackays of Chatham PLC, Chatham, Kent

I'll tell you what Mum, the truth of this story has got to come out one day, and as I said in the visiting box that one day a lot of people are going to get into trouble and I think you know who those people are.

Derek Bentley, 27 January 1953

INTRODUCTION

At six o'clock in the morning on 1 October 1992, Iris Bentley was woken from a dream by the insistent ringing of a phone. She pulled on her dressing gown and went downstairs.

The caller was Roger Corke, a documentary television producer. It was evidence amassed by Corke and his reporter colleague at Thames, Carole Peters, that had pushed the Home Office into instigating an Inquiry into the execution of Iris's brother Derek forty years before.

Now it looked as though the waiting was over. It had been on the early news, said Roger. A decision on the Bentley case would be announced later in the day.

It must be a mistake, said Iris. Surely she'd have heard. She told Roger she'd check with her solicitor. But Ben Birnberg was equally in the dark.

Two hours later however it was confirmed by the Home Secretary himself on Radio Four's *Today* programme. Kenneth Clarke was in jaunty, even jocular mood. But he refused to be drawn on the outcome of the Inquiry. It would hardly be right, he parried, to say anything before Derek Bentley's sister Iris had been informed. 'I always promised that she would be the first to know.' All he would say was that the decision had taken a long time to reach, as it involved not only assessing new evidence but weighing up the conduct of the trial itself.

In the kitchen of her small south London house, Iris Bentley listened to the radio. Although there was no second-guessing a politician, it sounded optimistic. Clarke's reference to 'the conduct of the trial' was positive. Even if all the new evidence was rejected, everyone accepted the trial itself was a travesty.

After forty years, it seemed, justice would finally be done in the case of Derek Bentley. Perhaps with the righting of this *cause célèbre* the litany of miscarriages of justice which had so dented British

1

belief in their legal system over the last few years, might finally be put to rest.

By twelve thirty Iris Bentley was sitting in her solicitor's office in Southwark, just a few hundred yards from where she and her brother had been born. It was now official. Details would be delivered to Iris before Kenneth Clarke spoke to the press at 1 p.m. Her own press conference would follow.

Roger Corke was already pacing up and down Birnberg's office when Iris arrived. A few minutes later they were joined by Carole Peters who had made a dash across country from Somerset where she had been filming. Outside, the press – cameras and tape recorders at the ready – were waiting to record and celebrate a people's victory, the press who never let the public forget the story of the boy who was hanged because the boy who pulled the trigger was too young to die.

One o'clock came and went. Outside newsmen listened on earphones to Kenneth Clarke speaking on *The World at One*. Upstairs, Iris, Roger, Carole and Ben waited in silence. They didn't have a radio. Nobody had thought to bring one. After all, Iris would be the first to know. But it wasn't until six minutes past one that the Home Office courier had pushed through the crowd of photographers and newsmen and made her way to Birnberg's room on the second floor. The young woman had two large envelopes to be signed for. One for Iris, one for Ben.

With trembling hands Iris Bentley slit open the envelope. But the tension proved too much. 'I can't do it,' she said and handed the sheaf of papers to Carole Peters. Carole was a television reporter, used to reading ahead of herself and before she started speaking, she had scanned ahead. Out of the corner of her eye she saw Iris's expectant face, like a child waiting for the present to be unwrapped. In a faltering voice, Carole began to read:

Dear Miss Bentley,
I am writing to let you know that the Home Secretary has concluded that there are no grounds for him to recommend that a

Free Pardon should be granted to the late Derek Bentley, nor for him to commission a new inquiry into the case. I have been asked to say that the Home Secretary appreciates and very much regrets the distress that this will cause to you.

And Iris Bentley burst into tears. Carole put her arms around the sixty-one-year-old woman as a mother to a child as she wept. Wept for the wasted hours, wept for Derek.

Next up the stairs was Maria, Iris's daughter. She didn't need to be told. She had had to fight her way through the newsmen who knew already, who'd been on their mobile phones or listening to Clarke's announcement on the radio several minutes before the Home Office messenger had arrived. There were more tears. Maria called the then shadow Home Secretary, Tony Blair, at the Labour party conference in Brighton. But he was preparing his keynote speech on crime for the next day and could not be disturbed.

Iris got up and walked to the window, her face wet and mottled. Below the press were still waiting. Roger Corke stood up.

'Don't worry about them, Iris. I'll speak to them. They'll understand.'

Iris Bentley turned her head sharply towards him.

'What do you mean?' she said. 'I'm doing the press conference as planned. Do you think I'm giving up now? No way. The fight goes on.'

For forty years Iris Bentley has been seeking a posthumous free pardon for her brother. Her fight for justice began on 28 January 1953 when Derek Bentley, an epileptic with a mental age of barely eleven, was hanged for the murder of a policeman. A murder he didn't commit. He was condemned to death as the result of a botched attempt at breaking and entering. On 2 November, a scant three months before Bentley was executed, Police Constable Sidney Miles had been shot by Christopher Craig, the other boy on the roof of the confectionery warehouse in Croydon, south London, with Bentley that night.

In the trial that followed police evidence alleged that, even though Bentley had been under arrest when the fatal bullet found its mark, he had shouted encouragement to Craig twenty minutes earlier, to fire at another policeman, the shot that started the gun battle. In the eyes of the law that alleged encouragement – 'Let him have it, Chris' – bracketed Bentley irrevocably with any action that then ensued. Those words are the reason Derek Bentley hanged. By encouraging Craig he was equally guilty of murder.

In 1952 a verdict of murder allowed only one penalty, death. Not surprisingly the jury found Christopher Craig, the boy who had pulled the trigger, guilty. The lesser charge of manslaughter would only have applied if the killing had been accidental. In the case of Derek Bentley, the trial judge, Lord Goddard, Lord Chief Justice of England, directed the jury that if they believed the words 'Let him have it, Chris' to have been spoken by Bentley, they had no option but to bring in a verdict of guilty on him too. The three police officers who had sworn under oath that Bentley had said them, had been conspicuously brave, Goddard thundered. 'Are you going to say they are conspicuous liars?'

Guilty verdicts of murder were duly recorded on the two young men. But Christopher Craig was only sixteen, too young for the ultimate penalty. He was not to die, but would be detained 'at Her Majesty's pleasure', which in the event turned out to be ten years. But Derek Bentley was nineteen, and the under-age proviso did not apply. So, in spite of the recommendation for mercy attached to the jury's guilty verdict, Bentley was hanged. It is the only time in the history of British justice that a man has been executed when the person directly responsible for that crime was allowed to remain alive.

Much has been made of the ambiguity of that phrase that has gone down in history. The pundits of the day opined that 'Let him have it, Chris' had simply meant 'hand over the gun'. But this line of defence was never pursued in court, as both Bentley and Craig consistently denied the words had ever been spoken.

Until the verdict was announced, public sympathy, no doubt

troubled by the increase in lawlessness following the war and the rise of so-called 'cosh boys', was with the prosecution. But when on 11 December 1952 Lord Goddard donned the black cap and told Derek Bentley that he would be taken to a place of execution . . . 'and may God have mercy on your soul,' something snapped. Although the press continued to side with the establishment, the British public changed their minds. Enough was enough. They said 'No'.

They had little knowledge of the law involved, it was simply a gut reaction on an entirely human level. If Craig who had shot the policeman was to live, then it was inhuman to allow the bystander Bentley to die.

Petitions were signed in their thousands; Parliament was near revolt; the British public from the great and the good to the man on the Clapham omnibus signalled as never before and never since, their abhorrence at this example of *Alice in Wonderland* justice.

But it did no good. The wheels of the law could not be wrenched from their rutted path. Christopher Craig the middle-class boy with a higher than average IQ would live, because his chronological age was sixteen. Derek Bentley, the epileptic, working-class boy would hang, although his mental age was barely eleven.

William and Lillian Bentley and their daughter Iris were ordinary working people. Their knowledge of the law was then as limited as yours or mine. Their belief that Derek should not hang was only an extension of the general public's, based not on the law, but on natural justice. Against them were ranked the establishment who had other considerations on their minds than the life of one 'half-witted' boy.

But as the fight went on, a different picture began to emerge. Not only had natural justice been flouted, but justice according to the letter of the law as well. In 1990, thirty-seven years after the death of her brother, seventeen years after the death of her father and twelve years after the death of her mother, a dossier was presented to the Home Office on Iris Bentley's behalf by Carole

Peters and Roger Corke whose ITV documentary had unearthed new evidence. Evidence gathered from witnesses present at the scene of the crime, witnesses who had never been called. Evidence that refuted the damning police evidence given during the trial. In 1991 there was another film and another dossier, this time including irrefutable evidence from Craig himself. Evidence that everyone involved believed could only result in Derek Bentley's conviction for murder being quashed.

They were wrong.

But so, it turned out, was Kenneth Clarke.

In early July 1993, nine months after that distressing October day, three judges in the High Court ruled that Clarke's decision to refuse Bentley a pardon was flawed in law. He had erred in his decision making process and they invited him to think again. Kenneth Clarke had now been succeeded as Home Secretary by Michael Howard. And so, on 30 July 1993, a pardon was duly proffered.

However, the quality of this mercy was strained. It was not the free pardon that Iris sought, vindicating her brother's innocence, but a part pardon, a belated acknowledgement that Derek Bentley should not have hanged. In 1953 it would have been enough, for Derek Bentley would have lived, lived to clear his name of the crime he did not commit. But coming forty years after his death, this part pardon was as hollow as the jury's recommendation for mercy. The verdict still stands. In the annals of English law, Derek Bentley is guilty of murder.

The night before he was hanged, Iris Bentley promised her brother that she would not rest until his name was cleared. On that October morning in 1992 as Kenneth Clarke bantered so jovially on Radio 4 it had looked as though that aim had been achieved. Had it been so, this book might never have been written. But it was not.

Here then is Iris Bentley's story, not only the first-hand account of a moral outrage that still touches us today, but also a story of grit and courage, the story of a woman who wouldn't give up, a living testimony to the spirit of endurance that Harold Nicolson described as 'the slow grinding will power of the British people', who refused to be cowed by Hitler's blitzkrieg on their streets and their homes. But those obstructing the path of justice today are not the Luftwaffe, they are her own people, the authorities who still withhold documents and records that could dispel all doubt. But these authorities are only acting within the law. Above them are the politicians who now, as then, have their own private agenda, as disdainful of the plight of one of their citizens as they were in 1953.

She has fought them through the courts, she has fought them through the press, now Iris Bentley fights them through her own words.

Penelope Dening

CHAPTER ONE

I
n dreams it's the glass that I remember. Plate glass as thick as
your wrist. I still wake up, all these years later, sweating,
thinking if only I'd smashed that glass, it would have been all
right. But of course it wouldn't have made any difference. I know
now that the law is stronger than any glass. But it's a terrible thing
not being able to touch someone you love. There was this gap at
the bottom, like they have now in banks, which our voices went
through. In banks it's there to protect them from hold-ups. What
they thought we were going to do, I don't know. Dad, Mum in the
middle and me, just sitting on that bench like bottles at Battersea
funfair.

It was 27 January 1953. My brother Derek had been in the
condemned cell since 12 December when Lord Goddard had given
Derek the death sentence at the Old Bailey. It was due to be carried
out at nine o'clock the next morning. Looking back it's hard to
believe that we were still so hopeful. But we were. The jury had
recommended mercy. The papers were full of it. Tens of thousands
of people had signed the petitions. Everyone thought he'd be
reprieved. And so did we. Although he looked like a man, Derek
was just a soft kid. He needed looking after, not killing. They must
see that.

We always talked about the same things, never about the case,
it wasn't allowed. Although he was a little slow, Derek did know
what was going on. The day before he'd talked about dying and
said he wasn't afraid because he knew he hadn't killed anyone. But
this time, this last time, he was quite cheerful, as if he was trying to
keep our spirits up, rather than the other way around. Dad explained
to him that the reprieve wouldn't mean he could come home
straight away. That he'd done wrong going up on that roof and
that he'd have to go to prison on account of him being on private
property.

Derek asked the usual things; how we were, how the dogs were; asked me to stroke them for him. He said the lights were making his headaches worse. Even at night they never switched them off. But he never really complained. He just accepted it like he'd accepted everything in his life. He trusted us to look after him as we'd always done. I asked if he was still playing cards. He said he was. His favourites were Snap and Happy Families.

The condemned cell was different from other cells. We would see the others on the way in. As the warder led us past the cells the prisoners rattled their mugs and threw lumps of brown bread through the bars and shouted good luck. The condemned cell was high up in a tower. It even had a window and Derek said he used to watch us leaving in the car.

'And it won't be long before I'll be driving with you, will it?'

'No, it won't be long, son,' Mum used to say. We only had half an hour. So short, but it was difficult sometimes to know what to say.

It was up a spiral staircase. At the top was a door, and behind the door a small room, split in half by the glass. Three chairs our side and three chairs the other. Derek in the middle and a warder either side.

The only people Derek saw were his warders. They were kind to him, he said. I remember thinking how old they seemed. They were probably only about forty but when you're twenty-one everyone seems old. But they were too old to be any kind of proper companion for Derek, who was only nineteen. I didn't know then that warders had to be twenty-five to work in the condemned cell.

Dad told him that, after we'd seen him, we were off to the House of Commons. Derek smiled and said, 'Who'd have thought they'd ever be talking about me there.' He'd always had a beautiful smile, lovely teeth.

'Still smoking, are you, Derek?' I asked.

'Not a lot.' Then he smiled again. 'Dunhills, Sis. Not one of your old Weights, thank goodness, you know they make me choke.'

He told me I'd put on too much eye-shadow.

'Look at it, it's like war-paint. And I don't like the blue. You'll have to wash it off when I get home.'

I told him it was all the rage. Suddenly it was time to go. Dad said that in the new prison where he'd be taken when we got the reprieve, it'd be better. That we'd be able to visit longer.

It's terrible not being able to touch someone you love. You could see he was just crying out for Mum to put her arms around him. All she could do was to put her hand on the glass that separated us like a fish tank and Derek pressed his hand against hers and as she dragged her hand along, Derek followed with his, as if he was taking courage from her. But she didn't have much left herself. I don't know if it was just because my eyes were so full of tears, but as I looked back at him, his eyes which were usually a brilliant bright blue, seemed to have grown quite dark, almost black. Then my Dad said, 'See you tomorrow then, Son.'

And Derek just said, 'Cheerio, Dad, cheerio, Mum, cheerio, Sis. See you tomorrow.'

And we walked away.

I don't remember walking along that corridor. Suddenly we were outside the prison and in the middle of what looked like a riot. Nowadays Wandsworth Prison is surrounded by a wall as high as a house, but then the entrance area just led on to the street. Later I saw newsreels showing the crowds had been there all day, but I only remember them when we left. It was dark and, as we came out, we were blinded by hundreds of flash guns from the photographers who had been waiting. Behind them the crowd were shouting and throwing lumps of horse dung at the great wooden gate which was already banged shut behind us. Mum, Dad and I fought our way to the car but the press still wouldn't leave us alone, with their questions and their lights. All I wanted to do was cry. I couldn't stand any more and remember shouting at them as the car pulled away, 'Just bugger off and leave us alone.'

We drove straight for the House of Commons but soon realised that Mum couldn't take any more. She was in a terrible state, so we told the driver to turn round, back to Norbury to put her to bed. A friend stayed with her. Then Dad and I set off for the House of Commons. By now there was a huge crowd outside our house as well. We walked through them to the car in complete silence. No one said anything until just before we got in the car when a man touched Dad's arm and said that he was a bus conductor and that Derek had often travelled on his bus and what a nice boy he had seemed.

More letters and telegrams of support had arrived and Dad and I read them in the back of the car, letters from everyone from vicars and lawyers to film stars and ordinary people. The streets around the House of Commons were seething, not just people milling around but walking from every direction, up Victoria Street, Whitehall, up from Millbank, across Westminster Bridge and Lambeth Bridge, not like the organized marches you get today, but a people's army, marching on the House of Commons. In the light of the streetlamps we could make out our name Bentley written on the placards and the sheets hung between broom handles.

There was nothing we could do except wait in the Members' Lobby. It wasn't the first time we'd been there. Since Derek's case we'd been three or four times. But I'd been there long before that with my friend Lillian. She'd always lived in Norbury and didn't know her way around London like I did, so we did the sights. First the Tower, then St Paul's and it was when it began to rain I thought we'd have a look at the House of Commons. At the time I thought it looked like a church with all its gold and stained-glass windows.

It was ten o'clock when the MP who had taken up Derek's case, Sydney Silverman, came out. As soon as I saw him take Dad's arm and lead him into a corner, I knew. Dad's body seemed to sag. I ran over to him, to hold him, but in the end it was him who held me, as I collapsed in his arms. It was the end of the road.

In the back of the car as we drove home all Dad could say was, 'I'm a disgrace. I can't save his life. What kind of a father am I.'

The café round the corner had sent in food. But we couldn't eat. The two journalists who had driven us sat with us, but nobody had anything to say. We put Mum to bed. Somebody phoned saying they wanted us to lead a march on Buckingham Palace. Dad said no.

At one o'clock the phone rang again. I still don't know who it was. They said people were smashing windows at the Home Office and were threatening to throw police officers into the Thames. It was turning nasty. Could he help? So once again we set off for Westminster. I remember Dad lifting me up on to a wall above the crowds and he stood on a bench. He thanked them for everything they'd done but said that he didn't want any violence.

'These police officers have all got families and it won't save my son's life. He's in God's hands now.'

Then we moved on. It's hard to remember exactly where we went. At one place the crowds were singing 'Abide with me.'

We weren't used to demonstrations in those days. It was only a few months before that I'd taken Derek up to Westminster Abbey to see King George VI's lying-in-state. We went with some of the other usherettes from the Streatham Astoria where I worked, after the last performance. Derek had been the only man amongst us. There weren't many young people there at all. We'd had to queue for hours before getting in, shifting from foot to foot because it was so cold. It was freezing. It was two o'clock before we got in. We bought a rose off this man who was selling them to put by the side of the coffin. But in the end we didn't get near it. We just put the rose under the rope with the others. I remember how Derek kept asking me all these questions, about what the king would look like. He was worried about looking at someone who was dead. But when we got in there, the coffin was closed, not like the lying-in-state of George V, who my grandmother had taken me to see when I was three. I'd expected him to sit up and say hello to us. The shroud came up to his neck and his whiskers stuck out over it. But seeing him lying there was much better than the closed coffin of his son. It really did feel like you were paying your last respects. It might seem strange to take a child, but our family were like that. Great believers in royalty and in doing the right thing.

I remember that night now only in snatches. So many faces, no one I recognized, just the sense of being pushed by unknown people. A bit like it must feel if you're drowning. I remember one woman who came up, because she was so elegant. You could see the flash of sparklers underneath her veil. She told Dad that if money would help, he could have all he needed. He thanked her but said no.

'Money is no use now.'

It was only when she died in 1993 and they printed a photo of her as a young woman in the obituary that I recognized her face. It was the Duchess of Argyll.

At last the crowds began to break up and go home, so we got in the car and drove back to Norbury. It was now about four in the morning. As we sat together in the front room the phone kept ringing but we didn't answer it. We didn't speak, we didn't need to. It was as if time didn't exist. But that was just my imagination. Time did exist and when the clock on the mantelpiece struck nine Dad just said quietly, 'Nobody will ever hurt you now, son.'

Mum, who was as white as a sheet, cried out, 'They've done it, Will, haven't they?' and she just collapsed. The clock had stopped ticking. We took her upstairs and rang the doctor, who came and gave her an injection. But it didn't work. She just lay there, crying and crying and crying. My father showed no emotion. He just said, 'I never thought my country would do this to us. None of my children will ever fight for this country.'

Later that morning Dad went to Wandsworth Prison, which was only a few miles away, to collect Derek's clothes and belongings. It was only when he came indoors that he realized they hadn't given him the new suit he'd bought him for the trial. And then, and only then, after all those weeks of torture did he break. I had never seen my father cry before. It was terrible. I will never forget it till the day I die.

It was then that I said again the promise I'd made to Derek on that last visit that I would not give up until he was proved innocent. I'll never forgive the Government for what they did. They just wanted a life for a life. They made up their minds that Derek fitted the picture and they didn't care about the cost.

I pulled on my coat and went out. It was just beginning to rain. A woman stopped me on the corner. 'I'm very sorry,' she said. Then, as she patted my hand, I saw a red light land on our house like a beautiful red ball that's been kicked too high. The woman saw it too. I believe it was Derek, who'd come home. It was the only way he could.

There was one more thing I had to do. I telephoned Laurie, my fiancé, and asked him to come over. We'd got engaged at Christmas. The wedding dress I had bought from C & A's in Oxford Street was already hanging in my wardrobe. But it would never be worn; at least not by me. I would sell it and put the money towards the fight to clear Derek's name. When Laurie came in I just handed him my diamond hoop engagement ring. Although it wasn't what he wanted, he understood. He was in tears, but I felt nothing at all. Nothing. As I walked upstairs I heard Dad talking to him, but their voices seemed far, far away.

From now on there was only room for one man in my life. I would not rest until I had smashed that glass.

CHAPTER TWO

I can't really remember life without Derek because I was not even two when he was born. We were so close, people sometimes thought we were twins. We weren't, but both of us had lost a twin at birth. Sometimes when we were older we'd talk about it. Wondering how like us our twins would have been. But at least we had each other so perhaps that was God's way of not making us go through life alone.

I was born on 5 August 1931 in York Road Lying-in Hospital, opposite Waterloo station, the same day as my father's father died. In those days you usually had your children at home but my mother had 'complications', she was expecting twins. I was the first out and weighed over ten pounds but my twin was barely three pounds. She only lived six hours.

Derek was born on 30 June 1933. This time there was no talk of complications and so like Joan, our older sister, Derek was born at home. Imagine my mother's shock when a second baby appeared a few hours later. By then it was the middle of the night and the midwife had already gone home. My father had trained with the St John Ambulance Brigade, so he did what he could, but Derek's twin brother died later that night. Through all this Derek was just sleeping in his crib and, with so much going on, Dad hadn't taken much notice of him. But when the doctor came to sort out Mum, he saw there was something wrong with Derek and took him to Evelina Hospital in his own car. It turned out he had bronchial pneumonia. They didn't have antibiotics then. The only thing was blood transfusions and it was Dad's blood that saved his life. For several days it was touch and go as to whether he would survive. Mum used to tell us how she would have to use a breast pump and Dad would take the milk to the hospital where they would feed Derek with a fountain-pen filler. It was six weeks before he came home.

Home then was number 13, Surrey Row, just off Blackfriars Road. I can't really remember it, but according to Dad it was terrible. There were just two rooms and the roof leaked so much that plaster was falling off the walls and it was the damp they said that had caused Derek's pneumonia.

It wasn't till Derek was two that Dad found something better. It was in Friar Street (renamed Webber Street just before the war) above a parade of shops. According to the sign above the front door, Priory Buildings were built in 1893. There were four floors and two flats on each floor, built around a central staircase. There were two blocks like this side by side. We were in the second block, number 9. We had three rooms. One, the smallest, we used as a kitchen, one was the living-room and one, the big one, was the bedroom, which Dad divided with a wooden partition which he'd papered so that it looked like a proper wall. Mum and Dad slept one side, Derek and I the other. It was to be our home for six years.

It might not sound much better than what we'd had before, but three rooms on the first floor, two of them big, dry, light and airy, was like a palace in those days when most working people had to share small, damp terraced houses. It was real luxury with gas, electricity, running water and our own toilet. There was no bath-room, but hardly anyone had bathrooms then and flats like ours were thin on the ground and it had been worth waiting for.

Over the years the people who have written about our family, in newspapers and books, liked to make out that the Bentleys were no good, that Derek was a delinquent because of how he'd been brought up. It makes my blood boil. We were poor and we were working class, but we were a respectable and decent family. And compared to some we weren't badly off. Dad was in regular work. The rent was always up to date and he was in charge of Priory Buildings, like a caretaker, collecting rents as well as keeping an eye on the place. Now, no landlord would trust just anybody to do that, would they?

My big sister Joan had never lived with the rest of us. The rooms in Surrey Row had been so bad that she had stayed with our grandmother round the corner, where Dad and Mum had lived after they were married and where Joan had been born. By the time we moved to the new flat, she was so used to having her own bedroom that she didn't want to squash in with us. By then she was eight and had what Mum called 'a mind of her own'. Joan had brains. But although she didn't sleep with us, she was still our big sister and we saw her every day as our grandmother was only round the corner. She would come home most days after school to have tea with us. She had this pair of roller-skates which were her pride and joy and she would skate round in less time than it takes to boil an egg.

Nan, as we called her, lived in a big house in Loman Street with Mum's sister, Aunt Rose, who was a nurse at Guy's Hospital. I loved that house. It was very old, built long before the railways came. It had iron railings you could run your hand along, a huge front door with a great black knocker in the shape of a lion's head and a shiny brass letter-box. And above the door the most beautiful fanlight with coloured birds. Today it would be worth a bomb but those old houses weren't appreciated then and it was knocked down just before the war and an office block put up instead.

Nan shared the house with her brother and sister-in-law, Uncle Joe and Aunt Lal and their son Joe, who was called Joeboy so you didn't confuse him with his dad, but we didn't have much to do with him as he was much older than us. Derek and I loved going round there. Wash faces and hands, then wave goodbye, out of Priory Buildings, turn left, past the pub, under the railway bridge, left down the alley, past the bacon factory and right into Loman Street. When Nan opened the door, her dog Shaggy would leap all over Derek, and I would go straight into the garden to see how Billy the goat was getting on. At the far end of the garden was the hut where you went to spend a penny. It was covered in roses and inside a wooden seat stretched right across. When you lifted the lid up, there were blue flowers and butterflies inside the bowl. How I longed for us to have one at home like that. It was wonderful and once I even fell asleep in there.

Nan was very old-fashioned and a great big aspidistra blocked out most of the window in the front room which she called the parlour. She had jet-black hair, and could sit on it, it was so long. Derek and I would take it in turns to plait it, then twist it into earphones. It had to be brushed forty times a day. Her hair never turned grey, even though she was sixty-nine when she died.

Nan's name was Sarah Cooper and she was a widow. Grandfather Cooper's name had been William, the same as our dad's. He was Australian and had been in the navy, his dad before him had gone out to Australia working on the convict ships taking prisoners out to Botany Bay. Nan would tell us these wonderful stories, things he'd told her. She'd been much younger than him; he was a widower and was forty-nine when they married while she was only twenty-nine. Uncle Joe, who still lived with Nan in Loman Street, was his son. Uncle Bob, his other son, had been killed in the First World War. Grandfather Cooper had been all around the world, she said, but when he'd married his first wife he'd settled in London and got work as a coal porter. But he'd done well and become quite rich with coal yards as far away as Kent. But one day a spike went through his boots and his leg became infected. He died fifteen years before I was born at the age of sixty-four.

When you're young you lap up these stories about your ancestors, but I've no way of telling now if they're really true. My dad and his brother Uncle Bert were always saying that their uncle, my great-uncle, was Bentley of Bentley cars. If he was, he certainly didn't pay much attention to his relations in Southwark. My mother used to talk about the legacy she'd been left by her father, Grandfather Cooper, and I imagined it was a fortune, thousands of pounds. But where it went I just don't know.

Legacy or no legacy it was the thirties and times were hard if you didn't have a job. There was no social security then. You had to chop wood or go to what they used to call the 'bun house'. When Derek was born, Dad was working as an apothecary, making tablets and pills for Smiths, in Borough High Street. But within a year he had lost his job. Somehow my parents managed to keep going.

They had a little money put by, it was kept in a china jug in the kitchen, and my grandmother did what she could, paid the rent and the 3/- a week (1/6d each for Joan and me) for the school, which you had to pay for in those days. But my father was a very proud man and wouldn't accept 'charity' from anybody, even from his own mother-in-law. But he was prepared to borrow her spare tables and chairs.

Just down from our flat, in Blackfriars Road, was The Ring, the most famous boxing ring in London. On the other side of the road, Dad noticed an empty shop under the railway arches. So with a few old card tables and chairs, cups, saucers and spoons borrowed from Nan, plus tea, milk and a shilling for the gas, Dad set up a café. His partner was an Italian called Roy. It wasn't his real name. It was too difficult he said. Soon they were going great guns, selling ice-creams and proper food which customers could either eat there, or send across for, and Dad would dodge the traffic with the plates piled high for the toffs and high-ups of the boxing world. I was not much more than a baby, but I remember the pigs' heads in the window like it was yesterday, two of them, one with an apple in his mouth, the other with a lemon. But mostly I remember the ice-creams. The ice-cream cart was outside and when things got busy, Mum used to help out. Once when she wasn't looking I thought I'd help myself. Next thing I knew I was upside down in the cart, legs in the air and howling. Ice-cream isn't as nice when it's on your face instead of in your mouth.

The café kept going right up till the war. Dad loved food, loved cooking but he thought of it more as a hobby that paid its way. He retrained as an electrician but times were so bad, all he was offered was the sewers. But that turned out quite well. He would come home with sixpences, sometimes even half-crowns, coins which people had dropped into drains by mistake. It went a long way in those days when wages were only about £2 a week and you could get a leg of lamb for 1/6d.

Our whole family loved food. We had a roast every Sunday either at Nan's or at home in Priory Buildings. The gas cooker was in the kitchen, but the oven was at the side of the range in the living-room and there always seemed to be a stew on the go. We would have roast on Sunday and cold on Monday. But stews were my favourite. My father would cut off the fat to feed stray dogs, then it was into the stew pot with split peas, pearl barley, celery and dumplings. The dumplings were something wonderful. Dad's stews were fantastic, out of this world. Although he loved the dumplings, Derek would never eat the meat. He was a vegetarian ever since he was a baby when he would spit out any bit of meat Mum tried to get down him. He mainly lived on Shredded Wheat. As for eating meat, he just couldn't understand it. 'How can you eat something that used to be running around?' he used to say. To Derek animals were more important than anything. And all the stray dogs and cats around us seemed to know it. Shaggy, Nan's dog, was his favourite. But even the butcher's dog who bit everybody else loved Derek.

On one side of the fender would hang the shoe brushes, on the other side the coal bucket, and as soon as we were big enough we'd have to fetch the coal from the bunker outside on the landing which coalmen would fill from their sacks. Now, that really was work. In the summer they would come about once a week but in winter they'd be there nearly every day. We'd hear them clattering down the street on their carts, pulled by these great horses, and shouting out 'Coal, coal'. People who wanted it would open their windows and call out, hundred weight, or half a hundred weight. And the coalman would stop outside and heave up one of these sacks on to his back. He had a hat on with a flap at the back to stop the coal going down his neck, laced boots up to his knees and his trousers puffed out and a leather jerkin.

Today it must sound terrible, but it wasn't. What was important was that everyone shared, and we learnt the lessons that would last us through our lives. One lesson I have never forgotten. It was summer and Dad was outside polishing up his bike. He was as fond of that bike as Joan was of her roller-skates. On Saturdays he'd be off into the country, to Kent, where Uncle Reg had a farm. (I don't think he was a real uncle, all grown-ups who were friends were called uncle or aunt. Everyone else was Mr or Mrs.) He'd set off straight after breakfast with Uncle Bert (a real uncle, Dad's brother) or George Jennings, his friend from work, and by half-past eight they'd be back laden with apples, damsons, pears or early Brussels sprouts. They'd even go in winter if it was fine and come back with nice fat cabbages. Sometimes the whole family would go, Mum, Dad, Joan, Derek and me, by train from Waterloo. I remember how we'd come back loaded down, but there would always be 2d for a bunch of flowers from the stall over the road from the station before we clambered on the train back home.

On this particular afternoon Dad was working on his bike when a man came up and asked him if he could spare him a few coppers for a drink. He said he was trying to get to somewhere to get a job. He was tatty and he smelt. My father said, 'The only way I can help you is with my bike but first come on in.' So Dad laid the table and sat him down and fed him. Derek sat quietly, as he always did. But I said to my mum, I don't want to sit next to that man, he smells. Dad heard me. He said, 'Don't you want your dinner, then?'

'Oh, yes,' I said.

'Well, sit there then.'

'No,' I said.

So he said, 'Right, go to your room.'

I must have been about six. Afterwards he explained that the man didn't have any money to go to baths or get washed and that was why he smelt. My father lent him the bike and three days later the man came back. He'd got the job and gave the bike back to my father. That was my parents. And they brought us up to be the same. If you've got a shilling then share it.

Living where we did you didn't need to go far for shops. Across the road was Blacks, the grocer's. You would take your basin over for a pennyworth of pickles taken out with a scoop. Pickled onions were a halfpenny for six, ham off the bone was a shilling a pound. Bread was from the baker Mr Miller. Masons was the butcher's, and the greengrocer's, Prices, was next door. The four Price sisters were our friends – Lily, Betty, Mary and Yvonne – and there were always speckly bananas and apples which their dad would give us to share. Then there was what we called Seven-Up, which was a sweet shop. Seven-up wasn't the fizzy drink it is now, but a domino bar made of chocolate. If you had the right combination of dots, you got the pick of the shop, an ounce of anything you wanted, bull's-eyes, toffee twist, cough candy. We would spend what we called our 'goody' money there but in the summer it might go on an ice. The Walls man would come round on his tricycle with the cold box in front. The lollies were diamond-shaped and you had to rub them with your hands to get the paper off. Then there was the toffee-apple man who came round with a box on his head. Derek's favourite was trebles, three small Cox's apples with thick crunchy toffee. He would come round every day just like the vinegar man, with a barrel on his cart. Mum would send me down with the vinegar bottle, a farthing to fill it up. I had a special passion for vinegar. It was delicious, it tasted of the barrel. I always used to take a couple of sips before I took it upstairs. It got so bad, Mum had to hide it.

I'd go back to those times any day. Nobody bothered to lock their doors, people would come in for a cup of tea. You all had respect for each other. There was a real sense of community. You didn't have much money but you appreciated what you had. It was a lovely life.

But it didn't last. When Derek was four and a half he had his first epileptic fit. And it was all my fault.

CHAPTER THREE

Before the war everyone who worked in the City thought themselves a cut above. Morning and night they'd pass above our heads on the maze of criss-crossing railway lines to London Bridge station, Blackfriars, or Waterloo in their thousands. The bridges over the river would be black with them, bobbing with umbrellas and bowler hats. But Dad used to say they were just shuffling paper. In Southwark it was real work, all wharves and warehouses and factories. There was the foundry next door to us, and Flack's the French polisher's, Pritchett's brush and broom manufacturers, Amalgamated Press printing works, Wild's machinery belting, metal workers, paper merchants and printers by the dozen. Squeezed between these factories and warehouses were streets where people lived. There were no gardens, no parks except Bedlam, now the Imperial War Museum, which was too far away for us kids to go on our own. The open spaces you see there now are just bomb-sites grassed over.

Our street was quite busy. It was more like a road than a street and we weren't supposed to play in it. Hopscotch on the pavement or skipping and that was it. At the end was a depot for the *London Evening News* and lorries loaded with great bales of paper were always going backwards and forwards to Fleet Street, which was less than a mile away, just over Blackfriars Bridge. Sometimes the men would play with us, lifting us up on to the lorries and we'd sit there, dangling our feet over the edge while they bought a packet of Capstan from the tobacconist's across the road. One day, Derek and I were just watching out of the landing window, where we often sat after school, our legs sticking through the bars put there to stop us falling out, when one of these newspaper lorries stopped right in front of us and the driver jumped down out of the cab and went off up the road to the depot. It was the spring of 1938, Derek

24

was four and I was six. They called me a tomboy and I was. I climbed everything, and the steps at the back of the lorry were too much to resist. So before you could say knife, I was off. Down the stairs, out of the door and up the high steps on to the lorry.

I knew it was wrong but it was so exciting to be up there on my own. Except that I wasn't on my own. Derek had followed me. I was tall enough to reach the handle of the front door of the flats, which was always closed. Derek wasn't, but in my excitement I'd forgotten to close it and he'd just followed me, right up on to the lorry. Suddenly I heard a shout. The driver was coming back. I jumped down and ran off, didn't give a thought to my brother, just knew I'd cop it if I didn't scarper. Next thing I heard was a thud. Derek had fallen off the lorry. He'd tried to copy me but was just too little. Going up's one thing. Going down's another. He just fell like a sack of potatoes. He was out cold. His lovely curls were thick with blood and he had this terrible bump on his head as big as an orange. I should never have left him alone. I thought he was dead and I howled. Then Dad rushed into the street from the paper shop underneath our flat where he used to lend a hand sometimes. He carried Derek upstairs and put him on the settee. I followed bawling my eyes out. He wasn't out cold any longer, quite the opposite. His little body was jerking and twisting this way and that and there was what looked like foam around his mouth.

An epileptic fit is very frightening the first time you see it, especially when it's your baby brother, and especially when you think it's your fault. I was terrified.

'He's not going to die, is he?' I wailed, to anyone who was listening, but to myself really. If my brother was dead, I was the murderer. Dad went downstairs to call the doctor, there was a box at the corner, and Mum continued to try to hold on to him. Derek was still struggling and making noises when Dad got back. The ambulance came a few minutes later and took him to Guy's. They didn't keep him in. There was nothing they could do, they said. Although there were drugs to control epilepsy they were too strong and Derek was too young. All we could do was avoid him getting any more bumps on the head or the back of the neck. Another bang and he might have another.

Derek had been going to school for about a year before the accident happened. We both went to the same school, Friar Street Elementary, just past the pub next door to where we lived. Joan went to the school in Orange Street, round the corner from Nan's. In those days in Southwark you went to school when you were three. It was unusual, even in London, but Southwark was a Labour borough and very modern thinking. There was none of this half-day to start off with. School started at nine, you came home for an hour and a half for dinner, then back to school for a lie-down, then lessons until four.

Derek hated school right from the first. He'd always been a mummy's boy. Mum had three children but only one son and she idolized him. It didn't help the school being so close. It was one of those great big Victorian schools made of brick, surrounded by concrete playgrounds and a high wall. But there was a hole in the back wall and all Derek had to do was just climb through it into our yard, up the stairs and home, back to his mum which was where he wanted to be. As soon as his teacher realized he'd gone, she'd send for me and I would have to run and fetch him back. I always went the proper way, along the street and in through the front door. Then back we'd come, me holding tight on to his hand. It was no use Mum bringing him, he'd just scream and howl because he couldn't bear to leave her. The only way he'd stay would be if I was with him. So in the end I was allowed to sit next to him in his classroom and I would just have to take my own work with me.

After that first fit Mum kept him at home for several weeks but when he came back to school things were even worse. It's hard to describe the change but he seemed to have slowed down. One minute he'd be awake, the next minute he'd have nodded off. As I was sitting next to him, I'd give him a great nudge in the ribs with my elbow and tell him to wake up. But he'd just say that he was tired and wanted to go to bed. With Derek being off school so often, Mum and Dad were anxious that he wasn't learning properly. Before the accident, the school had told them he was doing well. And although he'd been off, the teachers told my parents not to worry, he was still young, only five, and there was plenty of time for him to learn his letters. So Mum used to sit him on her lap and read to him, tell him the words.

For a while everything seemed to be all right. A year went by and there were no more attacks. He was more clingy than he had been but we just thought it was because he was fearful it would happen again. He didn't say as much, but we knew.

Of course the accident put an end to playing out in the street. So we just had to play on the landing, usually cowboys and Indians. We knew all about them because Nan would take us for treats to the cinema, the picture palace she called it, up at the Elephant and Castle. Whoever was playing the Indian could paint their face with colour from a gob-stopper or liquorice comfits. Guns we just had to pretend, as Dad wouldn't allow us to have real toy ones. Another game was pirates. Our ship was under the gateleg table in the middle of the living-room. Derek would always be captain as that meant I'd be off having the adventures and he'd be looking after the ship. He used to say, 'If I'm left on board I'll cry.' But I'd say, 'Don't worry I'll save you.'

In those days girls weren't supposed to play with boys' toys. But of course I did, especially as Derek was younger than me and since the fall, not too quick on the uptake. I only ever seemed to get embroidery sets and dolls but Derek had Meccano, model cars and trains. His favourite was a little coal lorry which used to chug across the lino. Dad would light a little thing inside and along it would go, puffing with real smoke. Derek could watch that lorry for hours.

When he was five he got given a tool set. Birthdays were always special in our family. Both Derek's and mine were in the summer and if it was the weekend we'd go off for a picnic, perhaps to the farm or to Box Hill for the day. We'd go by train and if it was Box Hill there'd be a bus to take us to the top and we thought we could see all over England. We were allowed to take one friend each.

Derek would take Pete Murray and I would take Nelly Murray who lived across the road. If it was a school day we'd have a little party indoors and ask our friends for tea. If Dad was there, or Uncle Bert, they would play the piano and we'd play games like aeroplanes where you would stand on a tray with a blindfold on. Dad and Uncle Bert would lift it up only a little bit, and then they would touch your head with a book and say it was the ceiling. Then you'd be told you had to jump, and you felt so frightened.

But Derek's fifth birthday I'll never forget. There was this special programme on *Children's Hour* on the wireless. Parents of children with birthdays would write in, and on the right day, the announcer would wish whoever it was Happy Birthday and tell them where their presents were hidden. This year it was Derek's turn. So just before the time Mum and Dad said they were going out. I was let into the secret and knew they were just going downstairs to chat to Mr Price. I turned on the wireless. The excitement when Derek heard his name, you would hardly believe, he danced around waving his little arms in the air as the man said, 'Happy Birthday, Derek William Bentley, living in number nine Priory Buildings. Go to the cupboard behind the settee and you'll find something special.'

We ran over to the cupboard and there was the tool set, with its own little mallet and saw. 'Think what we can do now,' I said. 'What do you say we mend the settee?'

Nan had given us a brand new settee about a year before but it wobbled and Mum was always on at Dad to do something about it. But all he said was, 'Don't worry, Lillian, I'll get round to it when I have time.'

But he never had. This was our opportunity to do something useful. So we turned the settee over on its side and as Derek held it steady, I sawed a bit of leg off. I was as quick as I could be because I wanted it done before Mum and Dad got back, so it would be a surprise. The window was open and I could see they were still chatting to Mr Price across the road.

I finished just in time. They were on their way back. After Derek had said his thank yous, I told them that I'd done that job. 'What job?' Dad said.

'The settee. I've mended one leg, but I think another one needs doing.'

They went mad. It wasn't the settee that was wrong, it was the floorboards.

I went straight to bed without my tea, and my 'goody' money was stopped for a month. That was the usual Bentley punishment for being naughty. Our parents were very strict about some things, about keeping our rooms tidy and not being rude but we hardly ever got smacked. Derek never, not after the accident.

So that we had somewhere safe to play Dad decided to turn the roof of the flats into a garden. He was the caretaker so he could. It stretched over the whole building, which was eight shops long, so it was big, bigger than Nan's garden, as long as a tennis court but not so wide. He made it safe by building the sides up with bricks where the wall was too low and fitting wire around. The other side was railings with spikes on them, so you couldn't climb up. He took crates up, and beer barrels cut in half and filled them with earth and made flower-boxes. We were so high we could see for miles, over to St Paul's one way, then up the river to the docks and Tower Bridge and the other way right down to the radio mast at Crystal Palace. And if we went right to the end we could watch Joan as she skated around to us after school.

Derek had a pedal car and Dad made him a garage with a petrol pump and a piece of hose to pretend to fill the car with petrol. Round the corner he rigged up another piece of hose which was our shower. This was real. It was attached to the water tank and worked with a tap. In the summer we would spend all our time up there. It was everyone's favourite place and all our friends would come up to play, including the butcher's dog, who Dad would fetch for Derek. After school they'd all be over, Derek's friend Pete Murray, my friend Yvonne and the other Price sisters, and we'd put on our costumes, scratchy woollen things they were, and lark around with the hose. If it wasn't baking hot we'd have to keep our vests on underneath. My costume was green. I could never work out which way round it went and once it got wet it never seemed to dry. That roof was our own wonderful world, a world away from our parents and we could run it as we liked. Provided we didn't get up to too much mischief that is.

Normal bedtime was half-past six but on summer evenings we were allowed to stay up late. We'd have tea first, bread and jam or salmon and shrimp-paste sandwiches. Sometimes with a bit of cake if there was any. Then we'd be up on to the roof till about seven, then bath and bedtime. We only had a tin bath which was always put in front of the fire. Mum would have heated the water on the gas cooker which she would have to lift up and lift off several times, a difficult enough job for anyone but much worse for her, with her bad back.

My mother's back was all bent over, from an accident she'd had at school. Curvature of the spine they called it. It was quite severe but Grandfather Cooper had got a Swedish specialist to see her and his hot plasters had saved her from a life of pain. Although the rest of her family were much taller than average Mum was barely five feet, and yet she had the strength of a lion. Dad wasn't tall either. He was only five foot six, so they might never have got married if she'd been her full height. But although he was small, Dad was as handsome as a film star. Nan used to say he was a 'real toff'. The only time you'd see him without an umbrella was on his bike. Although Mum never complained, Dad never let her do anything heavy or tiring if he could help it. Every weekend he'd do the shopping and the cooking.

'Nothing is too good for my Lillian,' he used to say.

Right to the end he loved her and cared for her better than anyone else I've ever known. He was a real gentleman until the day he died.

The part of London we lived in was very old and it may be because of that I've always liked history. We learnt about our past at school and even though we may not have understood much, we were very proud of our heritage. Borough High Street was busier then than it is today, full of bustle and life, but in the days when London Bridge was the only bridge across the Thames, before the railways came, it was the busiest street in London, lined with dozens of taverns and coaching inns, where people would stay the night before taking the Dover road.

The George was one of the last inns left. Everyone knew the George, and it's still there today, the last galleried inn in London. It's run by the National Trust now, but it was always somewhere special. Every summer great carts would be pulled into the courtyard and shows and plays would be put on. The audience would sit in the gallery and on benches in front, pint pots in their hands.

Rehearsals went on at Sunday school week after week after week, then the great day would come. Curtains would droop from the gallery to the carts to hide the actors (us) until we were ready. We did Shakespeare or Dickens mostly because they'd both lived in Southwark. *Little Dorrit* all happens in Southwark, and St George's is known as Little Dorrit's church because that was where she was christened (just like Derek and me) and married (like Grandfather Cooper and Nan).

It was only the older children, the brainy ones like Joan, that did the speaking. I always ended up playing a scruffy kid no matter what we were doing. Derek played urchins or angels. If he was an urchin there was no problem, but keeping him clean as an angel was easier said than done. Aunt Rose made all our costumes and just dressing up was fun. I remember thinking then that I might like to go on the stage when I grew up.

A year and a half had gone by since Derek's accident and just as he seemed to be getting a bit more confident, he had another attack. There was no warning. It was not long after his sixth birthday. He was just playing with my old dolls' pram. I'd grown out of it but it was where he used to keep his cars. Suddenly he collapsed on to the floor and started writhing around. This time I knew what it was, but that didn't make it any better as only a few days before he'd been really aggravating me. We'd had a pillow fight and I'd bashed him round the head. This time he was taken to another hospital in Lambeth and he stayed there for three weeks.

It was only a few days after he got back that war was declared.

CHAPTER FOUR

We were too young to know about what was happening in Germany. Munich, Chamberlain, Hitler, Nazis, were just words. But we saw what was happening in our street. The big iron school gates were taken away. Big metal bollards in the alley on the way to Nan's that I used to leap-frog over, they went. Even saucepans and handbells were collected in. We kept our bell as Dad had volunteered as an ARP (Air-Raid Precautions) warden. It would only be rung in case of a gas alert, and we all had our gas-masks. Mine had a snout like an elephant's and a window to look out of. The ARP ones were different, the 'trunk' was longer and the eyes were like goggles. The first time I saw Dad in his I was terrified and I ran away and locked myself in the toilet. I didn't know it was him. To me it was the devil.

The 3rd of September 1939 was a lovely day, warm and sunny. Everyone remembers what they were doing, like the day Kennedy died. It was a Sunday and we were going for a picnic. We usually left early to make a day of it but today we had to wait. Mr Chamberlain was going to make an important announcement at eleven o'clock. So we all sat around and listened to the wireless. Mum cried. It was war. The next minute an air-raid siren sounded. It was the first time we'd heard it, a strange wailing noise. But it was a false alarm. Dad said he wasn't going to let Hitler spoil our day, so we took the tram to Waterloo and caught the train for Hampton Court.

Then there was talk about evacuation. Children as young as Derek didn't have to go on their own and Mum was to be allowed to go with us. So the arrangements were made. The morning we were to go, Dad carried our bags into the school playground and we all said goodbye. Derek was crying. After he'd gone, we stood around waiting, not saying anything. Mum knew that neither Derek nor I wanted to go. Then suddenly she just picked up our things and we went home. Because Dad was an ARP warden, he had to stay in London. There was no way Mum was going to leave him and there was no way Derek would be separated from Mum. And where Derek went, I went. When Dad came home he pretended to be cross but you could see how pleased he was that we'd stayed. 'If we are to be killed, Will,' Mum said, 'we'll be killed together.'

That first year of the war, nothing much seemed to happen. Our windows were criss-crossed with brown sticky paper, like you put on parcels, to stop splinters of glass flying around. Everyone had to make blackout curtains which were supposed to stop any light. We weren't even allowed torches, but you had to have your gas-mask with you all the time. Everyone had them, even babies and horses. They were horrible. You could hardly see out, they misted up so quickly and Derek said he couldn't breathe and the smell of rubber made him feel sick. He had a special children's one, red and blue, which made him look like Mickey Mouse. We had to carry them with us everywhere in a brown cardboard box. Of course we put other things in the box as well, like sweets and biscuits, and they soon fell apart so Dad bought us smart new ones made of leather.

A lot of rehearsing went on. The London fire brigade had its headquarters a few streets away. They had these towers and Derek and I would watch them from Nan's attic through a beautiful round window. Houses would be 'borrowed' and they'd rehearse taking people out on stretchers through the windows. They'd rehearse putting out incendiary bombs. The real ones were hot balls that sizzled and fizzled as they came through the air. Even though they were not much bigger than tennis balls they were enough to burn down a house. You put them out with sand. Everywhere there would be men practising with buckets and stirrup pumps, with red faces and cheeks puffed out like hamsters. Piles of sandbags were delivered by the council outside houses and shops for stacking against windows. Uncle Bert had joined the ARP too, and he and Dad were at post number 1 in Blackfriars. The sky was filled with barrage balloons like floating elephants. But we never saw or heard a German aeroplane.

The hospital had said that Derek's fits would probably get worse before they got better. It was in May 1940, just after Dunkirk, when he had the next one. I remember it because it was the first time it really felt like war and the sirens began to wail more often. This time he went back to Guy's, but they said he was still too young to have phenobarbitone, a very strong drug which was the only thing that would control them in those days. He'd have to wait till he was fourteen. A long wait when you're just seven. The only way to prevent them was to keep him calm, they said, not to let him get upset or anxious. Fat chance of that, said Uncle Bert, with the war going on.

His headaches were getting worse. Whenever he felt one coming on he would cry. He was afraid it meant he would be 'sick' and he hated being sick, vomiting, which always happened when he had a fit. When he got a bad one he would just lie down on the settee and we'd draw the curtains and one of us would sit with him and put a cold flannel on his forehead. He'd say, 'Please take this head away, Dad,' and Dad would get oil of lavender and dab it on his forehead which seemed to calm him down. Then he would go to sleep.

At night he'd wake up, worrying about the war. It's no wonder really. It was all anyone ever talked about, even us kids, although we didn't know anything except what we heard our parents say. Most of it was just flags on the map. Dunkirk, then Paris, then France. A war map had come with one of the newspapers. We stuck it up on the wall with different-coloured flags which we cut out for the different countries and Dad would help me or Derek to move them across. No one could understand why the French had surrendered. According to the map, most of France was still left. Uncle Bert said it was because they drank wine instead of tea.

There were only two things we knew for sure: Hitler was evil and our boys would win. Even this was too difficult for Derek to understand. When I was asleep I'd hear his voice going on and on saying, 'Sis, Sis,' until I woke up.

'What's going to happen, Sis?'

Night after night.

'What's going to happen, Sis?'

'Nothing. Just shut up and go to sleep.'

Although the war frightened him, Derek's favourite book was a big picture book of aeroplanes. Dad used to sit with him and tell him their names: Spitfires, Hurricanes, Gloster Gladiator and the German ones, Heinkel, Messerschmitt, Dornier flying pencil and Stuka dive-bomber.

By now I was nearly nine and although Derek was two years younger than me I think I knew he should have at least been making an effort to read, but he was always too tired. He loved having stories read to him and every night before we went to bed we'd have one of his favourites: Aladdin, Ali Baba and the Forty Thieves or Bible stories. I would read to him. Mum and Dad would read to him. But he just didn't seem to have any interest in doing it himself.

School was still on and off. Probably more off than on. His teacher didn't help. Whenever he came back after being away, she put him at the back of the class. Just couldn't be bothered. I know as I was still sitting with him. Even if things were read out to him, unless it was really easy, he didn't understand. There were other things too. He couldn't co-ordinate properly. Once he came with me to Blacks to get half a dozen eggs and I handed them to him to let him carry them back and he just dropped them. We'd never ask him to do things after that. It was more than just being clumsy. He couldn't kick a football properly. He'd end up falling over. It was a long time before he learnt to do his own shoe-laces up, though he did in the end. But for all his life you could never ask him to carry more than one cup of tea at a time.

It was almost exactly a year before the blitz began. 'The battle of France is over, the Battle of Britain is about to begin,' Mr Churchill had said, so we knew it was just a question of when. First they said it was going to come in August, but in the end it was 7 September, a lovely Saturday afternoon.

During August the bombing had been creeping nearer. We'd even seen one or two German planes, but this was different. At first it didn't seem at all frightening, just exciting. Anyway, it wouldn't touch us, it was all the other side of Tower Bridge, well over to the east by the Docks. Dad took me and Joan up on the roof to watch. Derek stayed with Mum as Dad said it would frighten him and it would have.

It was out of this world, like the biggest firework display you ever saw. The sky was full of bombers and fighters, hundreds and hundreds of them. The noise was like thunder, but worse than thunder, like the sky was cracking in half. The sky glowed from the fires that the bombs had started in the docks. At first it had been so blue that afternoon, then it was covered with white vapour trails, but by late afternoon it had turned a dark red from smoke that poured upwards in thick columns from the burning buildings on the ground. After a break of a few hours they were back again but there was to be no more watching from the roof. This time we were safely down in the shelter.

Even before war was declared, shelters were being built everywhere. Huge trenches were dug in the park next to the Imperial War Museum, which we still called Bedlam. They even dug them in Green Park and St James's Park in front of Buckingham Palace, where Joan and I used to go to on our Sunday walks.

People who had gardens made Anderson shelters which were half-buried in the ground. You were given the corrugated steel roof and sides by the council but had to build it yourself. If you had a cellar then you used that. Some people just used to hide in the understairs cupboard. Then there were brick shelters, surface shelters they called them. In our area they were often built on to the sides of railway arches. Nan's shelter was like that. Her house in Loman Street had been pulled down not long before the blitz began and she, Joan and Aunt Rose had moved into a flat in Union Street, backing on to a railway line going to London Bridge station. Aunt Lal, Uncle Joe and Joeboy had moved too, to a flat in the next-door block to Nan's. Their shelter was built up against the embankment at the back. Even though it was so close, Nan didn't want to go.

She was sixty-nine and her flat was up two flights of stairs and she wasn't very good at hurrying. But Mum told Joan to take no notice. Nan must be made to go.

The shelter we went to was under a hop warehouse, opposite the Hop Exchange in Southwark Street. It wasn't that close to our flat, a good ten minutes' walk, but Dad's ARP post was now in St Thomas's Street, between London Bridge and Guy's Hospital. ARP wardens didn't use shelters themselves, but being near meant he could pop in to see we were all right. It was really just a big cellar and held about thirty people. Everyone seemed to know each other and I think it belonged to a friend of Dad's. Derek and I were the only children. Dad had made bunks for us and we felt very special because nobody else had them. We had sheets and blankets and for three months never slept anywhere else.

That first morning when we came out of the shelter what you noticed was the smell and the air which was still full of dust and bits which got in your eyes. We were used to smoke from fires and chimneys but this was different. Nothing much had been bombed near us that night, but the streets were full of people. When we got home we sat on the landing watching them stream by pushing prams and bassinets filled with babies and a lot more besides, carrying suitcases or boxes tied with string with saucepan handles sticking out. Refugees they were really, from Bermondsey and Rotherhithe, bombed out of their homes or just too frightened to stay anywhere near the docks another night. God knows where they went. There was no daylight raid that afternoon and I thought it was because it was Sunday. But there was to be no more watching on the roof. By five o'clock we were back in the hop cellar and by seven it had started up again. The shelter wasn't that deep and you could hear the rumble and feel the ground shudder with the bombs falling and we knew that they were coming closer.

The third night of the blitz, 10 September 1940 is the one date of the war that will live with me for ever. Dad finished his shift and came down to be with us. About four o'clock in the morning, another ARP on his post came down and said, 'Your mother-in-law's flat's been hit.' With that we all sat up and Derek and I began to cry. Mum was in a terrible state and said that she'd had a dream they'd all been killed. Derek and I just held on to each other, sitting on the side of our bunks and crying our eyes out. Dad said that they wouldn't have been in the flat, they'd have been down the shelter.

While everyone was rallying round trying to comfort Mum, Dad just put on his black tin hat with a white 'W' on the front and said he had to go. He didn't say where, but I knew. It was still all going on outside. When he got there he found that it was not only the flats that had got it, but the shelter too. The first people out were Aunt Lal, Uncle Joe and Joeboy, alive but all badly injured. Joeboy had been hit on the head and was never the same. Brain damage. Years later, when Aunt Lal died and there was no one to look after him, he ended up in a mental home. While they were taken off to Guy's Hospital, Dad carried on digging with the others, dragging out bodies from under the rubble. But when it came to the concrete slab that was on the top of the shelter they had to wait for lifting gear. Underneath they found my nan, my aunt and my sister. They took out twenty-eight bodies that night. Joan had had most of her head blown off and it was only when Mum and Dad went to identify her the next day that Dad realized from the clothes she was wearing and a ring, that he'd been the one who'd carried her out.

I find it hard now to remember what I felt. Dad managed to get a few things from the rubble. Nan's new dressing-table, an old doll of Joan's and her roller-skates. The bomb had cut down the side of the flats like a slice of bread and the kitchen dresser, the sort which was attached to the wall, was still there with our Jubilee mugs hanging on the cup hooks, and on the top shelf you could see the individual Christmas puddings with our names on which Nan always had made ready for our birthdays.

It was all so quick. Only three days before it hadn't felt like war at all. Derek didn't really understand. He was only seven. He cried because we cried and I think it took some time for it to sink in that Joan and Nan weren't coming back.

But the war wasn't about to stop just because our world had

been blown apart. The nightly bombing went on for over two months without let-up. For the first few days it seemed as if it was all going the Germans' way but soon our boys on the ack-ack guns were giving Jerry what for, and the night sky was lit not only by fires but by searchlights. Every morning the streets would be covered with a new lot of shrapnel, twisted bits of metal from our shells, and little heavy silver mushrooms – bullets that had flattened themselves as they hit the ground. All of which, of course, we used to collect in bagfuls on our way back home from the shelters in the morning. Sometimes we did swaps with our friends but only if you had a special piece which had a mark on it, but mostly we just collected. Our best souvenir was a wire from a crashed Heinkel. We found it when we were looking for new rubble heaps to slide down on the sledges we'd made from sheets of corrugated iron. Derek didn't do it, he just used to watch. By the time we had clambered up to look inside, the soldiers were back. But they let us have this piece of wire.

Nowhere was safe. There were holes in the road you could fall down if you weren't careful. I know because I fell down one. I was chatting to the Price sisters leaning against a barricade when it just gave way. We were round the corner from Friar Street, so while I was yelling, Yvonne ran for help. I had fallen on some wood which went up between my legs so I was taken to hospital to have the splinters taken out. I don't know which was worse, the pain or the embarrassment.

Raids weren't only at night, but in daylight they weren't so frightening somehow and as Mum used to say to Derek when he had to go to school, 'You can't spend your life underground.' There would be about six or seven air-raid warnings (red alerts, Dad called them) every day. You would go to the nearest shelter to where you happened to be. There were signposts in the street telling you which way to go. As the war went on people took more chances, and often just carried on what they were doing, unless the raid was really close. Trams would stop to let people off if they wanted, but otherwise just kept going. Even if you were down in a shelter, if the

Spitfires were up, you'd go out to watch. People would shout to the gunners to egg them on, things like 'get your eyes seen to'. But they were enjoying it really and everyone would be cheering, just like it was a football match.

I remember the first dogfight we saw because it was when Mum, Derek and I were buying black for Joan's funeral. We had gone to The Cut, where the Old Vic is, our closest big shopping street. Suddenly there was this terrible commotion. We rushed out into the street like everyone else. It was going on right above our heads. The bursts of ack-ack fire would grow in the sky like grey balls of cotton wool. Then the Heinkel flew right into a patch of grey cotton wool and came out the other side on fire. A great cheer went up. We cheered too. Then we saw the parachute floating down, it seemed so slow compared to everything else. The people in the street were waving knives and rolling-pins and were running towards Blackfriars Road, where it looked like he was going to come down. Luckily for him the soldiers got there first, otherwise he'd have been lynched. Mum just held on to our hands and we marched back to the flat.

It was about then that Uncle Bert came to live with us. His wife Dolly was one of the first casualties of the war. She was in Woolworth's at the Elephant and Castle when it had a direct hit early that August. They lived about five minutes away in Nelson Square, so Uncle was always dropping in to play the piano. He didn't have one at the Nelson Square flat. But after Dolly died, he hadn't the heart to go back to the flat where they'd lived. We hadn't heard from him for a bit and Dad was getting worried when he found out he was sleeping rough on Blackfriars Bridge. So he went and found him and said he should stay with us for a few days and he could sleep on the settee. Apart from when he worked on Pluto, the pipeline for D-Day on the Isle of Wight, he lived with us until he died on 3 March 1993.

Derek was now terrified that Mum or I were going to be the next to go. He couldn't bear to be out of our sight. School was still carrying on as usual, but keeping him there was getting more and

41

more difficult. Things seemed a bit quieter around Christmas. We decorated the hop cellar with paper chains and somebody brought a Christmas tree down. There was quite a party. If anything I think we had more presents that year because other people in the shelter gave us things as they all knew we'd be missing Joan, Nan and Aunt Rose. Or perhaps because they were missing their own children. I still have a poetry book that Derek was given by someone that Christmas. On the blank pages in the front there's a picture he's drawn of a gun firing and shells exploding. He used to draw while I was knitting, which was all I ever seemed to do. Squares for blankets, balaclavas, or socks. Socks were the worst. You needed four needles. Mum used to start me off, then I would do the long run, then she'd have to turn the heel and the same when I came to the toe. She did try to teach Derek but for every six stitches she put on, he'd drop three. He was all thumbs.

Just as life seemed to be settling down to some sort of routine – shelter, home, school – bad luck struck again. It was towards the end of March. Derek and I had gone to sleep in our bunks, the same as usual, but I woke up to the most almighty roar in my ears. The warehouse had taken a direct hit and the whole lot had come crashing down into the cellar. I couldn't see anything. It was black and muffled. My first thought was for Derek. I groped around and found his hand and gave it a squeeze. I could hear people moving about and tried to shout but my mouth was full of dust. Eventually we were dug out. I was all right but Derek's head was cut. We were sure it would lead to another fit, and it did.

Since the beginning of the blitz, the paper shop underneath us had been empty and Dad had begun to build an Anderson shelter in it. I say begun because with all the work he had as a warden, he'd not had the time to finish it. With the hop cellar gone, there was no choice now but the deep public shelter at London Bridge. There weren't many deep shelters as none had been specially built before the war. This one was left over from when they built the tube. It was huge and hundreds of people camped out there every night. It was disgusting. The walls were dripping wet, people were lying around on old sacks and coats. We ended up on the stairs. Not like the nice bunks we'd had in the hop cellar. And the smell, it was like a public lavatory and Jeyes fluid mixed. The air was thick enough to cut. After a few minutes you got used to it, but every evening when we went back in it was the same. We were there less than a month. By April Mum said she'd had enough. That the deep shelter was unhygienic and that as the worst of the blitz seemed to be over she'd rather go home and 'take our chance'.

So every night we would go to bed in the half-finished Anderson shelter under the flat. Then on the night of 17 April 1941, a bomb marked Friar Street school was dropped. With it went the back wall of our house. The sandbags Dad had stacked up around the shelter had saved us. Mum took us to the doctor to check we were all right and it was then that he saw my rash. Scarlet fever. The risk of epidemics in the shelters meant Derek and I were taken by ambulance to Grove Fever Hospital in Tooting. A few days later Derek was covered too. After that it was Dad's turn and Mum was left on her own. She wasn't really on her own though, as when Aunt Lal, Uncle Joe and Joeboy had got out of hospital they'd had nowhere to live so Mum had arranged for them to rent the room the other side of the landing to us in Priory Buildings.

The isolation hospital was not only for scarlet fever and just as we were coming out of quarantine, we got chicken-pox. Then there was a diphtheria alert. By the time we went back to Blackfriars, the summer of 1941 was nearly over.

There was still no back wall to our flat which was just covered with a tarpaulin. Since May there had been no more raids so Mum hadn't bothered going to a shelter but had just put the gateleg table on its side in front of the window to stop the glass from blowing in. The Germans had given up knocking the stuffing out of London for the time being and were now attacking Russia. Friar Street school next door was just a mountain of bricks and rubble. A Catholic convent agreed to let me go there but the nuns wouldn't take Derek as it was girls only. But by then we knew it was only temporary. With no more air raids, Dad's work was easier now and he'd decided enough was enough and that we had to get out of London.

CHAPTER FIVE

The country, the country! We were going to live in the country. Derek and I held hands and danced when Mum and Dad told us. The country to us meant Uncle Reg's farm, or Box Hill or Hampton Court. In fact the house Dad had found was in Edgware, on the north side of London, through a cycling friend of his, Eddie Doe, whose mother lived there. Edgware may not sound like the country nowadays, and it probably wasn't even then, but it was to us. Compared to what we'd just been through it was the garden of Eden.

Pembroke Place was a cul-de-sac. The houses weren't made of brick, or joined together in a row like London houses, but pebble-dashed and painted different colours. Ours was speckledy beige. I think Nan must have left Mum some money when she died because our new house had all new furniture, new beds, new chairs, new settee. We took hardly anything with us from Blackfriars, only the gateleg table and Nan's dressing-table and chest of drawers. To us number 1 Pembroke Place seemed brand new and it was probably only a few years old. It had parquet flooring, a front doorbell and best of all a bathroom with a huge white bath in it. We could have a bath every night if we wanted, we didn't have to share and we didn't have to wait till the water boiled, but just run the taps. But because of the war effort we were only allowed four inches. It was like a dream come true.

Then there was the garden. There were hollyhocks as high as a house and apple trees big enough to climb and roses that went right up into my window.

There were no guns, no air raids and it was so quiet it was hard to remember the blitz had ever happened at all. But we hadn't left the war behind altogether. Dad was still with the ARP in Blackfriars. Since September 1939 he had stopped being a volunteer. Being a warden was now his job. Edgware was the last station on the

45

Northern Line, so most nights he would be back with Mum, Derek and I and on summer evenings we would all walk the mile or so to the station to meet him.

The garden was Dad's kingdom. I don't know where he learnt about vegetables, but he knew how to make things grow as sure as cabbages is cabbages. Nan's garden had been surrounded by high walls which Dad had planted with vines and roses. Here we had beetroots, carrots, broccoli, spinach. Behind the Anderson shelter were rows of potatoes and Brussels sprouts. The shelter was our den and Derek and I would play there for hours, melting down candles, colouring them and making new ones by dripping the wax along a piece of string. We thought we were helping the war effort. We hardly ever used the shelter for its real purpose. In Edgware it was back to going to bed and pyjamas next to your skin, not on top of layers of underwear 'just in case'. Derek was always pestering Dad to make the shelter into a pond. But Dad said no, 'just in case' and the shelter still had a store of biscuits and special water, tins of food and a tin opener, a small bag of clothes, mainly socks and knickers, and a tin pot hidden behind a curtain which Dad had made for privacy.

No sooner had we got there than Mum was expecting again. New house, new baby. It was ten years since she'd had Derek and as she used to say, 'I'm not getting any younger'. So with Mum not having so much energy, Dad being away and Edgware being so countrified, Derek and I could come and go like we'd never done before. The Sunday after we heard about the new baby being on the way, the church bells rang out for the first time since the war began, and we thought it meant the end of Hitler. Suddenly everything seemed to be going our way.

Our first Christmas in Edgware was just wonderful. There weren't any toys worth having in the toy shops but Dad made us wonderful jigsaws out of wood, a teapot for Derek and a more difficult one just of spots for me. Plus we were each given a National Savings book with a few 6d stamps in it already. From then on we would buy savings stamps with our goody money. Rationing meant that we couldn't get many sweets anyway. But we were lucky because our friend Eileen's dad worked at Rowntree's, and she always had plenty to share. Christmas dinner that year was roast pork and apple sauce made with apples from the garden and lots of crackling. The roast potatoes were from the garden too. But potatoes weren't rationed and you could eat as many of them as you liked.

Although we missed our old friends, we soon made new ones. There was John and Alan Lindsay who lived at the end of the road, their dad was a policeman. Then there were John, Freddy and Dulcie Hazlegrove, and Eileen whose father worked for Rowntree's Fruit Gums, Clifford Pullen, Margaret, and Hazel the girl who lived on the corner. Everyone knew about Derek's illness and about him being slow, but nobody made fun of him and he was included in everything we did, even if he didn't join in. He was more contented, living in the country. He was still having his 'heads' but seemed to be more calm about them and coming out of them more quickly.

In those days hardly anyone had a car. Only the doctor or someone like that. No one in Pembroke Place had one and the road was our playground where we played tennis or football or mucked around with carts made from pram wheels. But mostly we would just sit on the kerb and chatter. There was no shrapnel to pick up, no crunch of broken glass on the pavement.

But the war hadn't disappeared completely. We still played at being soldiers. Derek had a tin hat Dad had brought him from Woolworth's, but just like in Blackfriars, nobody wanted to be a German. Sometimes we'd take out our gas-masks and put them on but Derek and I didn't like playing war games, perhaps because we'd been through it. We'd rather go to the park where there was a see-saw and swings, and that was something Derek loved. He couldn't do it himself, but nobody minded giving him a push.

All our new friends went to the same school, Camrose Avenue. We'd been used to going to school around the corner, so this new school felt like it was miles away. In the morning we would hurry, me worrying about being late, and it would take about ten minutes to walk there. But on the way home we'd be all together with our friends, mucking around so it was more like half an hour. We would always stop at the large round water tank at the side of the road between the recreation ground and our house. It had been put there in case of incendiary bombs. I don't think it had ever been used and the water was covered with green slime. It was about twenty feet across and five feet high. To get up you had to climb on a crate. There was wire mesh over it to stop children like us falling in. We had races, boats made of paper, or if we hadn't made any, bits of wood and twigs.

Everyone hated that school, and everyone especially hated the headmaster whose name was Mr Beeching. I called him Beechnut. He was a vile man. He kept Derek in nearly every day. Not for doing anything bad, just for being late. I would be punished for talking in class which you can understand, but Derek never said anything. They had prefects on the gates and even a minute late meant you missed your playtime and had to go to the punishment room. If you were late back from dinner it meant staying late after school. But time was one of the things Derek didn't understand. He'd see a cat on the pavement and he'd be so busy stroking it he'd forget all about going to school.

He was all right with the friends from home, but in the playground other boys would taunt him and he'd go away and hide, or even run home. There were two gates into the school and he would come in one and go out of the other. Then he'd hide in our garden until I got home, curled up with Flossie, a black and white cocker spaniel that had attached himself to Derek one day at the allotments and been with us ever since. I don't know why the Edgware kids picked on us, whether it was Derek's not being able to read or just because we came from London. I think it was just because we were different. They told us straight out they didn't like cockneys, they thought they were better than us. But I think they were just jealous that we'd been through the blitz and they hadn't. Once when I was giving Derek a see-saw in the park a girl from school grabbed my hair and was about to go for Derek's but I pulled her off him and gave her a pasting. 'How dare you hurt my brother,' I yelled. She soon ran away. She hadn't counted on me being a fighter. But I am. And always have been.

I'd always enjoyed school until I came to Edgware. And this was nothing to do with Derek. Perhaps it was because I was younger when I was in London but there the teachers really seemed to care. If you didn't understand anything, they'd put their arm around you and explain it again. Here they just expected you to know. I hated that place.

'I wish that school would get bombed.'

But Mum would say, 'They don't have bombs up here, Iris.'

There were allotments about five minutes away that you got to through an alleyway by the scout hut. Allotments were where people who didn't have enough space in their own gardens would Dig for Britain. At the far end was Edgware Town football ground and at the other side was a stream, Silver Stream it was called, with branches dipping in and crumbly banks, just like real country. It was our favourite place to play. Derek and I would spend hours lying down in the long grass watching the fish, just tiddlers, minnows and sticklebacks going up and down and hiding under stones. In the spring it was a mass of tadpoles and frog spawn. One day Derek decided he wanted to go fishing. Mum was resting so we borrowed a net curtain from the cupboard and Derek stood one side of the stream and I stood the other, holding the ends. The net came up full of jellied frog spawn. Just then it started raining.

'They can't stay out in the rain.'

Derek looked as if he was going to cry. So we put the curtain in a bucket, went home, filled the bath up and put them in. Mum was still resting. Then I think we must have forgotten about them and just got on with having our tea. Next thing we knew, we were in bed and Dad was yelling the house down. He'd got back from work, had his dinner then turned on the tap for a bath only to find it full of this green mushy stuff with black wriggly bits in it. He made do with a wash that night and we took them back next day.

The new baby finally arrived on 18 August 1942. He was two

weeks late. Dad had taken a week off from work to be there. When the midwife shut the door of Mum's bedroom, Derek and I just sat on the stairs and listened. We knew exactly what was going on. We'd had our birds and bees talk with the doctor. Of course when we heard what really happened we were well and truly shocked. It was even more unlikely than a gooseberry bush. The midwife had arrived at half-past eleven and by two Denis was born. He was named after the doctor who delivered him. The other Dennises we knew had two 'n's, but not this doctor. Mum had got everything ready, she'd crotcheted a beautiful white shawl and a little first outfit, but the midwife couldn't find them. Denis had to wear something, so she found a red and white check tablecloth in the chest on the landing and put him in that. How we all laughed. He looked so funny with his shock of red-blonde curls poking out of that tablecloth.

Two hours after Denis was born the sirens went and we all rushed down to the shelter. Talk about timing. It was the very first air raid we'd had in Edgware. No sooner had the All Clear gone than Mum was in the kitchen making dinner. My dad nearly had a fit.

'Get back into bed, Lillian.'

'Don't be so silly, Will. I've had a baby, not an illness.'

Halfway down the allotments there was a huge old tree, perfect for a tree-house. It was so big that even I couldn't get up it on my own so we made a rope-ladder by plaiting string until we had a good thick plait. The cross pieces we made the same way. Derek couldn't climb so we had to lift him up. I was always a bit worried that he might have a fit but he never did. The floor was a platform of planks nailed together with long nails I'd got from home. We put up shelves for the larder and there would be tins of fruit cocktail, a tin of condensed milk. Everyone would bring some bread and jam or whatever they liked. We might buy a fruit pie which we'd break up into sections and have a mouthful each. Sometimes we'd do a show. One of the girls would tap-dance and I might sing.

Shows were what I loved most. I even did them in the front

garden. I put on an old white wedding dress, put chairs and cushions on the lawn and charged children a farthing to come and listen to me sing. Opera I called it. The music hall was what Mum and Dad liked but Nan had taken me to an opera, *Carmen*, and ever since I'd had this idea I could be an opera singer. Or if I wasn't good enough I could always marry one.

We'd use old clothes for dressing up but for one show Derek needed long trousers. Boys didn't wear long trousers then, they wore short trousers, made of the same itchy stuff, but which only reached down to the knees. Luckily I remembered Dad had a suit which he never wore. We could borrow that. The trousers were far too long so I folded them over so that Derek wouldn't trip up, but they didn't stay tucked up. By the time we got home they were caked in mud. You could pick off the lumps of clay. I tried brushing them but it was no good. The only thing to do was to hang them in the wardrobe and hope Dad didn't notice. Nothing happened for a while as he always wore his uniform. But a few weeks later we were all going to the theatre and he'd decided to wear his suit. Then came the voice I knew so well. The only person who called me by my second name.

'Pamela, come up here.'

They went to the theatre, I didn't.

We had nails hammered into the branches of the tree-house for cups and the tin opener and one day I slipped and caught my eye. Clifford Pullen wrapped my head in an old sheet and led me home. It should have been stitched, but I wouldn't go to hospital. The last time I'd been I hadn't got out for three months. I've still got the scar and my eyebrow has never really grown back properly. But with Derek the way he was, I knew better than to cry over nothing. I knew I had to be that much stronger to look after him.

On 1 January 1943, just after our second Christmas at Edgware, Dad's call-up papers came. Derek said he didn't want him to go and that he could hide under the floorboards so no one could find him. Dad explained that they needed more soldiers so they had to take younger ones and older ones. He left for training in Aldershot the day after his thirty-eighth birthday in May. We thought it was the beginning of the end, but it was just the end of the beginning. After Dad had gone it felt like the war was going on for ever.

We knew all the shapes and sounds of German aircraft but we never saw them in Edgware. What we did see were allied planes. Not long after we'd left Blackfriars the Japanese had bombed Pearl Harbor and soon after that the Americans came into the war. Edgware was only a few miles from Hendon airport, which had been turned into an American air base. Over the last year we had got used to seeing GIs queuing for the cinema in Edgware or Burnt Oak. Flying Fortresses and Liberators had joined the Spitfires and Lancasters and Hurricanes on the ceiling of Derek's bedroom which was covered with model aeroplanes that he would make with Dad. The German ones all had red cotton wool coming out of the tail.

Every evening about half-past four, 'our boys' would set off on bombing raids into Belgium and Holland and as we lay on the lawn, knees bent up and our legs swinging back and forth, Derek and I would watch as they tipped their wings to us. They flew very low and we knew they could see us. We would count them out and count them back the next morning. If they came back early and we were still in bed, I would rush to the window and try and get the numbers. When some didn't come back, we would make little crosses out of balsa wood left over from the model kits. I would cut them and Derek would rub them round with sandpaper and I'd help him glue them together. If we knew the number of the plane that had been lost, we'd mark that on. Then we'd stick them in the ground, one for each one lost. Our own war memorial. If there were clouds we'd lie on our backs and imagine that the dead pilots were angels sitting on the clouds and watching us.

Months and months went by. All people could talk about was the invasion, the invasion. But it never seemed to happen. Then, when it did on 6 June 1944, nothing seemed to happen either. The dads, including ours, still didn't come back. The only change was Hitler's secret weapon. There had been lots of talk about it, but no one really seemed to know. Then all of a sudden we did and it was more frightening than anything we'd had before because you had no real warning. We called it the doodlebug, shaped like a plane but with no pilot. It just stopped when the fuel ran out. Then down it would glide to earth without a noise, until it hit something and, bang! There was nothing you could do.

One evening in October, when Dad was home on leave we all went to spend the night with Mrs Doe, who'd found us the house and who didn't live far away. Next morning as we walked back to our place Flossie began to growl. Something was up, she knew. Then I knew it too. There it was, that familiar smell. Dust, fire. Bomb.

A doodlebug had landed in the gardens between Pembroke Place and the next road. Twelve houses were destroyed. Ours was one of them. The shell was still there but everything inside was shattered. You couldn't live in it. It had happened at about eight o'clock the night before, 5 October. There had been a warning, but only about four minutes. Most people had had time to get to their shelters, but six people had died including a mother who'd gone back to fetch her newborn baby from upstairs after putting her other children under the Morrison shelter, a thing like a metal rabbit hutch, in the kitchen. And my friend Eileen, whose dad worked for Rowntree's Fruit Gums.

CHAPTER SIX

D erek and I just stood there and stared. We didn't cry. I don't even think we were surprised. In some strange way we might even have expected it. It was just what happened. Nobody said anything much. What was there to say? The Does' house wasn't far, so we all just turned round and walked back. It was lucky Dad was on leave. He put the word out and within a week he'd been offered a flat just the other side of the Elephant and Castle. A fortnight later we were back in London.

Although we'd been away for three years, we'd never lost touch with Blackfriars. With rationing you had to register with one particular grocer, like you do with doctors, and we'd always stayed with Anne and George Colman whose shop was down an alley just opposite Priory Buildings. The Colmans were friends, which came in handy when coupons were running thin. As Derek didn't eat meat, we all shared his ration and he got our cheese in return. It still wasn't enough, and shopping at George and Anne's there would always be another 2 ounces of cheese or a couple of extra rashers of bacon. Cheese, potatoes and carrots were all Derek lived on, plus Shredded Wheat and milk. Milk was one thing we never went short of. At school we'd have those little bottles at playtime and during the holidays we'd go up and fetch them.

While Dad was still at London Bridge, he would do the shopping once a week. After his call-up it was down to us. Every Friday we'd take the pushchair with Denis in it and take the Northern Line to Waterloo. From there it was only a seven-minute walk up Webber Street to Blackfriars Road and the Colmans' shop. Going back to Blackfriars made Mum come alive. It wasn't that she didn't like Edgware or hadn't made any friends, but Blackfriars was where she was born. For her it was a chance to hang up her pinny and put her glad rags on. We would always stay and have a cup of tea with George and Anne round the back and then we'd pop in to see some other friends. Lily was one. Lily was born without any arms and did everything with her feet. It was incredible what she could do. I was fascinated just to watch her. She'd not long had a baby and would even do his nappy with her feet.

When Mum first saw the flat in Hillingdon Street she was broken-hearted.

'What on earth made them put us in this dump?'

'Never mind, my love, we will find something else soon.'

But we didn't.

I hated it. Derek hated it. It was vile. After Edgware it was like the slums. All Derek wanted was his stream. All I wanted was to run away. But in some ways it was good to be back in the land of pie and mash. Hillingdon Street was just off the Walworth Road, about a mile to the south of where we used to live. It was one of the worst bombed streets in the area. The house next door was just like a black walnut shell. The stairs were still there but they went up to nothing and being a daredevil my great trick was soon 'tightrope walking' across the burnt beams.

We were back to living in a flat, but at least it was big. It looked nothing from the front but it went back and back. We had four bedrooms, plus a sitting-room and a living-room next to the kitchen. But as there was no electricity and no bathroom it was back to gaslights and the same old tin bath, which like Nan's dressing-table and Joan's roller-skates seemed to have supernatural protection from the Germans.

It was also back to shelters. There was an Anderson shelter in the garden which we shared with the Austins from the flat down-stairs. There were four narrow bunks between six of us and the Austins didn't like children. Derek and I shared the top one and Mum and Denis had the one underneath. But often ours was empty because of the chickens.

The chickens came from East Street market, the other side of Walworth Road to Hillingdon Street, where Derek and I would spend hours just wandering around. The market was wonderful, just like before the war, with everyone shouting out what bargains they had. One day we saw this man selling chicks. Derek was very careful with his goody money, always saving it up, hoarding it you might say, usually to buy little presents for Mum and Dad. But when he saw these chicks he had to have them. He already had one chicken. June she was called and he'd got her in Edgware. June had belonged to some people across the road in Pembroke Place and one afternoon, Derek was hanging around when this neighbour came over for a bit of a gossip and was telling Mum how her chicken had broken its leg and that rather than waste it they were going to have it for dinner. Derek didn't like the sound of that. The thought of anything dying always upset him, so he said could he buy it for 1/6d, which was a lot in those days. The neighbour said, well, if it means that much to you then you can have it. So he collected this bird with the broken leg, which was white, and took it upstairs. Mum was worried that it would die on him. Its feathers were all smeared with blood and it didn't look long for this world, she said. Next thing Derek's down again and the chicken, June, had a great bandage around it. He'd made a splint with a matchstick. We didn't think it would last the night but it lived for about another six years. It must have known Derek had saved its life because it was as faithful as a dog. It didn't live outside, it was a pet, and at night perched on Derek's bedpost, where there was a tray to catch the droppings. It sounds rather strange now but Nan had had a tame chicken in Loman Street that just wandered around the house, so perhaps it was quite common then. June finally died when she couldn't push out an egg that was bigger than a Size 1 in Tesco's. Derek tied the egg with a black ribbon and kept it on his window-sill, in remembrance.

There was a chicken run in the bombed-out garden next door. Dad had dug it over and planted it up before he went away. Our own garden was taken up with the Anderson shelter. He put in everything you'd want, onions, broccoli, potatoes, and left me instructions about what to do with them. He hadn't touched the chicken run. So the chicks went in there. One day a cockerel, a Rhode Island Red, came wandering down the street, so we tore up an old crust and put it on the pavement and while he was eating it, grabbed hold of him and put him in with the rest. Stray animals were always around in the war. That's how we'd got Flossie, Derek's cocker spaniel in Edgware, but she died not long after we arrived in Hillingdon Street.

The chickens were Derek's new pets. We fed them on potato peelings, ends of carrot, old shells and things like that, plus they were always scraping around in the dirt. Of course Derek wouldn't stand for eating what he called 'unborn babies', so we gave most of the eggs away, except those Mum put in cakes which Derek didn't know about. Derek loved those chickens. He refused to go into the Anderson shelter unless he could take the chickens with him. Of course the Austins wouldn't stand for that. So Derek and I draped the chicken run with blackout material and we spent night after night out there. So as we could see, we had a candle in a glass chimney to stop it going out and we collected wood from bomb-sites and made a fire so that the chickens wouldn't get cold.

That winter was the coldest since records began, they said, and to make it worse there was a flu epidemic. Derek was the first to get it. He was too ill to go down to the shelter and anyway Mum said she didn't think the Austins would thank us for his germs. So we just stayed upstairs and once again 'took our chance'. As well as doodlebugs there were now V2s, rockets that were completely silent until they hit the ground and exploded. We found out later that they only took four minutes to reach London from Holland where they were launched, so it was no wonder there was no warning. They killed hundreds of people. There was nothing you could do about them.

One day not long before Christmas an incendiary hit the roof of our house. The first we knew was a great crash as Derek's ceiling fell down on top of him. He was covered in rubble and plaster but otherwise all right. He was still ill and moved into Mum's bed until the roof was mended. Then Denis came down with the flu, then Mum, until they were all in bed and I was the only one who could do anything. There was nothing much in the larder, except for some bottled pears from the tree out the back which Mum had done in saccharin, and potatoes from the next-door garden. But the ground was so hard I hardly got any up. The worst thing was not having money for coal. Dad's army pay came in an order book, which only Mum could cash. He had written to us from Scotland but that was all we knew. I didn't know who to ask for help. The Austins downstairs weren't the kind of people you could ask for anything.

Then a girl I knew from school told me her mum had been helped by the SSAFA, the Soldiers', Sailors' and Airmen's Families Association. She found the number and I went to the box round the corner and phoned them. Two days later there was an American jeep outside our window with the driver beeping his horn and Dad sitting next to him. They'd called his regiment and arranged compassionate leave. He'd been in Scotland with the Americans and he didn't come empty-handed. We knew they had more money than our boys but this was like finding treasure. Our eyes were out on stalks. There were tins of fruit, tins of Spam, powdered milk, chocolate and even caviar which I'd never even heard of before, but with my liking for vinegar, I soon got a real taste for it. Fish eggs sounds horrible but for me caviar is out of this world. But there was no short cut to getting coal. Dad gave me the money and I went off with the pram down to the coal market. I queued for four hours and got half a sack.

It was just before Christmas, and one of the presents Dad had brought for Mum and me, which he'd got from the Americans, was nylon stockings. At school we had to wear thick woollen lisle ones, a horrible beige colour. It was part of the uniform. White blouse, blue gymslip and a yellow sash. You could get nylons on the black market, but they cost about 10/- a pair, and that was a fortune. But the best Christmas present was having our father home again.

When he heard about the chickens Dad went mad. He gave them to a man up the road for a promise to let us have a few eggs in return. As far as the shelter was concerned, from then on there was to be no argument, we had to go underground. In the early days of the blitz, they turned everyone away from the tube. But it didn't work. People just bought tickets as if they were going to go somewhere, and just didn't come up again. Now with the V2s, the tube was the only place you were safe. Some of them were properly organized with bunks, like Kennington and the Oval. We tried those two first, but they were full to bursting. That first night we travelled up and down the Northern Line with Dad just looking for somewhere where there was room. We ended up at Leicester Square, which was about five stops away. Even this was jam-packed but as we walked up the platform, a woman said she could make a bit of space by her, but only for three. Dad said that was all right as he wouldn't be staying, and Denis was still a baby and didn't count. So Dad and I put down the ground sheet and arranged the blankets. There was a white line drawn about three feet from the edge and you didn't move over it because trains were still coming through and this was Leicester Square and people were still getting on and getting off, going to the cinema or dancing, especially dancing. Dad was in uniform and people in uniform weren't allowed to go down the shelters so he spent the night up top. It was his last night with us and the next morning I saw him off at London Bridge. So many dads had died since D-Day. And I remember wondering if I'd ever see him again.

From then on we went to Leicester Square most nights. We would arrive at about five. Everyone was regulars, so our places were saved. All I had to do was collect our bedding from upstairs and settle down on the platform for the night. We never took much with us, just a bottle of water and a Thermos of tea. Someone near us had a little stove where you could boil a kettle. Everything was shared. I think it was about half-past ten when the last train had gone through and only then could we spread out over the platform, over the white line. Mum would lie holding Denis, then Derek in the middle and me on the outside.

The first train was called the ghost train. It would come through at about five o'clock in the morning. There was no one in it but it meant we had to get up, easier said than done in the case of Derek. I would pull him along the ground on his blanket and only when he saw the escalators would he jump off. Then I'd dress him and while Mum was seeing to Denis I would tie the bedding up like a bale of laundry and take it up top where it was kept. They'd give you a ticket and you'd collect it again when you came back. It cost 1/- a week. On a Wednesday Mum would take it home for washing and we would lug a clean lot down that night. There were no sleeping-bags, only sheets and blankets. But it was so hot down there you didn't need much. In fact you fried.

On our way home one morning we saw that the pub on the corner of our road had been hit. Everyone was killed, including the landlady's new-born twins. The laundry was just around the corner and when I took our washing in, there were these laundry bags lying on the counter. I was waiting to hand ours over when a man came in. He'd come for the bodies, he said, and picked the bags up off the counter. It was only then I realized they were the dead babies. I'd seen some terrible things. There was the horse that was sliced in two. It was at the beginning of the blitz. This horse and cart were sheltering from an air raid under a railway bridge. But a piece of shrapnel flew in and split the horse in half. I was sheltering there as well, and it happened in front of me. One side of the horse fell on the left of the road, the other fell on the right while the driver just sat there holding the reins. The stench was terrible. When the raid was over I ran home. I couldn't stop crying. I told Derek what I'd seen. He said it would be all right.

'We can just go back with a needle and thread and sew the horse back together.'

Then there was the time I saw a woman running down the street with a plate of glass right through her. Derek was with me that time. I don't know what happened to her. But she seemed like a mad woman. Her eyes not seeing anything. Just running. But those two little bags like lumpy pillowcases, with blood oozing out finished me off. I left our washing and ran. I don't know what happened to it or whether we ever saw it again. But after that I couldn't eat or sleep for a week.

The Leicester Square shelter had a life of its own. There was the black market. Men would come into the shelter with suitcases which would be full of things like chickens, tea, sugar, butter, not to mention nylons. But the prices were quite beyond Mum's purse. A joint that you might get at the butchers for 1/6d they'd be charging £3 for. What she did buy was extra coupons. You sometimes had the money but not the coupons. Clothes rationing had been going on for three years and they didn't go far, especially if you had three growing children like Mum did.

Sometimes I'd go up top to get a pennyworth of chips for me and Derek from the fish shop in Charing Cross Road. There was always a Military Policeman standing at the entrance to check up on the troops. There was one I really liked. He was very appealing, about nineteen or twenty, but although I was tall for my age, I was still only thirteen. But any excuse and I was up chatting with him. I probably went up there more for the chat than the chips. He would put me on the escalator and say, 'Now, young lady, no more up tonight.' I often wonder what happened to him.

A bit of me might have been a young lady but most of me was still tomboy. I was taller than all the boys my age and if it came to a race I could beat anyone around our block which was about half a mile. After school we would play cricket with the stumps chalked up on a brick air-raid shelter in the road. I wasn't much good at hitting but could I run. The first time a boy tried to kiss me was at a friend's thirteenth birthday party. It was the spring and Dad had a few days' leave. She didn't have a cake so Dad had made one for her. What with I don't know, something like carrots and condensed milk. He was never short of ideas. I had always loved parties and party games but that afternoon we played something called Postman's Knock. It was a game where you ended up kissing someone and I didn't like it. Next day this boy whose name was Stephen, knocked at our door and we went out and sat on the wall with some other friends. This time the game was Dare Truth Kiss or Promise. I didn't like that either. It was the same thing. You always ended up having to kiss someone. Soon after that there was a different boy called Kevin, quite good looking, with a bit of Italian in him. He knew my roller-skates (Joan's) were broken and said his father would weld them for me and he asked me up to his house for dinner. His dad would bring me back, he said. But even with the promise of mended skates I said no. I was happy in my little world and I wasn't about to let any nasty boys into it.

I lived in those roller-skates. In spite of all they'd been through they were still in good working condition. After Dad came back with the Americans, I had made Derek what we called Derek's Jeep. It was an old wooden box at the back, with a piece of wood with string attached to steer with at the front. The wheels at the front were small, the ones at the back were big, off an old pram. In spite of its name there was no hill at Hillingdon Street, but with my roller-skates on, I could push the 'jeep' really fast and we'd rattle down the road. I once took Denis with me to get fish and chips, skating all the way. It wasn't till we were back sitting down and Mum said, 'Where's Denis?' that I realized I'd left him in his pram outside the shop. I was so busy thinking of my tummy I'd forgotten all about him.

'Those skates are coming off for errands. I'm fed up with seeing them under the table on your feet when we're having tea. You only seem to take them off when you go to bed.'

Then Derek had his three pennyworth.

'She wouldn't even do that if you didn't look.'

By now Dad was in France. And like everyone else we spent all our spare time listening to the news. I used to listen for the secret messages. Things like when the newsreader would say, 'Hazel is doing well.' You could tell from the slow way he spoke the words, each one quite separate, that it was nothing to do with anyone called Hazel. Radios needed electricity and for people like us who didn't have any, there was a special cable running from house to house which you would plug into, run by Radio Rentals. You had to pay for it, but not much. That was at the back. In the front room we had an accumulator, it was white, about the size of a shoe box and worked like a car battery which we would get charged up over the road. Apart from the news our favourite programme was *Dick Barton*, special agent. We were always allowed to stay up for that.

Although he was now eleven and tall for his age, far taller than our little mother, Derek was never sent on errands, not even to fetch the accumulator. Instructions were a bit much for him. We did try once or twice, but as he could never remember what he was sent for it wasn't worth the bother. Also although his fits seemed to be dying down, we were always worried to let him out alone in case he had one and nobody knew what do do. One afternoon in April, Mum sent me over the road to buy a pot of jam for tea. I was just crossing the pavement when a plane came out of nowhere. I knew it wasn't English by the noise. British planes roared, German planes sounded more like hiccups, as if they would be lucky to make it back to the airport. We all knew what to do, you had to lie down on the ground and put your arms under your chest to protect it. So that's what I did. I was flat on the pavement so couldn't see anything but suddenly the plane dived down and the machine-gun opened up, ratatatatatatat. It shot all the way along the pavement and the last one fell at my big toe. I just stayed there, I didn't move even after it had gone, not until I heard Mum's voice. Of course, everyone ran out to see if I was all right.

'She's very lucky, the bullet stopped at her big toe.'

Of course, after that I was a real hero with my friends wanting to know what it was like, being shot at. The plane had just been one on its own. Nobody knew why they came. Some said they were reconnaissance planes taking photographs of the damage the V2s had done. When Dad finally arrived home he dug the bullet that had just missed me out of the pavement. It's lost now. And if you want to know, being shot at turns you ice-cold.

Something like that happening frightened us more than the blitz in some ways. The war was nearly over, yet this could just come out of nowhere. Like they say, out of a clear blue sky.

The Elephant and Castle had always been our Piccadilly. It had everything. It's terrible what they've done to it now. There were loads of cinemas, the Trocadero had been the largest in London before it was bombed. Going to the pictures was something that everyone did, even in the middle of the blitz. It was about the only think left that made you forget what was going on outside. Not for long perhaps. But it was better than nothing. Sometimes Derek and I went on our own, sometimes we'd go with my cousin Juliet, who I only got to know when we moved to Hillingdon Street. We would wait till we were out of sight of the flat and then out would come the lipstick and the powder which I hid in the bottom of my handbag because Mum didn't approve. Then off we'd go, arm in arm, down the Walworth Road up to the Elephant, dressed up to look like film stars. No more ribbons in my hair. Now I rolled it up in the front like Betty Grable. The back went in a thing like a crocheted hair-net, called a snood. All the rage then, which Mum made for us.

Derek always came with us to the pictures, even when I went with Juliet. The last thing most of my friends wanted was to be with their brothers. Brothers were like the enemy. Brothers were a pain. Always wanting to do things their way. Always wanting to be boss. Derek wasn't like that. He always did what he was told. He was quiet. He didn't talk back. He wasn't like other boys. And my friends seemed to know it. They treated him more like somebody's baby. They petted him. Sometimes he was so quiet I forgot he was there. Except that I always knew he was really. There was still so much he couldn't do or understand. Even things like crossing the road you couldn't let him do on his own. And since Denis had been born, Mum didn't have the time. With Derek you had to be patient. Rushing him only made things worse. That's when his temper flared up. It was just frustration really. But I understood him. I could calm him down. We'd always been together and it wouldn't have felt right leaving him behind. After all, what difference did it make to me? He couldn't go anywhere by himself and I was used to taking him. He was no trouble and Juliet didn't seem to mind.

We usually went on a Saturday afternoon and had to be back by a certain time. There were still no streetlights but the blackout restrictions had stopped by then and we could use a torch. Mum would pay for the tickets but we'd spend our own money on nuts and pumpkin seeds. There were no ice-creams, just peanut butter in a cornet which was vile. Mum would give us sandwiches of bread and jam and a bottle of coloured water which we shared. Sometimes she and Denis came too. I remember us all going to see *Bambi*. I used to take him to all kinds of films, most of which he probably didn't understand but *Bambi* – Derek cried his eyes out. He cried all the way home.

Films had always been my passion, ever since Nan took me up to see one of Shirley Temple's at the Trocadero when Derek was still a baby. But when I told Mum that I wanted to be an usherette, she hit the roof. I suppose I thought that working in the cinema I'd get to meet the film stars. I loved losing myself in the adventures, perhaps I even thought I would have adventures there myself. Because when you went into the cinema you went into a different world.

It was about April when we heard that Dad was coming home. He'd been injured. The letter didn't say how, or how bad. It turned out to be his rear end and not serious. When he got back Mum used to make jokes about it, but it just meant he had to do a lot of standing up.

Once the V2s stopped then we knew that Germany was being defeated. We were playing out in the street more. Some of the dads started to come home, injured like ours, or prisoners of war. There'd be Union Jacks around the front door and banners saying 'Welcome Home Dad' and even if you didn't know them, that night you'd be in there celebrating with all the other mums and dads. Rationing was worse than it had ever been, but they'd rake up the food from somewhere. We'd all help towards it. We might say, you can have half a pound of sugar. There were all these little parties going on, building up to the big celebration on 8 May, VE day, when the whole street, the whole of London, had gone mad with bunting and flags. The war was over and so was my childhood.

CHAPTER SEVEN

The war was over. It had lasted nearly half my life. You can't live through such a violent time without it changing you, but it changed me the opposite way to what you might think. It taught me tolerance, understanding, not to have hatred. The worst thing was losing my sister. Joan was much cleverer than me, not because she was older, Joan was different. Joan had brains to burn. She had left Friar Street school and moved on to her next school two years early. If Joan had lived she'd have made something of her life. But she never looked down on me, just like I never looked down on Derek. We were good friends as well as being sisters and we'd done so much together. She was only twelve when that shelter was hit.

As the war went on you noticed it was never people who had lost loved ones who were vengeful. If you'd lost someone yourself, you could never wish such suffering on anyone else. It's not wars that kill people, it's governments. If governments want wars then they should be like chess, not use us humans to fight their battles. No. The war taught me that life is too short to fight and argue. I can't hate anybody. God is the only one who can set the punishment. That's why I feel no hatred about Derek.

England had won the war, Labour was in, and life for working people could only get better, they said. But after the street parties stopped, things carried on much as before. In fact, they got worse. Bread was never rationed during the war, but it was after. The meat ration was cut. At one time I remember it was only 8d a week. Everything was make-do, makeshift and mend. But no one ever mended our roof.

Dad was still in the army. He wasn't demobbed until a year later, when we were miles away from Hillingdon Street. He was a chef in what he called 'the cage', a prison for German officers, but he wasn't allowed to tell us where it was. Dad wasn't vengeful either and he got on well with the prisoners. One of them even gave him a little box with two jewels in it and a note saying thank you and that if Dad ever went to Germany he should get in touch.

In November 1945 we left Southwark for good. George Jennings and Dad had known each other since they were born. Before the war he and Uncle George, as we called him, were forever going off on their bikes. He'd married his wife Anne during the war and we'd only met her once or twice. George was a mechanic, doing well for himself, he said, and even had his own car. One Sunday they dropped in at Hillingdon Street for tea and said they had this big house in Norbury with more room than they needed and what about us sharing it. Hillingdon Street still had only half a roof so with winter just around the corner, we went to have a look. It had everything you could want, a garden, electricity, inside toilet and a bathroom. And as Dad said, Norbury was a real step up.

Moving was a thing in itself. Everything went in the removal van except us and the cats. Since Dad got rid of the chickens, Derek had been looking after five strays and they'd all had kittens. We now had eighteen. There was no way Derek was going to leave them behind, so we put them into two big packing cases and they came with us on the number 16 tram. What George hadn't said was that he had a Dalmatian, called Bob. He was vicious. He'd go for anybody. When we opened the cat boxes, Bob began to bark and chased the cats up the curtains. It was nearly a week before they calmed down.

Norbury was about twelve miles from central London, halfway between Streatham and Croydon. But there was no way of telling where one ended and the other began, except for the Common on one side of the road. It was quite hilly but Norbury didn't feel like the country like Edgware did, but then it wasn't as far out. Norbury had grown up around the station but it felt like living in a village. Everyone was so friendly. Plus there were all the shops you needed, three pubs and the Rex cinema. But for a night out people would still go to Streatham or Croydon, which were only ten minutes away by bus.

Fairview Road ran along the back of the shops opposite the station. Number 1 was the first up on the left. We didn't split the house, but both families had rooms that were 'private'. The Bentleys had the front lounge and the Jenningses had the dining-room with French windows that led on to the garden. Mum, Dad and Denis shared the big bedroom at the front, I had the box-room over the hallway and George and Anne had the back bedroom. Derek slept in the lounge. We all shared the kitchen and the breakfast room. We'd take it in turns to eat. Anne worked on the trams and was out most of the time, so the arrangement was that Mum would do the clearing up.

Derek and I both started at Norbury Manor school. But because I had only a few weeks to go before leaving, I was really a helper. It was the same as at Edgware. Nobody wanted to know us. They treated us like scum, except for a girl called Lillian and she's been my friend now for forty-eight years. At least I didn't have long to go. You left school at fourteen in those days. Unlike Derek I hadn't had long gaps away, but with having spent so much time out of my own class sitting with him, reading and writing still didn't come easy. When I think now how little I was helped, I see red. I now know that I'm dyslexic, but then nobody knew or even cared. At least I could get by. Derek couldn't even write his name. All he wanted now was to be home with Mum.

But I didn't think like that in 1946. Those last few days, I couldn't wait for school to end. The world was my oyster. I imagined I would soon have so much money I wouldn't know what to do with it. But with the war over, munition factories laying everybody off, and the streets full of men in demob suits looking for work, all I could find was what I hated most, sewing.

Miss Gathercole lived about five minutes' walk from Fairview Road. She was what was called a 'court' dressmaker. The female equivalent of a tailor. She didn't make ordinary clothes, just wedding dresses, bridesmaids' dresses and evening wear. But Miss Gathercole was far from being a walking advertisement for her slinky silks and satins. She was small and bulky and looked like

Humpty Dumpty. Aunt Rose had taught me to use a treadle sewing machine. She had a real knack with a needle and made all her own clothes and dresses for Joan and me, not to mention costumes for the plays we did at the George. They were beautiful and Aunt Rose was a lot to live up to. There were four of us apprentices and Miss Gathercole was very strict. We weren't allowed to talk and the only sound in that room was the sound of the treadles or the sound of the brides complaining as I jabbed a pin in them just to hear them scream. If I thought work would be better than school I was wrong. It was worse. Far worse. I would always be the one to make the tea in the morning and afternoon, just to get out of that room because of Miss Gathercole's leg. It was ulcerated and even though it was as bandaged up as an Egyptian mummy it always smelt something terrible. Now I feel sorry for her, but to a young girl the smell was so vile, I just couldn't stand it.

You were supposed to stay at Miss Gathercole's for five years. The wages were 13/- a week. I gave Mum 12/- and kept a shilling for myself. It was nothing even then, but you put up with it because it was training and you knew at the end of those five years you'd be a 'court' dressmaker and could get a job in any of the top couture salons.

Now Derek was at school on his own, without me to keep an eye on him, it wasn't long before there was trouble. The headmaster Mr Bonnetto knew about his epilepsy and Dad had explained what to do when he had a fit and Derek never went anywhere without the stick in his pocket which had to be put between his teeth to stop him biting his tongue off.

One day, not long after I'd started at Miss Gathercole's, he came back from school crying and with his knuckles bleeding. Mr Bonnetto had caned him for being late. Now he went to school on his own and didn't have me to tell him to hurry up. And at Norbury Manor being late meant getting the cane. But as I said, time had no meaning for Derek. It wasn't that he couldn't tell the time. I'd taught him myself and Dad had even got him a watch. Being in the army, Dad was a great one for being punctual. And whenever we did anything, we'd always had to be ready ten minutes before the off, but Derek just didn't understand.

'What are you worried about, Sis?' he'd say when I told him to hurry up. 'They'll still be there.'

Dad was all for marching up to the school and saying something, but Derek said no.

'Don't interfere, Dad. It'll only make things worse.'

But it wasn't just the teachers. Not being able to read and write made him a laughing stock with the other boys. Although he wasn't the only one by a long chalk, with them it was just because of the war, not because they weren't up to it. They were fly enough to hide it. Derek wasn't, so it was easy for the others to take the rise.

But we didn't know it had got so bad until that April when the school board officer, the 'kid catcher' came. Derek had been 'hopping the wag' for three weeks and we knew nothing about it. My friend Lillian had got a job as a mother's help to some children who lived near Derek's school. She had a soft spot for him and couldn't bear to see him crying his eyes out and had felt so sorry for him that she'd taken to hiding him all day until it was time to come home.

The school board decided he should go to another school, some sort of special school in Ingram Road in Thornton Heath. It was further away, about ten minutes' bus ride, but not so much would be expected of him, they said, plus he would be given extra lessons for reading. He moved at the beginning of the summer term. I think Derek was a bit happier there, especially as he soon made friends with a boy called Philip Stevens, who lived on the way. Like Derek, Philip was a bit slow. But there was nothing wrong with his brother and sister Robert and Wendy. But Dad didn't like this new school and complained that he wasn't learning anything and it was too far away. The next term he was back again at Norbury Manor.

One day when everyone except Mum and Denis was out there was a knock at the door. It was the landlord. He had come for the three years' back rent the Jenningses owed him. Mum was completely taken aback as George and Anne had always made out the house was theirs. She told him she knew nothing about it, but that our rent, the rent she paid George and Anne, was up to date and showed him her rent book to prove it. The man said they'd never been able to get near the door before as Bob, who could be quite vicious, would be set on anyone who came through the garden gate.

Now Mum found out not only that they didn't own the house, but worse, they had no right to sublet. We hadn't been there that long and she was in a terrible state waiting for Dad to come home. Dad just didn't believe it.

'There's got to be some simple explanation.'

There was a simple explanation. What the landlord said was true. When Dad tried to get some sense from his old friend George, Anne turned on him and for the first time showed herself in her true colours.

'It's none of your business,' she nearly spat the words. 'You had no right to open the door to him.'

From then on things went from bad to worse. Anne turned really nasty. Dad tried to sort it out with George but he just shrugged his shoulders. It made us very uncomfortable. The house was big, but not that big.

What was big was Mum. It was fibroids the doctor said and he gave her an appointment for the hospital. A few weeks later Mum said to Dad, 'Funny fibroids, Will, they're moving.'

It wasn't fibroids at all. Mum was pregnant. She went mad. She was forty-four.

'Far too old for all that bother.'

But it had happened again. New house, new baby.

One Saturday a month or so later, it must have been about May, Dad couldn't get the front door key to work. We'd all been out for the day with friends and were tired and ready for bed. I think Denis was even asleep. He tried knocking in case George and Anne were in. But there was no reply. Luckily the front window was open, it was a lovely summer evening and no one worried about leaving windows open in those days. One by one we climbed in, first me so

I could help the others, then Derek, then Mum, then Denis was lifted up and finally Dad. He went straight to see what was wrong with the door.

'What the hell . . .'

Dad hardly ever swore.

I was right behind him. The lock hadn't jammed. Dad hadn't been able to open it because planks of wood had been nailed right across. Then he tried the door into the breakfast room but found that was locked as well. Anne and George weren't out, they were there, hiding in the back and as Dad turned the handle, Anne shouted, 'Get out, we don't want you any more.'

It gave us all a terrible start. Denis woke up and started crying and Dad sent us upstairs to get ready for bed while he and Mum tried to think. Upstairs nothing had been locked except the back bedroom. But without getting into the kitchen we had nowhere to cook. They also had the fuse box their side of the locked doors and switched our circuits off.

Next day Dad bought some coal and a leg of lamb which he tied up with string and made a spit with a dish underneath to catch the drips and put it in front of the fire to roast. For light we had two hurricane lamps. Derek and I could only see the funny side and we sang 'By the Harbour Lights', but for Mum and Dad it was dreadful. The only way to get in and out was through the front window. Mum being pregnant made it worse. We even had to empty the teapot outside in the drain. When the neighbour across the road heard what was going on, she cooked us some meals. And Mrs Leppard is the silver lining to this story. After this she became Mum's best friend.

This farce went on for nearly two months. Through the walls we would hear George and Anne rowing, and all the time Dad would be trying to get some sense out of George, but as he could only talk through the door he couldn't get him on his own. All George said was, 'Sorry, Bill. There's nothing I can do. She's the boss.'

But things couldn't go on like this for ever, especially with the baby being due.

'Climbing in and out of the window is all very well for you lot, but to put Mum and baby through all this is quite out of order.'

When it came to a toss-up between his friend and his family, family won. In spite of his pride, Dad realized that he couldn't get it sorted on his own. He knew that's what the British Legion were there for, to help people who'd been in the forces, so he decided to go and get some advice. But he got more than that. I was there when Dad and the officer climbed in. When he saw the planks on the door, he didn't say a word, just went straight outside again, checked the door was unlocked, put his foot up and smashed it open. Then with a hammer he knocked all the planks off. Dad could have done it himself but he wouldn't stand for any kind of violence and had gone on hoping that George would see sense. Also he'd been worried that we would have nowhere to live. Bad as things seemed to be, at least it was a roof over our heads. But the officer said we were not to worry.

He stayed with us till the Jenningses came home and read the riot act. Next thing we knew the Jenningses were given notice to quit for three years' non-payment of rent. As they were subletting to us, which they had no right to do, Dad was convinced we'd be shown the door too. But the British Legion organized everything with the landlord. As long as we could afford the rent, we could stay. The day they left, Derek and I were in the garden feeding the chickens and Anne Jennings picked up a brick and threw it at us and shouted, 'I curse this house and the whole family.'

Dad still didn't have a job, which was lucky considering the state of the house. The whole of the back was disgusting. The settee in the back dining-room was alive with fleas and had to be burnt. Since Derek and I had stopped taking Bob for walks, he'd hardly been out at all and the whole place stank like a toilet. It all had to be soaked in disinfectant before Dad could start decorating. But now we had the whole house for ourselves. Derek moved up into the back bedroom, which he shared with Uncle Bert, who had finally seen sense and stopped paying rent on his flat in Southwark. He'd never lived there since Dolly was killed in August 1940. For the last few years of the war he'd been in the Isle of Wight working on Pluto.

Although Derek was back at Norbury Manor, his best friend was still Philip Stevens, who he'd met at Ingram Road. With Derek and Philip being friends, and with me taking Derek to their house to play, I soon made friends with the Stevenses too. Robert, Philip's brother, was older than Derek but younger than me, their sister Wendy was quite a few years older. Mr Stevens had not been home long. He'd been a Japanese prisoner of war and looked terrible. He couldn't get about at all and as he liked to be with his children, we would often go over to their place. He looked much older than he was and the only way he could eat was to suck things through a straw. It was nice that Derek had his own real friend now and Philip was a good friend to him, right up until the end.

Just after Christmas, on 28 December 1946, Roger was born. Mum had a difficult time of it, and she had to be taken to hospital. He was what used to be called a mongol, what they now call Down's syndrome. But I still don't know if that was right because Mum said he was like he was because his leg had got caught when he was being born which had stopped oxygen going to his brain. There was nothing wrong with the way he looked. He was a beautiful bouncy baby with a mass of ginger hair, the only thing wrong with him that I could see was his wheezy chest.

Meanwhile I'd begun to have my fill of Miss Gathercole's. One day we were round at the Stevenses and I was saying how much I hated it when Wendy said there was a job going where she worked, at a radio-component workshop in Croydon. It was a good laugh, she said, and they had the radio on all the time. That did it. I had the interview on the Thursday, told Miss Gathercole I was leaving on the Friday and started on the Monday.

After Anne and George had left, Dad had turned the garden shed into a workshop. He built on a whole extra bit so it ran right across the bottom of the garden. It was full of electrical parts, bits of radios and televisions, given him by Mr Fife down the road who, like Dad, put together radios and things as a hobby. Derek and I used to help him at weekends. It was more fun than sewing dresses. It probably helped me in getting the job as it meant I'd had a bit of experience.

Derek's fits were getting worse. It was another accident that set them off again. One morning we were just having breakfast when we heard this crash. We rushed out to the hall and there was Derek, at the bottom of the stairs, out cold again. One of the banisters had broken and he'd fallen downstairs and knocked himself out. Although we never knew for certain which happened first, the fit probably started at the top of the stairs and then he broke the banister with his flailing around. He was still bad when the doctor arrived. He gave Derek an injection, I don't know what it was. He was thirteen. But after that he was on phenobarbitone morning and night and if he got one of his 'heads', then we'd give him another pill. He wasn't allowed to have the pills himself. Phenobarbitone is a dangerous drug that works by depressing the central nervous system. He couldn't be trusted with them. He might take too many or forget to take them at all.

I don't know how much good they did, whether they stopped him having so many fits. But they did seem to help his 'heads' – at least they didn't seem to last quite so long. But they also made him even slower, even more 'spaced out', as we'd say these days. I've never had bad headaches and he was never very good at explaining, but I think his were like migraines. When he got one there was nothing he could do except take one of his little blue pills, lie down on his bed and go to sleep. After a couple of hours I would take him up a cup of tea and he'd be all right.

At the end of that summer term in July 1947 Derek was sent back to Ingram Road school. He'd only been back at Norbury Manor for two terms. The reason they gave to get rid of him this time was that there had been some sort of trouble with a younger boy and they wanted to split them up. And this time, to avoid trouble with Dad, they got an official magistrates' order. It was just before his fourteenth birthday. He still had another year of school to go. Derek didn't mind going back to Ingram Road, as he was with his friend Philip, but Dad did.

That November, even before he was a year old, Roger died. His chest had always been bad ever since he was born. His lungs were all clogged up and we would have to keep steaming kettles, sometimes just water on its own, sometimes with Friars Balsam to ease his breathing. Someone had to stay with him all the time. During the day his cot would be downstairs so Mum, Dad and me could take turns to sit with him. You got used to the noise of him breathing and you listened out for any change. I was with him when he died. Mum had just popped out to the shops. I called Dad in from the shed and he tried to massage his heart. But it was no good. He just took one final breath and then no more. He was gone.

Derek took it very bad. He didn't like anything to die. The garden at Fairview was like a cemetery with cross after cross marking everything from chickens to cats. He would even try and save birds with broken wings and bandage them with splints like he'd done with June his pet chicken, who still slept on his bedpost and would fly on to his shoulder when he came in the front door. He'd be beside himself and think it was his fault when any animal died. Roger was his baby brother and he couldn't make out why he had to die. I can hear him now, asking the same thing over and over again.

'Why, Mum? Why did Roger have to die, Mum?'

'He's gone to Nan and Joan, son. He was too beautiful for this world.'

Mum took it bad too. She had the little white coffin upstairs on her bed, with him lying in it. After the funeral she still didn't move his cot out of their bedroom. It was heart-breaking seeing her go to it each day, unfolding and folding his clothes.

All the neighbours sent flowers, they knew what a lovely little fellow he was. We only needed one car for the funeral. They laid the coffin in between the driver and the mourners. He was buried at Nunhead cemetery with the rest of the family. Dad said it would have been better if he'd died at birth. Mum said no.

'We must be grateful we had him to love for a little while.'

That Christmas was terrible. What made it worse was that Dad had won the latest round in the battle of the schools and Derek was to go back to Norbury Manor in January. Dad might have been pleased, but Derek wasn't. He hated Norbury Manor.

It was spring 1948. Derek was fourteen now, but he looked older. He was already taller than Dad and taller than me. He'd been taller than Mum since he was about eleven. Like with Juliet at Hillingdon Road, we'd often go out the three of us, Derek, my friend Lillian and me. Music halls were our favourite then, and they're still mine today. The Croydon Empire and the Empress theatre at Brixton were where we went. There's never been anything to touch the music hall. There was the comedian Issy Bonn, he always ended with a very sad song called 'To Mother with Love'. I could sit there and be hypnotized by his voice. Then there were the Maxes, Max Wall with the funny wigs and the leggings, big boots and frock coat. I can't remember why he made us laugh, but he did. And Max Miller. All jokes which you could take the wrong way if you'd a mind to. Max Bacon was another comedian. He told jokes in between playing the xylophone. Then there was Max Bygraves, singing the same old songs as he does now. There was Teddy Brown, a huge man weighing twenty-two stone, and Phyllis Dixie, the 'lady with the fans'. Great things as big as palms they were which she hid behind. You were supposed to think she was naked, but I don't think she was. Then there was Old Mother Riley and her daughter Kitty, and Arthur Askey and Tommy Trinder. It wasn't all comedians. There were always the 'acts', acrobats and men on unicycles, girls roller-skating, and Henry Hall's big band and his singer Betty Driver. She had a lovely voice. There's never been anyone to beat her. She's still going, behind the bar now in *Coronation Street*. There was Joan Rhodes, who used to tear telephone directories in half. But for us it was really the comedians, and top of the Bentley bill was Jimmy Jewell and Ben Wariss.

77

Then, with no warning that I can think of, came the bombshell. One afternoon when Dad and I were at work, Mum opened the door and it was two policemen. They'd got Derek with them. They said he and another boy from Norbury Manor had been arrested for stealing some bus tickets and 10/- from a conductor's till plus attempting to break into a shop.

When Dad heard he went mad.

'Why did you do it? Why, son? You know you only have to ask me if you need anything.'

'Only did it for a dare, Dad. Don't get mad.'

It was the Norbury Manor boys, he said, who were picking on him.

'They dared me, I thought if I did it they might stop taking the rise.'

On 18 March Dad, Mum, Derek and I all went up to Croydon Juvenile Court. Derek and the other boy were both fined £2 and bound over for two years. Derek was also ordered back to Ingram Road school. Dad paid the fine. But Derek got his punishment. Dad 'gated' him for three months, which meant he couldn't go out, not even with me and Lillian.

CHAPTER EIGHT

Derek finally left school in July 1948, a few days after his fifteenth birthday. Because he still couldn't read or write finding a job was never going to be easy, we knew. He liked working in the workshop, but there was a limit to what he could do if Dad wasn't there, so he mostly just helped Mum with the housework, which he'd always enjoyed, ever since Blackfriars.

By now Dad was working as an installation engineer for the Croydon Electricity Board, where he stayed until he retired, aged sixty-five. As for me, life at the electrical workshop was as good as Wendy Stevens had promised. Within six months I could do anything they put in front of me. Every day was different depending on what had to be done, from winding radar coils as fine as hair, to wiring up those red, white and blue neon barbers' poles. There were seven men and three girls and we could chat as much as we liked and usually did. It was a real home from home. The radio was on all the time, I think it made you work all the faster. You got a rhythm going. They were just the old favourites, like Bing Crosby and Frank Sinatra.

If we thought life would get easier for Derek now he'd left school, which we did, we had another think coming. It wasn't long before it happened again, the knock on the door and Derek standing there with a policeman. This time the charge was stealing tools off a building site. It was the afternoon, when only Mum and Denis were at home, so I only know what Mum told me. She said that without so much as a by your leave, not to mention a search warrant, the policeman barged straight past her upstairs to the back bedroom which Derek shared with Uncle Bert. Then, finding nothing there he went down to the shed which was full of tools, batteries on charge, broken-down radios and televisions. Dad never locked up. You didn't in those days. When Dad heard what had happened he was beside himself. I only caught the tail end of it, but he was angry all right, at Mum for having let them in, at the policeman for having ransacked his workshop and at Derek for not having more sense.

'Another dare, was it?'

'No, Dad. Just mucking about, shying at an old paint tin. We didn't take nothing.'

So next day it was back to Croydon Juvenile Court. The police had been tipped off by a woman living opposite. She hadn't seen anything special, just two boys mucking about. She just decided they were up to no good. In the court, it turned out these tools Derek and this boy were accused of stealing were only worth nineteen shillings, less than a pound. But even if they'd only been worth less than a shilling, I'd still not believe Derek took them. Not because I'm his sister, but just common sense. If Derek and this boy were going to steal tools – and Derek did know that taking something that wasn't yours was wrong – it stands to reason they'd have made themselves scarce. Not hung around in broad daylight waiting for the police to turn up. And where were these tools anyway?

To help them make up their minds, one of the magistrates asked Derek to spell 'fluorescent'. I must have seen that word every day on cardboard boxes at work for weeks, but could I spell it? No. What chance had Derek? And what sort of a question was that anyway? A chance for the magistrate to impress us all with his brains? If he'd really wanted to make fun of Derek he should have tried getting him to spell 'justice'. When I think of how people like that kept black-market spivs in business, it makes my blood boil. There's no way that a magistrate like that was living on 8d worth of meat rations a week.

Needless to say, Derek and the other boy were found guilty and remanded for further reports. Whatever these reports said (and nobody has ever found them) they were both sentenced to three years at an approved school. Three years. The magistrate said that it would be an opportunity for Derek to learn to read and write.

Uncle Bert reckoned it would be an opportunity for Derek to learn bad ways.

Kingswood Approved School was just outside Bristol. It was hard on Mum and Dad. They were determined not to let Derek think we had forgotten him and once a month they took the train from Paddington to Bristol. It was their only way of keeping an eye on him, because, as he couldn't write, he couldn't send letters. As it turned out Kingswood was not too bad. Derek settled down quickly. For once it appeared he was being treated with understanding and kindness. On their visits, Mum and Dad were allowed to stay in the Governor's house and they didn't just sit around. By the time Derek had left, Dad had wired up a hall they used as a theatre. He did everything, from start to finish, even down to a microphone, stage lighting and all the controls.

Although he was happy in himself that first year, Derek's headaches had been getting worse. Kingswood didn't seem to be doing anything about it so Mum and Dad took him to see our GP Dr Reynolds when he was home on holiday in June. She decided it was time he had more tests at Guy's. The report, by Dr James Munroe in the Department of Psychology, was sent on to Kingswood. We didn't see it then, but did later, though not till long after Derek's case was over. It is dated 11 August 1949 and says:

> There is no doubt that Derek is very backward intellectually and
> that most of this is the result of congenital lack of intelligence.
> The father thinks it was wrong to commit Derek to an approved
> school and he looked forward to having the boy at home to work
> in his electrician's business. In due time I think that would be a
> satisfactory solution.

Dr Munroe also said Derek should be examined by the Bristol Child Guidance Clinic.

Back at Kingswood Derek was sent for an EEG on 16 November 1949. This is an electroencephalogram which they use to check brain-wave patterns. They attach electrodes to the head and it picks up things like brain tumours or epilepsy. Derek had never had one before but it was medical proof of what we'd always known, that he had epilepsy. It showed up positive. He went for another one in February, and it was positive again. What we didn't realize at the time, but which again we found out later, was that they also did an IQ test on him. He came out at 66, a level described at the time as 'feeble-minded'. Now he would be called educationally subnormal. He had a reading age of only four and a half, and a mental age of about ten and a half although he was now seventeen. But, as I say, we never knew about any of this at the time. But they did.

I gave up the electrical workshop in the summer of 1949. I wouldn't have left except a job came up that I just couldn't say no to. It turned out that the sister of one of the girls at work was married to the doorman at the Streatham Astoria and he'd heard there was a vacancy going for an usherette. The deputy manager was called Mr Crossley. It was a funny interview. I sat down the other side of the desk to him, like you do and the first thing he said was 'Stand up.' So I did.

'Show me your legs.'

After the war, skimpy clothes were out and we were all wearing the 'new look' skirts which were full and well below the knee. I remember I was wearing a navy and white dress. So I did what he asked and lifted up my skirt.

'You'll be ideal.'

I didn't tell Mum or Dad about that part of the interview. Naïve as I was, I knew well enough they would disapprove. They disapproved anyway and I wasn't about to give them more ammunition. Working at the Astoria meant working on a Sunday and that was something Dad didn't believe in. Sunday was for church and family. I told him that the Astoria didn't open till 4.30 p.m. on Sundays and that I could go to church in the morning. In the end he gave in.

'If it will make you happy, Pam, then you do it.'

Dad always called me Pam, never Iris. Pam was my middle

name, but to this day I don't know why he did it. The day after the interview I bumped into Roy, the doorman, in Norbury High Street.

'Iris, I think you've got the job.'

The Streatham Astoria was a dream come true. There was a cinema in Norbury, the Rex, but it was a poky little place with none of the glamour of the Astoria which was huge, a wonderful picture palace built in the thirties. The job of the usherette was to show people to their seats. The lights didn't come up between films like they do now. You could stay in all day if you wanted to and see the programme round again. Prices depended on where you sat. The cheapest was at the front, the most expensive downstairs was back row of stalls where courting couples went. The front row of the balcony was the smartest. There were about six different prices. We each had a 'post' and we'd check the tickets as people came in and then show them where their seats were. Then we had other duties like answering the phone and telling people what was on. Or door duty, tearing tickets in half and putting them on the needle to check against the takings. Then there was selling ice-creams which was good because you made a bit extra with the commission.

We all wore uniforms, which we were given, and high-heeled shoes which we had to buy ourselves. High heels were compulsory, they were part of the image, part of the glamour of a night out at the pictures. We changed in a big dressing-room backstage, behind the screen. It was just like a proper theatre dressing-room, with mirrors and lights like ping-pong balls around them so you could see properly to do your make-up. Mr Crossley liked us to wear plenty of make-up, Max Factor Pan Cake, bright red lipstick and false eyelashes. Dad didn't approve of make-up so I hadn't used much until then. But the other girls showed me what to do, how to take the colour right down your neck, so it didn't leave a tide-mark. It ruined your uniform. The white dicky front got thick with it. You had two so you'd always take one home for washing and bring a clean one in the next day.

We kept our uniforms and shoes in lockers. Sometimes, if you were in a bit of a hurry to get away at the end of your shift, you put your uniform straight on top of what you were wearing. But if Mr Crossley found out, you were for it. Every day we'd have the parade before we went on duty, standing in a line with our hands out in front while Mr Crossley walked up and down inspecting us: the state of our nail varnish, whether our hands were clean, our hems, whether the seams on our nylons were straight. Everyone else wore suspender belts, but I couldn't stand them. I just wore garters. Then there was your hair. I wore mine down and got it done once a week by a boy called Peter whose father owned the hairdresser's across the road. He didn't charge the full amount as I was always on show and people were forever asking where I'd had it done.

After the film had started we were free to do what we liked, just so long as we were at our posts ready for the next one. A couple of us had to stay in during the film in case of emergencies. We took that in turns. Sometimes if we had time we would go back to Fairview, it was only five minutes away on the bus, or another girl's house, otherwise we would go backstage to the canteen. In the summer we might go to the Common. After I'd been there a year or so I did relief cashier work which I enjoyed. My ambition was to become head cashier because the cash desk always closed at nine. Otherwise it was half-past ten or later by the time you'd checked the seats and taken the uniform off. And then you had to get home.

My social life was definitely improving. Being an usherette you got to know the regulars. And if someone liked the look of you he soon became a regular, even if he wasn't before. The speedway boys appealed to all of us. The Wimbledon speedway track was not far and soon we were quite a crowd. Although they raced motor bikes they weren't the sort of bikes you could ride about on, but quite a few of them had cars. Then there were the ice-hockey boys from the Streatham Ice Rink. But nobody got serious. It was all good clean fun. There was Rita and Pam and Molly and Joyce and Peggy and Norman and Alan and Robert and Michael. We would go to watch them race, or dancing at the Locarno, or even for a spin down to Brighton if the weather was fine.

On 28 July 1950 a letter from Kingswood dropped on to our mat at 1 Fairview Road. By now Derek had been there two years and still had another year to go, so this letter came like a bolt out of the blue. Derek was being released, it said. A year early.

> We hope Derek will do well and we shall be glad to see him or
> hear from him. Please endeavour to see that he writes as often as
> possible to let us know how he is going on, and we shall always
> be glad to see him at Kingswood if he is able to visit the school.
> Always remember that it is our job to help Derek, and we are
> anxious to do so.

The letter was signed by the Deputy Headmaster, John Fidoe.

The sentence the magistrates had handed down was for three years and the letter said he would stay in the care of the managers of Kingswood until three years *after* the sentence had run out – 'until 29 September 1954'. And right up until Derek was arrested, in November 1952, a man from the Home Office, Mr Towes, came to see him regularly. He saw Derek thirty-two times in two and a bit years. If Derek was the menace to society that the court at the Old Bailey made out, why didn't Mr Towes get wind of it and send him back to Kingswood? He wouldn't have needed anyone's say so. Derek was on licence and Mr Towes could have done it just like that.

But that morning there was no denying it – Derek was coming home for good! It was the best birthday present ever. In two days, on the 30th, he would be seventeen. He was being released fourteen months earlier than the magistrates had ordered. That would show them! Dad felt so proud of Derek, we all did. He must have done so well to earn that sort of remission. Mum and I were in tears, crying for joy. Dad had a smile on his face that could have cracked it in half. The next day I was working, so Mum and Dad went down to fetch him on their own.

I hadn't seen Derek for a few months. I'd been down to Kingswood once or twice, with Mum just for the day because I couldn't get a whole weekend off. So when I came in that night and saw him, it was a real shock. He had lost a lot of weight and looked so pale. He was like a shadow. Not like our Derek at all. We had a celebration dinner with his favourite Christmas pudding, even though it was midsummer. It was one of Dad's specials made without suet. But even that didn't seem to cheer him up. He was more down that I'd ever seen him.

So it was back to Dr Reynolds. She had always had time for Derek, always been understanding. She wasn't married and lived with her mother in a big house just across the main road. The surgery was at the back and you would sit in this big lounge and she would come and get you herself when she was ready. She put him on phenobarbitone again. I don't know what had been happening at Kingswood. I remember asking Derek, but I didn't get any sense out of him. He should have been on it all the time. It might have helped his headaches but it didn't help his state of mind. Looking back now, I would say Derek was depressed. I'm no doctor but I've seen people who are depressed. They can't seem to get started on anything, even people with jobs, they just close up. That was just how Derek was when he came back from Kingswood. Nowadays there are antidepressants but not then.

He refused to leave the house. He said everyone would just point and say, there he goes, that thief, that approved-school boy, Derek Bentley. So he just stayed inside, doing nothing much, just helping Mum with the housework during the day, and sitting with Dad in the workshop when he got back in the evenings or watching TV until it went off at ten. We were the first in our road to have a television because Dad could put them together himself. Most of the time Derek just stayed up in his bedroom with only his tortoise Julie for company, listening to the radio or playing records on the old wind-up gramophone. His favourite was 'Wheel of Fortune' by Kay Starr. When Uncle or I was at home, he'd play billiards. Or sometimes table tennis. By now we had a billiard table in the dining-room. When I got back from the Astoria at about eleven I'd go up and sit with him and talk. I say talk. I'd do most of the talking. Derek had never been a great talker, but this wasn't the Derek I knew.

I can't remember exactly how long it went on, this not going out. About six months I think. The Home Office man, Mr Towes, was still coming to see him but a lot of good that did. Whatever the magistrates might have thought, those two years hadn't done anything for Derek's reading and writing. Although he had picked up smoking, a habit Dad couldn't abide, Derek still couldn't even spell his own name.

I tried everything to get him out. We had a brown lurcher then called Bob. The other Bob, the Dalmatian belonging to the Jenningses, they'd taken with them. This Bob belonged to a friend of mine, Maurice Burton, who lived in the next street. I'd got to meet him through the Astoria where he was the assistant projectionist. He was very good looking so when he asked if we could look after Bob for him while he was away doing his National Service, I'd said yes. I suggested Derek should take Bob for walks.

'Someone has to do it, I don't see why it shouldn't be you.'

'I don't feel like it.'

'Well, neither do I. I've been at work all day. You do it.'

But it was no good. Then whenever there was a good film on, something I knew he'd like, like a musical, with Jane Russell or Betty Grable, I'd try again.

'Come on, Derek.'

'Come on, Derek' was all I ever seemed to say. It was all anyone ever seemed to say. Dr Reynolds was very patient and said it was understandable, that we must try and let him take his own time to settle down, that pushing him wouldn't help.

'Take each day as it comes,' was her advice. Even now I still think that when it comes to GPs, a woman is more caring than a man.

What finally got him out of the house was a searchlight display on Streatham Common – to show people how they had worked in the war. It was a cold night in January 1951 and Uncle Bert and I were all wrapped up ready to go, and we just said to Derek, as we so often did, 'Coming, Derek?'

It was a real shock when we saw him putting on his coat and scarf. Uncle and I looked at each other, of course, but didn't say a word, just in case he should change his mind. And that was that. It probably helped that it was dark, that he wouldn't be recognized.

The next thing was getting him a job but he was still wary of seeing anyone who knew him. He would walk around with his head bent over and his coat hunched up. At the end of Fairview Road were some garages and one was rented by Mr Hutchings, who had his own house-clearing firm in Croydon. His warehouse was at Reeve's Corner in Croydon but Mr Hutchings himself lived in Norbury. Dad knew him quite well. Sometimes when he needed a bit of a hand, Dad and Uncle Bert would help him out for a couple of hours on a Saturday afternoon. We'd got the billiard table from Mr Hutchings. It was a proper full-size one and he'd sold it to Dad for a knock-down price.

Now that he was coming out of the house a bit, Derek began to help too, sometimes just giving the lorry a wash down and a polish, sometimes going out on a house-clearing job. He was tall, just under six feet and quite strong, even though he was more wiry than heavily built.

After a while of just helping out, Mr Hutchings offered to take him on full time. Derek had never worked before and for him to have proper wages of his own made all the difference. He took home £4 a week, gave £3 to Mum and kept £1 for himself, as much as me. Being taken on by Mr Hutchings was the making of him, Uncle said. Suddenly he was back to the Derek we knew, only better. Mr Hutchings told Dad he was really pleased with him. Girls started hanging around our house because being so tall, and with his lovely curly blond hair, he wasn't short of admirers. He was quite happy now to go to the shops for Mum and coming to the Astoria was soon a regular thing. Before National Service, Maurice had worked as a projectionist and when he was back from camp he sometimes filled in at the Astoria. At the interval, if I was doing ice-cream duty, Maurice would train the spotlight on me, like he was supposed to. It blinded me. He was only supposed to keep it on for two minutes but, being Maurice and it being me, he kept it on longer. Derek thought this was the funniest thing and I would hear his laugh echoing round the cinema. I had a free pass for two every week and he'd come with his old friend from Ingram Road school, Philip Stevens, or sometimes Mum and Dad would come, but it was usually Derek. When he got used to the other usherettes, he began going out with us, especially if Rita came along. He thought she was wonderful. Nobody minded him being around, not even the speedway boys.

It was when Derek was on a house-clearing job in Thornton Heath with Mr Hutchings that he found Judy. The owner of the house had died and Mr Hutchings would only have taken her to Battersea Dogs' Home, so he said Derek could have her. She was lovely. A brown Manchester terrier. What we didn't know was that she was expecting pups. But as far as Derek was concerned, the more the merrier. She ended up having them on Derek's bed. He woke up one morning to this heavy weight and wriggling around his head. Judy was everything to Derek. She didn't die till 1973, twenty-two years since Derek first gave her a home.

One of the things Derek needed working for Mr Hutchings was a knife. Not all the furniture they got was good enough to be sold so some was broken up and this knife was for ripping open upholstery to salvage horsehair and suchlike. Everything was still make-do and mend and even horsehair had a price. Derek was happier than he'd ever been before. I never met the people he worked with. I think they must have been older, but he seemed to get on with them. The days of being picked on were gone. The work wasn't easy and sometimes he'd come back knackered after a twelve-hour day, but at last here was something he could do, something he was good at. And all the time he was getting stronger. That summer he got me to take silly photographs in the garden with him pushing his muscles out, looking like Tarzan.

That January 1952, Derek got his call-up papers for National Service, which everyone had to do. When he went for the medical in Kingston, he took along a letter from Dr Reynolds explaining that he suffered from epilepsy. But because so many people used excuses like that to get out of the army, the letter wasn't enough by itself and he had to do an intelligence test. He got the lowest grade possible, Grade IV, which meant not only that he couldn't be a soldier but he couldn't even be trusted to do labouring jobs on the camps.

From then on, Derek's new life began to fall apart. One day in March he must have lifted something the wrong way and his back went. He was in terrible pain for about a week, and Dr Reynolds said although it would get better, it would only go again unless he stopped all the heavy shifting and carrying. There was nothing that could be done. Derek didn't show much, but I knew what it meant to him. He just sank back into himself again. Mr Hutchings was sorry to lose Derek. He said so then and later on to the newspapers. He was one of the people on the list of visitors allowed in the condemned cell.

Then in May, just a month or so after leaving Mr Hutchings, Derek was in trouble with the police again, this time over some missing petrol. This time it was only questions. I mean, what would Derek have wanted petrol for? Derek had nothing to do with it. Like before, there were two of them. This time the other boy's name was Christopher Craig.

CHAPTER NINE

Everyone knew Christopher Craig in Norbury. At least by sight. He hung around street corners wearing a black coat and a trilby hat. The rest of the time he was an apprentice garage mechanic. The Craigs lived in Norbury Court Road. You'd often see Craig and his friends hanging around at the off-licence at the corner of Tylehurst Road, a couple of streets away. He fancied himself as a little Al Capone. He was known as the Kid, or Kiddo, the little gangster, because he was only fifteen and everyone knew about his older brother Niven being in trouble.

You couldn't help noticing Craig. He set himself apart. He wasn't tall, but he wasn't as short as some people have made out. He had dark greasy hair which he plastered with Brylcreem. He was so full of himself, he would come into the Astoria talking with that stupid American accent of his, all lip. Gangster films were his favourite. He'd always be there, downstairs in the 1/8s. One evening there was some trouble in the gents. Craig had been found with two guns in his pocket. The doorman was called to sort it out.

Once when I was doing cashier duty, Craig came over to the till.

'If I put a gun up to the cash desk, would you hand the money over?'

'You'd have the biggest shock of your life if you did.'

And he just shrugged his shoulders and backed away. The shock I was talking about was an emergency bell under the counter, but I wasn't about to tell that little gangster about that. I remember once seeing him with something that could have been a gun, but I thought it was made out of liquorice. It never crossed my mind it might have been real. Real guns were just in films, or for special security, like at Buckingham Palace. I know now that there were more guns around in those days than there are now. Mainly ones that dads and uncles had brought back from the war and hadn't

91

handed in. They weren't going to use them, they were more like souvenirs, something to collect. If they did fire them, it was like kids with air rifles today. They took pot-shots at rabbits on the Common. Or so everybody thought. After all the business with Craig it turned out he wasn't the only one to collect guns. Lots of boys used to do it and swap them like cigarette cards.

I don't know exactly when or how Derek first met Craig. But Norbury was a quiet hole. They used to say if you farted in bed you'd be found out. They'd both been to the same school, but there was three years' difference in their ages, and that's a lot when you're young. I remember him telling us about a boy at school that had guns, but that was before he went to Kingswood. It might have been Craig, but then again, it might not. Derek's friends were always dropping round to Fairview Road but I had never heard Craig's name nor seen his face till that summer of 1952.

But Craig would have known about Kingswood. As I say, Norbury was small. And Derek being at an approved school would have impressed Craig. His brother Niven had been to an approved school and he idolized him. According to Mum he was always going on about Niven.

'I tell you that boy Craig's got a vivid imagination. He was telling me that his brother Niven goes around with all the gangsters but if he gets in prison the gangsters will look after his mum.'

And she just laughed. Although there was twelve years between them it seems Niven had a lot of time for his baby brother. During the war he'd got twelve military convictions. In spite of all that, the Craigs thought themselves a cut above people like the Bentleys. Craig's dad liked to be called Captain Craig and he worked in a bank.

In any case, Christopher Craig wasn't the sort of person who needed any introductions. He was all lip, thought he was really big, mostly because of his brother who everyone knew was a bad lot. Craig was good looking if you like that sort of thing. He was well built for his age, they say he was good at sport. And he was sharp-witted. But it was more than that. He had this arrogance that made him different from anybody else that Derek knew, that any of us knew.

How much of Craig's mouth was just showing off, how much thieving he actually did, I can't say. I've never spoken to him, not since Derek died. But he's said since that while other boys wanted to be engine drivers or generals when they grew up, all he ever wanted to be was a villain, a gangster. He knew that's what his brother already was, so perhaps it was just copying him. Craig's father had been a captain in the army. He was a war hero in the First World War. His hobby was guns and one way or another Craig had got his hands on a whole collection. It turns out he had had forty or fifty and when he was arrested they found stacks of ammunition hidden in his loft. He said later he'd picked up the ammunition from firing ranges. That's why most of it didn't fit. How he'd got so many guns I've no idea. In Court later he said he'd swapped them. Swapped for things he'd stolen probably. When it was all front-page news, a teacher at Norbury Manor was spouting in the press about how Craig used to bring guns in to school. So why didn't he do something? This teacher claimed that if it'd been knives he'd have confiscated them, as they were dangerous. Guns were different. Guns were for collecting, for showing off, not for firing. But, as I say, we didn't know any of this then.

Dad never liked Craig from the first and I certainly didn't. He was always bragging about 'jobs' he'd pulled or Niven had pulled but I didn't take much notice, after all he was six years younger than me, just a stupid kid.

One day he went too far. Derek was washing down Lady Casson's car. She was a widow and lived in Craignish Avenue the other side of the main road. There was no garage there, so she rented the one next to our house for her Hillman. Lady Casson had seen Derek when she came to get the car and one day he'd asked her if she wanted it cleaned. He'd done a bit of driving at Kingswood and so she gave him the key so that he could drive it outside to clean it. She liked Derek and had started giving him driving lessons. For Derek, driving was his dream. Ever since he had that pedal car on the roof of Priory Buildings, he wanted to drive for a job, like an ambulance driver for a hospital, but he knew it was impossible because you can't if you've got epilepsy. In those days you didn't have to take a test and Lady Casson said he could take the car out providing he had a passenger in case he had a fit. The roads in Norbury were empty then and Derek used to drive me around the back streets. He was in his element. He once drove Mum and Dad to Eddie Doe's but that was all a bit of a strain, not the driving but finding the way. They didn't do it again.

One day Dad and Derek were cleaning Lady Casson's car in the side alley and up comes Craig, bold as brass, and says he wants to borrow it to 'pull a job'. Dad nearly blew a gasket. Derek told Craig to push off or he'd thump him. But from then on Dad banned Craig from coming anywhere near Derek. Not that that stopped him. He just carried on hanging around the end of our road. Derek and Philip would nip down the side alley to dodge him on their way out. I asked Derek what it was about Craig. He was only a kid, yet it was like Derek was afraid of him. I asked him straight out why, but he never said. But it was probably about Derek being at approved school. Derek couldn't bear anyone knowing. That's why he'd not gone out for six months, because he thought everyone would be pointing at him. Craig was always harping on about it, Derek said. Later, after it was all over, Mum told me how Craig would taunt her when she answered the front door to him.

'Surely you don't think I'd get him into trouble, Mrs Bentley.'

He just wouldn't take no for an answer.

We didn't know it then, but Craig already had a police record. A few months before the business of the petrol when he and Derek had been questioned by the police, Craig was picked up in Hove with a gun, a .45 Webley revolver. He'd been trying to run away from home and had this idea he could catch a boat to France from Brighton. When Dad went with Derek to Norbury police station about the petrol the Sergeant there, Sergeant Reed, gave him what he called 'a friendly word of warning'.

'Keep Derek away from Craig.'

But he made no mention of the Hove business, the business with the revolver. Derek told Sergeant Reed that Craig just pestered and pestered him.

'My advice is to ignore him. Just ignore him.'

After leaving Mr Hutchings' house-clearance firm, Derek got himself a job with Croydon Corporation, on the dust carts. Mum and Dad thought it was a good sign, because he did it all on his own. It was his idea. The wages were good, over £6 a week. It went a long way then and after what he paid to Mum, most of it went on clothes. Derek was always a snappy dresser. But his back wasn't up to it and they moved him to road sweeper. That didn't pay as much, only £4 something. Even that didn't last. This time it was nothing to do with not being able to do it, but the same old story of being late. I wouldn't be surprised if he was forever stroking cats and forgetting about the sweeping. At Mr Hutchings' place everyone understood. They took account of him. Derek was Derek. Derek was a person. At Croydon Corporation he was just a number. They just wrote him off. He left there in July 1952, just before my twenty-first.

On 5 August 1952 I was twenty-one. Two other girls in my street had just had their twenty-firsts and someone had hand-carved a great big key that we all were given in turn. I got to keep it as I was the last of the three. We had the party in the house. Dad was like a kid planning it. Uncle Bert was a printer with Nuttings, so he did the invitations at work. They were really smart, all in gold and silver lettering. We sent out a hundred.

Maurice and I were now courting. He was still in the RAF, so it was mainly weekends. He was very handsome, lovely dark curly hair, but a bit fast with it, always coming up behind me at the Astoria and putting his arms around me. I soon found out that he was a bit of a Fernandel with other women, so I stayed wary. During the week I just went around with the other girls and the speedway boys. 'All right, Pop, if we take her out?' they'd say. Dad liked all of them, especially Norman, who was a bit of a dasher.

Even though it was my birthday, I still had to do the early show, but I was let off early and because so many of my friends worked at the Astoria, the usherettes and the projection boys, the manager arranged it so they didn't have to stay late. As it was Saturday, I'd done the children's show. Mr Crossley had come on stage.

'Now, children, it's Aunty Iris's birthday today. And what do we do on birthdays?'

'The bumps!'

'That's right, the bumps. Up you come, Iris.'

There was no escaping. I had to go up and be thrown into the air by Mr Crossley and someone else. He took the leg end, as I knew he would.

Maurice and his friend Roy Birchill came to the Astoria to pick me up. Maurice had got me a pink carnation for my dress, and when we got on the bus he planted a gold locket and chain round my neck. It was the most beautiful thing I'd ever had. We went to the pub, the William IV, for a birthday drink and I arrived back at Fairview carried by the pair of them in a 'chair' made by their hands, then off I went upstairs to change into my dress, off-the-shoulder, china blue taffeta. Mum put a white carnation in my hair, then she led me down, into the back dining-room. The table was groaning and in the middle was a birthday cake to top any in the world. It was so huge, I just cried.

You could hardly get in the room for the barrels of beer and Mr Hutchings had got hold of a bankrupt stock of soft drinks. Dad's famous punches soon claimed a few victims, including Mum and Lillian. She only came to with the cutting of the cake and even then her husband Bert had to help her downstairs. A friend of Maurice's who was already a bit the worse for wear made a lunge for Rita, Derek's favourite among my usherette friends. This boy was a stoker on the trains and it turned out he hadn't washed his hands properly before coming out. Rita spent the rest of the evening with two great hand marks on the back of her white evening dress, but not before she'd given as good as she got. She lashed out at him, but he ducked. Instead she knocked a shelf of glass ornaments with her hand and Derek, who happened to be passing, got the full benefit. But my brother had his eyes on another girl that night, I remember, Doris. He was always one for the girls and when we got his wallet back there were a couple of photographs and a letter from Doris. I wonder if he ever got to know what it said.

Mum and Dad really pushed the boat out. The piano was playing non-stop. When the pianist had a break, someone would shout, 'How about giving us a tune, Bert.' And Uncle would sit down and out they'd all come, the old favourites 'Nellie Dean', 'Show Me the Way to go Home', 'Old Johnny' and 'My Old Dutch.' The piano was my present from Mum and Dad. We hadn't had one since Blackfriars.

And still they kept coming. We'd sent out a hundred invitations but in the end we counted 134. There were the speedway boys, the ice-hockey boys, the Astoria lot. One friend of my mother's was asleep on the floor by the beer barrel which was dripping on her face while Derek's dog Judy was just lapping it up.

At midnight came the cutting of the cake, but not before I'd said 'Yes' to Maurice. I'd had two proposals that night. Maurice I'd been expecting, but Ron the speedway boy was a great surprise. And they all sang 'Twenty-one today'. I can remember standing there as if it were yesterday. Just before, I'd gone upstairs to tell Mum that we were about to cut the cake and all she could manage was 'What cake?' She was out cold on Derek's bed.

Then Dad led the conga from our house all the way down Norbury High Street. Dad was so happy. At about four in the morning, he said he was all done in and was going to sleep. Two girls were asleep on the bed, but he was so tired, he just got in anyway. It was baking that night and in the morning he woke up to find the two girls stark-naked. What a shock.

It's no exaggeration to say the party went on for a week. Everyone was invited in, even the dustmen. It was the only way we could get rid of all that drink.

I couldn't have had a more perfect twenty-first if we'd been millionaires. I had Maurice's locket around my neck and the most beautiful platinum bracelet round my wrist, my present from Derek. I was engaged to be married. It was the happiest day of my life.

Now that Derek had lost his job with the Corporation, he turned back into himself again. He carried on doing bits and pieces in the workshop, but there was a limit to the things Dad could find for him to do on his own. I was working so I couldn't keep much of an eye on him but even so, he didn't go out much. By this time Dad had done up the loft, planked it over so we could go up there and muck around. It was still used for storage and we'd forever be going through our old junk, saying remember that and remember that. It had a bench, chairs and a wind-up gramophone. I would play Mario Lanza. I loved Mario Lanza and I once took a whole week off work because of *The Toast of New Orleans*, his first film. It didn't come to the Astoria, it was at the Rex in Norbury and I sat through it twice a day, every day, for a whole week.

Derek preferred the Andrews Sisters, or Issy Bonn's 'To Mother With Love', or 'You May Not Be an Angel' by The Inkspots, or 'ABCDEFG' by Cab Calloway. Then there was 'Red Roses for a Blue Lady' by 'Hutch' – Leslie Hutchinson – and of course 'Wheel of Fortune' by Kay Starr.

Sunday at the Astoria was different. Every film was on for a week, starting on Mondays and the last show on Saturday night. Sunday was just old films. On Sunday, 2 November they were showing *The Lady from the West*, an old film starring Betty Grable. The week before it had been that Bob Hope film *Paleface* with Jane Russell. Any film with Betty Grable or Jane Russell Derek would always go for. On Sundays there were only two programmes, so we opened later and finished earlier. I was up in the circle when I got the flash from one of the girls that Derek was downstairs. We had a whole code of flashes. You held the torch down, never like normal. I never got out of the habit and still hold a torch like that now.

He was with Philip Stevens. I put them in the front circle, the 3/1s. I was usheretting in the 2/8s – back circle – that afternoon. I watched the film for a bit, as I hadn't seen it before, but around six o'clock I whispered to Derek that I was going to supper in the canteen and I'd see him later.

'Is the canteen open on a Sunday, then? Bring us some chips back.'

I was back in about half an hour with a portion of chips. But he gave them to Philip. Derek said he couldn't eat anything. He wasn't feeling well.

'It's a blinder of a headache. Got your handbag with you?'

He wanted his tablets which I always carried. So I went back to the dressing-room for them. They usually worked quite fast but perhaps being in the dark with the flashing screen didn't help. I stood at the back, a bit anxious as I could see him against the light of the screen with his head down. After a bit I went to see if he was feeling any better.

'It's no use, Sis, I can't sit here any longer. It's not easing off. I'm going home.'

The film had nearly finished and Philip said not to worry, he'd see Derek got home all right. So they left.

It was nearly eleven by the time I got back to Fairview Road. Television had closed down for the night but the radio was on in the background. Mum and Dad were sitting in the front room. Mum was on the settee doing a bit of crochet, Dad was reading the evening paper.

'How's Derek?' I asked.

'He's all right. He's gone out for a bit of a walk with a friend of his called Norman Parsley. Do you know him, Iris?'

'No.'

'Ever such a nice boy. Well-spoken, educated. Ideal for Derek. He didn't take any money or even his key so he won't be long.'

I went to the kitchen and made myself a sandwich and a cup of tea and took it back into the living-room and we sat talking for a bit. They said that Craig had been around earlier. But that Dad had opened the door and sent him packing. He'd come looking for Derek the night before, but he was out. Denis had opened the door and when Mum went out to see who it was, there was Craig waving this horrible metal thing in the air on his hand trying to impress Denis, who was only nine. It was a knuckleduster. Mum told him to put it away, that it was frightening Denis and that he'd get into trouble with the police. Dad had sent him packing.

But you couldn't get rid of him for long. He'd been back this lunchtime. Again Denis opened the door. This time Derek was home, and Craig made him go outside to talk so that Denis couldn't hear. But Denis listened at the door and overheard Derek saying, 'I don't want anything to do with it, leave me alone.' Denis told Dad, of course. But Dad couldn't get anything more out of Derek. He just clammed up.

If only I'd been there. The last time I'd seen Craig was a week before. This time I opened the door and I wasn't about to let him in.

He said he'd got tickets for the Rank staff dance in Leicester Square.

'A little bird told me you and Del'll be there.'

Craig always called Derek Del. Nobody else did.

'You just watch it, Christopher Craig. I've had just about enough of you.'

By now Derek had come downstairs. 'Lay off it, Kid.'

'You too, Del. You watch your step. Don't say I didn't warn you. Anyone dances with my girl and they'll be for it. And that includes you.'

It was horrible. I told him to get out and not to come back. I told Dad what had happened as soon as he got in. Dad said we shouldn't go to the dance. But I'd paid for the tickets. There was no way I wasn't going. And why should Derek miss out just because of that stupid kid?

As long as I stayed with Derek, I said, Craig wouldn't get a look in. Dad finally agreed but said he was going to try and get the police to do something to stop Craig having anything to do with Derek once and for all. So on the Monday morning, before he went to work, Dad went back to Norbury police station and asked to speak to Sergeant Reed, the policeman who'd warned him about Craig after the stolen petrol business. But Sergeant Reed had said there was nothing he could do except 'keep an eye on him'.

That was Monday. Now it was Sunday, six days later. Dad told me that when he had got rid of Craig earlier on, Derek was relieved. Derek told Dad he never wanted to see Craig again. As we sat talking it felt like a great cloud had lifted. Derek had a new friend now, he'd gone for a bit of a walk with some nice 'college' boy called Norman Parsley. I told Mum that she and Dad should go to bed.

'I'll wait up for Derek, you go on up. I don't expect he'll be long.'

It was nearly midnight. I started putting my hair in pin curls and turned the radio up. You could see the end of the road from the front window so I kept getting up and looking out. It had been raining earlier and it was miserable and cold. I began to get a bit worried. Where had he got to? Had he had a fit? His last attack was only a month ago. I moved Dad's armchair to the window so I could see without getting up. Still no sign of him. It was gone one when I went up and knocked at Dad's door.

'He's not in yet.'

'I know. I can't sleep, but don't worry, I'm resting.'

I went back downstairs, really anxious by now. Derek's sense of time was always a bit weird but it wasn't like him to be out this late.

Not long after I'd been up to Dad, there was this loud bang, bang, bang at the door, hammering, not letting up. It wasn't Derek. Although I knew he didn't have his key, I'd hear him whistling long before I'd hear a knock, and he'd never knock like that. We were taught never to open the door at night, so I asked who it was.

'Police officers, open the door.'

I took the chain off and was about to stand back to let them in when they just pushed at the door and sent me flying into the hall-stand.

'Where's your parents?'

'In bed . . . is this to do with Derek?'

They didn't answer, just went tearing up, the three of them, all plain clothes, and barged into the front bedroom and I heard my dad, his voice tense and angry.

'What do you think you're doing? How dare you. My wife is in bed. Even my children knock when they come into our bedroom.'

I stood at the bottom of the stairs, shaking. I could see Dad pulling his dressing-gown on. He never slept with a pyjama top.

The loft was open and the ladder still up and one of them went up there.

'Which is Derek's room?'

I can't remember now whether Dad said anything or just pointed to the back bedroom. In they charged and of course Uncle Bert is still fast asleep. He soon woke up. They went through all the cabinets and drawers, flung everything in a pile on the floor. Uncle didn't have any idea what was going on. He said later he thought at first it was a dream, a nightmare. It was. But one we would never wake up from. I could just hear his voice behind the thumps and crashes of the policemen. Mum had joined Dad and he stood with his arm around her. Then the police were back on the landing again. They had Derek's upholstery knife. They'd taken it out of its sheath. This time Mum spoke up.

'What do you want that for? You're not going to say he had that with him.'

'Don't worry, it won't be used in evidence, you'll get it back.'

'Make sure we do.'

We never did. We did see it again, though. In court. Without its sheath. They claimed Derek had it with him on the roof. It's now in the Black Museum at Scotland Yard. They claim they found it on Derek when they searched him. I know they found it in the bedroom that he shared with Uncle Bert.

But we didn't know any of this then. I was still standing at the bottom of the stairs. There was no room on the landing. Then Dad came down with the police. Mum went back into her bedroom.

What was going on? What sort of trouble was Derek in this time? I followed the police into the front room. But they barred the way.

'Not you.'

Dad gave me a look, so I let them shut the door.

I was feeling very angry. Knocked over, pushed out, shut out. So I did what anyone would have done, knelt down and listened at the keyhole. Dad had kept asking, 'What's happened? Where's Derek? What's he done?' It was only when the door was closed in my face that they answered.

'Your son has killed a policeman, Mr Bentley.'

'Never.'

I can hear the gasp in my father's voice.

'My son wouldn't even kill a fly. If I kill a fly he tells me that I shouldn't. That it had life in it.'

My hearing seemed to go funny. My mouth was dry. I felt so cold. In my head I said those things like, am I dreaming, did I fall asleep on the settee, will I wake up? I was shivering with cold. I felt like bursting in but I couldn't move. Like I was glued.

'Where is he?'

'Croydon nick.'

'Well, I'm coming to see him.'

'You can't see him tonight. You'll have to wait until tomorrow after he's been charged at Croydon Magistrates' Court in the morning.'

'What's happening, Iris? What's going on?'

It was Mum, calling down to me. She was still upstairs, sitting on the landing.

I knew she had to know. Had to be told. So I went up and sat down beside her. My mouth was so dry the words could hardly come out.

'They say Derek's killed a policeman.'

'My son wouldn't kill anybody.'

She started crying and so did I. She had her hands in the air. She was always one for waving her hands about when she got upset or excited.

'My boy wouldn't do things like that. My darling boy, what have they done to him?'

I tried to comfort her but she would have none of it. All she wanted was Dad. I helped her downstairs. The police were coming out of the front room. They pushed past us on their way back upstairs. They didn't give Mum and me a second look. Then it came over the radio. A gun battle in Croydon. Two youths had been arrested.

No sooner had Dad taken Mum into the lounge when the door went again.

Another man, on his own. 'Miss Bentley? Sorry to trouble you at a time like this but my name's Vic Lilley. I'm a crime reporter from the *Express*.'

As the police officers walked out, he came in.

Dad looked like an old man.

'They say my son has killed a policeman.'

'No, they've got it wrong,' said the reporter. 'I don't understand why they said that. It wasn't your son, it was a young boy, a sixteen-year-old called Craig. He shot a policeman and then jumped off a roof.'

This was all new. Until now we'd been told nothing. Nothing about a roof, nothing about Craig. So Vic Lilley told us what he knew. That Derek and Craig had been spotted on the roof of a sweet warehouse in Croydon and that when the police had got there Craig had shot one policeman dead and winged another one.

To my mind there can be only one explanation of what those police said to Dad. 'Your son's killed a policeman.' Over and over they said it. Because they had made up their minds that that's what had happened. They knew they couldn't get Craig, because he was only sixteen. He had even taunted them on the roof that he was too young. Derek would have to do. The police had found him guilty there and then. There was no need to go to court. Derek was convicted that night, 2 November, on the spot at 1 Fairview Road.

CHAPTER TEN

By now two other journalists had arrived and they offered to take Dad and Uncle Bert down to Croydon police station in their car. Vic Lilley stayed with us and I made some tea. Mum was feeling a bit calmer now she knew that Derek hadn't killed anyone. But it wasn't long before Dad and Uncle were back. They hadn't been allowed to see Derek. Dad was very anxious.

'I said to them, "Don't question him on his own, he gets confused," but they took no notice.'

We didn't go to bed that night.

Next morning we were at Croydon Magistrates' Court. The place was surrounded by crowds of angry people. Like a lynch mob they were. But it wasn't Derek they were after, it was Craig. And he wasn't there, he was too ill from his fall from the roof and was still in hospital. I didn't get to speak to Derek. But he could see us and asked me to get Mum to buy him a packet of cigarettes. I learnt to lip-read at school. You weren't allowed to talk in class, and passing notes was always a bit tricky because you never knew if someone would hang on to it, or not pass it on, or just drop it for the teacher to find out. Derek tried to do it, but he never really got the hang of it. But he knew I could. When they charged him with murder he said, 'Not me, sir.' They then asked if there was anything he wanted to say and he just said, 'I will see my father.' And that was it. It was all over in about five minutes. We never got to see him.

There are so many versions of what happened in Croydon on that night of 2 November. Newspapers went to town. Most of it was wrong. Even reporters who talked to Dad got it wrong. They just wanted a story, the more sensational the better. CHIGACO IN CROYDON in the *Daily Mail* said it all. They even said they had machine-guns up there. But the truth. What was that? There was the police version, the version they put forward in court, under oath. And there was Craig's version which was probably the closest to the truth.

Derek's version doesn't really exist. His police statement is just how the police wanted it to be. But for what it's worth, here it is.

statement of: DEREK WILLIAM BENTLEY, aged 19

1 Fairview Road, London Road
Norbury

Electrician

who saith:

I have been cautioned that I need not say anything unless I wish to do so, but whatever I do say will be taken down in writing and may be given in evidence.

(signed) Derek Bentley

I have known Craig since I went to school. We were stopped by our parents going out together, but we still continued going out with each other – I mean we have not gone out together until tonight. I was watching television tonight (2nd November 1952) and between 8 pm and 9 pm Craig called for me. My mother answered the door and I heard her say I was out. I had been out earlier to the pictures and got home just after 7pm. A little later Norman Parsley and Frank Fazey called. I did not answer the door or speak to them.

Signature D. Bentley   Signature witnessed by J.S.

My mother told me that they had called and I then ran out after them. I walked up the road with them to the paper shop where I saw Craig standing. We all talked together and then Norman Parsley and Frank Fazey left. Chris Craig and I then caught a bus to Croydon. We got off at West Croydon and then walked down the road where the toilets are – I think it is Tamworth Road. When we came to the place where you found me, Chris looked in the window. There was a little iron gate at the side. Chris then jumped over and I followed. Up to then Chris had not said anything. We both got out on to the flat roof at the top. Then someone in a garden on the opposite side shone a torch up towards us. Chris said: 'It's a copper, hide behind here.' We hid behind a shelter arrangement on the roof. We were there waiting for about ten minutes. I did not know he was going to use the gun. A plain

Signature D. Bentley   Signature witnessed by J.S.

clothes man climbed up the drainpipe and on to the roof. The man said: 'I am a police officer – the place is surrounded.' He caught hold of me and as we walked away Chris fired. There was nobody else there at the time. The policeman and I went round a corner by a door. A little later the door opened and a policeman in uniform came out. Chris fired again then and this policeman fell down. I could see he was hurt as a lot of blood came from his forehead just above his nose. (signed) D. Bentley

The policeman dragged him round the corner behind the brickwork entrance to the door. I remember I shouted something but I forget what it was. I could not see Chris when I shouted to him – he was behind a wall. I heard some more policemen behind the door and the policeman with me said, 'I don't think he has many more bullets left.' Chris shouted 'Oh yes I have' and he fired again. I think I heard him fire three times

Signature D. Bentley   Signature witnessed by J.S.

altogether. The policeman then pushed me down the stairs and I did not see any more. I knew we were going to break into the place, I did not know what we were going to get – just anything that was going. I did not have a gun and I did not know Chris had one until he shot. I now know that the policeman in uniform is dead. I should have mentioned that after the plain clothes policeman got up the drainpipe and arrested me, another policeman in uniform followed and I heard someone call him 'Mac'. He was with us when the other policeman was killed.

tis as B

This statement has been read to me and is true. Sgd

Derk [sic] Derek W. Bentley

Statement taken by me, written down by Det Sgt Shepherd, read over and signature witness by J. Smith DI.

At first glance that might look all right. But in court the police said Derek had just come out with it, just like that. Spontaneously. Not in answer to questions. Derek couldn't remember anything long enough to run an errand for Mum. How could he remember all that? And at five in the morning after everything that had happened? No way. Plus I'd given him that extra lot of phenobarbitone, for his headache in the cinema, only a few hours before. Only a few hours, but as far away now as his dreams of driving an ambulance, or even working quietly at home in the workshop with Dad. And Constable Sidney Miles had died at his feet. Derek couldn't even cope with a cat dying. I've seen him come back from school so terrified of the taunting that he couldn't speak at all. He must have been in a terrible state.

And then there's the signatures. Police statements usually get signed twice. Once at the beginning after the caution and once at the end. Why all those signatures? And so many different versions. Derek Bentley, D. Bentley, Derek W Bentley and Derek W. Bentley. Not to mention 'Derk'.

The 'Derk' is more like it. And the 'Tis as be' – that's Derek's attempt to write 'This statement has been'. If policemen were prepared to forge Derek's signature (which is what all those different signatures mean, to my mind, and what Craig's barrister, John Parris, also reckons) what else were they prepared to do?

Derek did give another version of what happened up on the roof, to his solicitor. But, like so many other things, it's been lost. He did it later, when he wasn't so het up. He said how he had 'given himself up' to the 'plain-clothes man' (whose name was Detective Constable Frederick Fairfax). He said how after Fairfax

108

had been shot he had helped him up, looked to see how badly he was hurt and called out to Craig, 'You bloody fool.' That sounds more like Derek. Also when Miles was killed he said Craig had called out, 'Is he dead?' and Derek had said, 'Yes he is, you rotten sod.' The jury never heard any of that. Derek's barrister Frank Cassels didn't refer to any of it.

But there are so many versions of what happened that night. The police version goes like this.

They were called with a 999 call from a phone box, by a man called Mr Ware who lived in a house opposite Barlow & Parker's, a confectionery warehouse in Tamworth Road, Croydon. His daughter had seen two suspicious-looking men outside. His wife had seen them climb over the gate.

(That just goes to show just what 'professional villains' Derek and Craig were. They'd gone all the way into Croydon and ended up trying to rob a warehouse just round the corner from Croydon police station in Fells Road. So it only took a few minutes for the police to get there after the 999 call.)

DC Fairfax was first up the drainpipe, the same way Derek and Craig had got up on to the roof. He saw them on the far side, about seventy feet away disappearing behind a lift shaft. Fairfax ran across the roof and called to them to come out. Said the place was surrounded. He then collared Derek and pushed (or pulled – Fairfax changed his memory when he was cross-examined) Derek in front of him, round in front of the lift shaft. Craig went round the back. It was when they had just got around the lift shaft, that Fairfax said Derek shouted, 'Let him have it, Chris.' Craig fired at Fairfax, from only six feet away, Fairfax said, and winged him on the right shoulder. Fairfax said the shot knocked him to the ground. Craig fired again and missed. Then he got up, grabbed Derek as a shield, and took him back towards the front of the roof where the stairs came up.

As everyone knows, this shout 'Let him have it, Chris' was what did for Derek. It's called incitement. Egging on Craig to fire at point-blank range would have made Derek just as guilty of murder as Craig. Just like the person who hires a gunman to kill someone is just as guilty as the person who pulls the trigger.

Derek always said he didn't say it. Craig always said he didn't say it. But the police say he did. Three of them: DC Fairfax and two other policemen. One, PC McDonald, was in an alleyway alongside the building – halfway up a drainpipe – the other one, Constable Harrison, was on the next roof. Both said they heard the words *before* the gun first went off and Fairfax was hurt. (*But what they didn't realize, was that Derek never called Craig, Chris, he always called him Kid, or Kiddo.*)

Then the police say that McDonald climbed the drainpipe up from the alleyway and joined Fairfax and Derek, who were now hiding behind where the stairs came up. Fairfax said he searched Derek and found a knuckleduster (the one Craig had shown Denis the night before and which Derek said Craig gave him that night as a 'present'. Anyway, it was in his right-hand pocket where Craig had put it. Derek was left-handed and said he had never even touched it.) There was also a knife, which Fairfax described as a 'dagger type'.

Fairfax then said that when McDonald had asked him (Fairfax) what kind of gun Craig had, Derek butted in and said, 'He's got a .45 Colt and plenty of bloody ammunition too.' This, for the prosecution's case against Derek, was very important as it showed Derek knew Craig had a gun before he had been arrested, which made him a party to the whole thing. Derek said he didn't say it. (I don't think he did either. For a start, Derek wasn't one for butting in at the best of times, so up there, with policemen and being under arrest, no way. Not to mention being terrified. Second, he wouldn't know one kind of gun from another. And third, nobody except a policeman would say .45 Colt. Any normal person who's heard of them would say a Colt 45. That's what they say in films. Craig lived films. If he had told Derek what kind of gun it was, he'd have said Colt 45, wouldn't he?)

Then a uniformed policeman, Constable Sidney Miles, came up the stairs to the roof. They had found the son of the owner of

Barlow & Parker's to come and open up. They'd got the key to the roof door off him. The door opened the 'wrong' way, towards Craig. It was stiff and needed kicking. When Miles finally got it open and came out on to the roof, Craig shot at him and got him just under the peak of his cap, just above his left eye. Death was instantaneous, they said.

Next on to the roof was Harrison and another policeman called Jaggs. Harrison came up by the stairs, Jaggs up the drainpipe. Then they all rushed Derek around the door to take him downstairs. As they did so Derek shouted, 'They're taking me down, Chris.' Then they all left the roof, leaving the dead PC Miles lying there and Craig still hiding behind the lift shaft. But by then the whole place was crawling with police plus all the crowds who'd come to see what was going on. Then Fairfax went back on the roof, this time with a gun and he said there was a shoot-out. When Craig ran out of ammunition, Fairfax said, he decided to kill himself and dived off the roof. It was thirty-three feet up. But Craig didn't die. He hit the edge of a greenhouse and ended up with a fractured back and other broken bones.

All of this was just from Fairfax's and the other police officers' accounts. Fairfax told the court that he hadn't made any notes. It was his 'memory' of the events of that night, his 'memory' of what Derek said, and his 'memory' of when he said it (because if the 'Let him have it, Chris' was said *after* the shot that hit Fairfax, it wouldn't have been incitement) that was going to convict Derek of murder. No notes. You'd think he'd make notes after something like that, wouldn't you?

The other important evidence for the prosecution in proving Derek knew what was going on, was that in the car going back to the police station the officer in the front, Sergeant Roberts, gave evidence that Derek suddenly came out with 'I knew he had a gun but I didn't think he'd use it.' Nobody said anything else in the car, of course. Not a word. Except the official caution, that is. Well, they wouldn't, would they? There they were, the first chance they'd had to pump this 'villain', first they caution him but then they don't ask him anything. No. Derek just came out with this remark 'I knew he had a gun but I didn't think he'd use it.' Tell me another. The officer sitting next to Derek in the back of the car, PC Alderson, was never called as a witness, neither was there anything from him in writing. Yet, for Derek's case, this evidence was just as important as the 'Let him have it, Chris' as it contradicted what he said later in his statement and in court about not knowing about the gun.

But none of these things were queried by the judge, Lord Goddard, the Lord Chief Justice of England, in his summing-up. Not one. And there were so many of these things, these little contradictions. Nothing on their own, but together enough to pull down the whole case against Derek, which was just a house of cards, even if we didn't know all the ins and outs of it at the time.

At the beginning, like all the thousands of people who petitioned against Derek being hanged, we just believed that it was wrong to hang Derek when it was Craig who had pulled the trigger and he was only going to prison. It was a crime against natural justice. What we didn't realize then was that it was a crime against legal justice as well. But as the years went by, as the evidence given by the police at the trial fell apart, we realized, just like Derek told us in his last letter, that it wasn't just morally wrong, it was a pack of lies. The more we found out, the more it gave us hope that someday, someone would get to the truth. The trouble with lies is that people usually forget exactly what they said, what they agreed between them. With the truth there's not that problem.

As I said, Craig's version of what happened that night is probably the closest to the truth. First he was asked in court about what happened before they climbed over the gate and up on to the roof of the warehouse. Craig told them they had gone to rob a butcher's shop but there was someone there, so they didn't. He said it was planned by Derek. But the Derek I knew wasn't capable of laying the table, let alone planning a robbery.

When it came to what happened on the roof there were four important differences to the police version. First, that Derek never said 'Let him have it, Chris'; second, that Craig had shot at Fairfax from a long way away, more like forty feet, not six feet. Third, that there was no gun battle on the roof. He said all this at the trial. The fourth difference, perhaps the most important of all, never got mentioned at the trial. It was this. Derek was sent by Fairfax to try and get the gun off Craig. Craig said that Derek had walked more than halfway across the roof with his hand out, asking Craig to give himself up. Craig had then threatened to shoot Derek too if he didn't back off. So Derek went back to the police.

We never knew about this till years later. But Derek's barrister Frank Cassels knew. Craig had told his barrister John Parris. Parris knew it wouldn't help Craig's case but realized it was crucial for Derek. So Craig agreed to Parris telling Cassels. Why Cassels didn't ask Derek about it, we will never know. Why the police didn't mention it is obvious. Because it didn't fit in with their story. Would they have asked him to leave them and go over to Craig if they thought he was still in it with Craig? No way. They knew Derek was with them. Why Derek didn't come out with it off his own bat at the trial was because he had no idea what was going on. It was all he could do to answer, yes and no. As for not mentioning it in the police statement, it just goes to prove that the police statement was what the police got him to 'say'. If anyone had asked him, reminded him that it had happened, he would have said it.

It might sound like the trial was easy to follow. But how I've explained it here has taken me years to understand. I didn't understand it then because I didn't even hear it. Mum, Dad and me, Derek's own family who knew so much about him, who could even have prompted the barrister when we heard something we knew was wrong, we heard *none* of the evidence, *none* of the case at all. We weren't even in the court for the summing up. We were in the passage outside. Dad thought we would be called as witnesses and so we couldn't go in until after we'd given our evidence. It makes me weep when I think how patiently Dad sat there, waiting to give evidence about the coat. Derek was very careful with his clothes. Always a sharp dresser, like I said. We'd been told that Fairfax had claimed he'd pushed Derek to the ground on that wet, tarmacked roof. If he had done, then where were the marks on the coat? It was spotless. Even Dad knew it wasn't much, but as far as we were concerned it was proof that Fairfax was lying. And if he was lying about one thing, what about the rest? And at that point, we didn't even know how much of 'the rest' there was. Also Dad was going to give evidence about Derek's epilepsy. About the pills he had to take and how slow he was. But he was never called.

In those days the barrister for the defence didn't get to make an opening speech, and if he wanted to make the final speech before the jury went out, he wasn't allowed to call any witnesses, except his client, the accused. If he did call any witnesses, the last speech went to the prosecution. So that's what Frank Cassels, Derek's barrister, decided to do. He didn't call us, or Mr Hutchings or any medical evidence. But then, we heard later from Craig's barrister Mr Parris, Frank Cassels had said at the beginning that he thought 'both the little fuckers should swing'. That from Derek's own barrister. We found out afterwards that Cassels had hopes of becoming a judge and he didn't want to blot his own copy-book.

But Cassels never told us he wasn't going to call us as witnesses. He used to stalk past us. Never used to talk to us. It was like he was shunning us. Dad said perhaps it's part of the system that they're not allowed to talk to us. I know different now. So we just sat there, in the corridor, for two whole days. Not knowing anything about what was going on except what we read in the newspapers. So the jury never heard about the coat and, although they knew Derek was illiterate, because of not being able to read the oath, they never heard about his epilepsy or anything about his medical or mental history at all. Not one single word.

Up until the trial started on 9 December, five weeks after the shooting, Derek was kept in Brixton Prison. We visited him most days. The Astoria let me off work. Croydon Electricity Board gave Dad compassionate leave. The Bentleys just began to draw in together.

The first time we went for a visit, Derek's face was all bruised and puffed up. He'd obviously been done over. Dad asked how it happened. But a warder stopped Derek answering the question. You could tell he was frightened of saying anything that might set them off again. But later on he told us that it was DI Smith, the officer who'd witnessed the statement. When he'd got to Croydon police station, Smith told him to take his shoe-laces out and when Derek bent over, he booted Derek in the head. He said he couldn't remember anything after that. Chances are he had a fit. That's what happened when Derek had a fit. Just didn't remember anything. It makes you wonder when they did the statement. Before or after the kick. Plus it was strange that they had him in the hospital wing in Brixton if nothing had happened. It wasn't as if he'd broken any bones like Craig. Anyway, we weren't allowed to discuss what happened. From beginning to end we were never allowed to discuss the case at all.

But generally Derek seemed quite cheerful. After all, he knew he'd done nothing worse than try to break into the warehouse. Though he didn't even admit to that. He probably didn't want to let Dad down. Derek was like a child who starts eating his Easter Egg before dinnertime and swears blind he's never touched it, even though he's got chocolate all round his mouth. Because Derek *was* like a child. When he couldn't cope, he'd just hide in the loft, or like he used to do in Edgware, hide in the garden, just pretend things hadn't happened. He hadn't the wit to realize that it was no use, that everyone knew they were breaking in. It was the worst thing he could have done. In court he carried on denying everything, even when he'd heard Craig say about the breaking in. But then he changed his tune and said that he did know. But it was too late. When he said he never shouted out 'Let him have it, Chris' and said he never knew about the gun, no one believed him. It was like the fairy-tale of the boy who cries wolf. But that's just it, Derek might have had the body of a man, but he was just a child.

It was while Derek was in Brixton that they did the medical report and he went for tests at the Maudsley which was a psychiatric hospital. This was important because in English law you can't stand trial if they don't think you will understand what's going on, what

115

they called then 'feeble-minded', or if you're insane. The tests were done by Dr Hill, but the report was written by the Brixton Prison doctor Dr Matheson. We didn't get to see it till years later. In fact, Cassels, Derek's barrister, also claimed even he was never shown it. This medical report is just like one of those 'spot the differences' competitions in a paper. Most things seem to be there but if you look carefully, the things they left out make all the difference. Here are just *some* of the things they left out or got wrong. The report claims Derek had only had a few epileptic fits in his life, the last one when he was eight. Eight? How did they work that one out? He'd had one only a month before. (Not to mention the one he probably had in the Croydon police station.) It doesn't mention he was on phenobarbitone (and he'd had an extra dose the night of the shooting). It claims Dad said Derek's falls were not bad ones. How could Dad have said that? How could anyone say that the fall from the lorry, and his head all bleeding, wasn't bad? Dad would never have said that. It doesn't mention Derek having been turned down by the National Service. It doesn't mention Derek's depression when he wouldn't go out for over six months when he got back from Kingswood.

It wasn't that Dr Matheson didn't know. He did. He had all the information, reports from Derek's past, the new report from Dr Hill of the Maudsley psychiatric hospital. But Matheson left out the bits that would have shown Derek was not fit to stand trial. And leaving things out that did happen is just as much a lie as making things up that didn't happen. The ending he had decided was that Derek was fit to stand trial.

CHAPTER ELEVEN

At 11.15 a.m. on 11 December all the talk was over, all the evidence, all the speeches, all forty-five minutes of Lord Goddard's summing-up. Years later, when they debated Derek's case in the House of Lords, they said the trial was a travesty. Most of this was down to Lord Goddard who kept on interrupting both Derek and Craig's barristers. They say he interrupted over 250 times. When it came to the summing-up it was worse. In the House of Lords Debate Lord Arran called it 'manifestly biased'. The only mention Lord Goddard made of Derek's defence was two sentences. 'Bentley's defence is "I didn't know he had a gun, and I deny that I said 'Let him have it, Chris'. I never knew he was going to shoot and I didn't think he would."' But he had plenty of time for the knuckleduster. 'Have you ever seen a more horrible sort of weapon? You know this is to hit a person in the face with who comes at you. You grasp it here. Your fingers go through – I cannot quite get mine through, I think – and you have got a dreadful heavy steel bar to strike anybody with: and you can kill a person with this, of course. Then did you ever see a more shocking thing than that? You have got a spike with which you can jab anybody who comes at you; if the blow with the steel is not enough you have got this spike at the side to jab. You can have it to see, if you like, when you go to your room. It is a shocking weapon.' He spent the rest of the summing-up waving it about in the air. The knuckleduster was nothing to do with what happened and nothing to do with Derek. Craig had made it to fit his small hand. Just like Lord Goddard's, Derek's hands wouldn't even have fitted in. Before the jury had gone out, they'd asked to take Fairfax's coat and jacket with them. Fairfax had said Craig had fired at him from only six feet away, but the ballistics expert had said there was no sign of burning which there should have been if the gun had been fired from so close. Craig's barrister John Parris had been going for manslaughter, trying to make out that none of Craig's firing had been aimed at anyone, and that the bullet that had winged Fairfax had just ricocheted off the roof. They wanted to look at it to see for themselves what the hole looked like, if there were any burn marks. This is why Craig couldn't stand up for Derek. Because Parris was claiming Craig wasn't shooting at anybody but if it came out that he was threatening to shoot Derek, then the manslaughter defence was out of the window.

According to someone who was in court at the time, a young barrister, Anthony Samuelson, Lord Goddard went berserk when he heard this and shouted at the jury, 'You will remember that you are not considering the wounding of Sergeant Fairfax. You are considering the murder of a policeman,' and he smashed the knuckleduster on to the bench. But, says the barrister, 'Only a few of them heard and saw this frightening display.' But Goddard saying 'murder' when Craig was going for manslaughter was against all the rules and when it came to writing the transcript of the trial, they changed it from 'murder' to 'death'.

Goddard was famous. He was known as the Hanging Judge and as a Law Lord he sat in the House of Lords. After the war the Labour Government wanted to reform the law and they put forward a Criminal Justice Bill which, amongst other things, abolished flogging and birching. Later Sydney Silverman, a Labour back-bencher, added an amendment to abolish capital punishment itself. When it was debated on 15 April 1947 in the House of Commons, Sydney Silverman's amendment was carried by 245 to 222. It didn't abolish capital punishment altogether, but just suspended it for five years, to see how things went.

On 27 April the Bill went over to the House of Lords and Lord Goddard made his maiden speech. Although he'd been a Lord for four years, this was the first time he'd spoken and he attacked the abolition of capital punishment and birching for all he was worth. It was just what the Lords wanted to hear, and they rejected the whole thing. It went back to the Commons, who then decided to compromise and tried to limit the kinds of crimes that would result in hanging. They also *raised* the minimum age for hanging from eighteen to twenty-one. Back it went to the House of Lords. But Goddard was at it again and was responsible for defeating that too and keeping the minimum age for hanging down to eighteen. In the end the House of Commons decided it was better to get the original Bill passed without any more fuss from the Lords, so all the capital punishment part was dropped. It stayed exactly as it was.

That was in 1947. If it hadn't been for Lord Goddard, I believe capital punishment might have been abolished there and then. Even if that's just wishful thinking, without Goddard the amendment to raise the age from eighteen to twenty-one would probably have got through. Either way, Derek would have lived.

Now, with Lord Goddard's summing-up over, the jury went out. Anthony Samuelson, the young barrister who saw the business with the jury asking for Fairfax's jacket and waistcoat, said that the jury were terrified of Goddard. 'Too terrified to acquit.'

As I said, Mum, Dad and I hadn't heard any of the summing-up or the business with the jury. We were still sitting out in the corridor. One of the ushers pushed through the crowd and told us we could go down and see Derek. We were allowed to see him twice a day, at dinnertime and before he was taken back to Brixton. The prisoners weren't given anything to eat. You had to get them food yourself. If they didn't have any family, then they went without. Dad had Derek's dinner sent over from the café opposite. He had the same both days, cabbage, cauliflower, potatoes and gravy, followed by rice pudding.

The first morning of the trial we had to give Derek the bad news that Philip Stevens's brother Robert, who was doing his National Service out in Korea, had been blown up by a mine. Derek was shocked.

'Robert, Dead? No. He can't be.'

But it was true. Mrs Stevens had told us that morning. He was only twenty. Philip was devastated. First his best friend on trial at the Old Bailey for murder, then his brother killed. Philip never forgot Derek though, and over those next few weeks he was always with us at Fairview Road.

Everyone back in Norbury was rallying round. Mrs Ruhe, Mrs Leppard, Mr Hutchings. Even Miss Margaret next door whose surname we never knew. But after the first few days, the press hadn't troubled us much. The Bentleys weren't in the limelight and we didn't want to be. Craig was the killer. It was his family the press were interested in. And they were a cut above, weren't they? Mr Craig working in a bank. The Bentleys, with Dad just being an electrician, were painted with a much rougher brush. To read about us in the papers you'd think we'd crawled out of the gutter. For the first few days it was the press who were crawling around, looking for skeletons in the Bentleys' cupboard, but when they couldn't find any they left us alone, but not before Dad had issued a writ against the *Express* for libel.

The Craigs had sold their story exclusive to the *Sunday Pictorial* and they arrived at the Old Bailey every day in a Rolls Royce with the journalist Harry Proctor sticking to them like a private eye in case any other newspaper tried to talk to them. They were put up in a luxury hotel, the Angel, overlooking the Thames at Shepperton.

For the Bentleys it was a different story. We got the bus every morning from Fairview Road. Yes, we were working people, but we were decent, respectable people and proud of who we were, as anyone who saw us at the Old Bailey would have seen. Our clothes were not bought specially, they were just our Sunday best. Mum had bought a hat because she heard you had to wear one in court. I already had one, yellow that matched my yellow corduroy coat. I loved yellow. I had yellow trousers, a yellow cardigan. When I went into shops in Norbury where people knew us, they used to say, 'Here she comes, here comes the yellow canary.'

People always ask me whether Derek understood what was going on. If they mean what was going on in Court number 2 in the Old Bailey, the answer is no. But then none of us did. It was like playing a game where you don't know the rules. The lawyers and everyone else sitting there have been trained for it. They can put you in jeopardy because you don't know what's going on, you don't know what different things mean. It was all very bewildering. No, Derek didn't understand. When we saw him down in the cells, talking with him while he had his dinner, you could see he was frightened, so pale and his face twitched which it never used to do. His hand shook so much that when he tried to get up a piece of potato on his fork it would just fall off.

I think he was frightened more through not understanding than because he thought he might die. I don't think he had any notion that might happen, at least not until the end of the trial. He would keep asking why we weren't in court and Dad would explain about us giving evidence and about not being allowed in until we had. Like a child, Derek thought Dad knew everything. So Dad would do his best to explain. But how could he, when we didn't understand ourselves? All he would say was, 'It'll be all right, son. Don't forget British justice is the best.'

Denis came with us on that last day of the trial because Derek had said he wanted to see him. Being only nine, they wouldn't allow him to visit his brother in prison. There was only the summing-up that last morning, so we were allowed down in the cells to see him while the jury were out. Denis told Derek about his tortoise, Julie. How it was hibernating and how Denis had wrapped it in straw and was keeping it in the corner of Derek's room.

'Don't worry about Julie, Derek. I'll look after her until you come home.'

We stayed with him about twenty minutes, which was all they allowed and I think we had a bit extra because of Denis being there. When they said 'time', Mum gave Derek a cuddle, like she always did and left. We needed something to calm our nerves so we went over to the café. We didn't stay long, just long enough for a cup of tea and were soon back in our seats in the corridor within ten minutes.

While the jury were out, Lord Goddard had been doing another case. It was Norman Parsley, being sentenced for armed robbery with Craig. Yes, Norman Parsley. Norman Parsley may have been a college boy but he was not the 'nice friend' Mum hoped he was. No wonder Craig was so full of himself ten days before when he came round waving his knuckleduster in Denis's face. He'd just come from doing this 'job' with Norman Parsley. His victims were the couple who ran the greengrocer's Philip Stevens worked for, called Howes. It seems Craig had asked Philip something about which day had the most takings and poor Philip told him Saturday, not thinking anything of it. So that night Craig and Parsley break in and of course find nothing better than a few soft turnips. So then they went off to where Mr and Mrs Howes lived. They both had guns and pulled their scarves up over their faces. They pushed old Mrs Howes on the ground and threatened to shoot her if Mr Howes didn't hand over the money. So he gave them a paper bag with what he had. It was less than £5. Parsley got four years, Craig six years. Years later Craig said that he wanted Derek to go with them but that Derek had said no because Craig said they were taking guns.

Philip's name never got mentioned in court, and it was a good thing. It wasn't his fault that Craig had learnt the easy pickings there were to be had from someone who was a bit on the slow side. And what with having his best friend on trial for murder and his brother killed, Philip had enough crowding in on him.

It just shows how little we knew about what was happening, how little Derek's barrister thought about us, that Dad didn't realize that once the jury had gone out he couldn't be called to give his evidence. He still thought we would be called as witnesses. But when the usher came out and told us that the jury were coming back I said I'd had enough.

'I'm fed up with sitting here, I'm going in.'

And I did, Mum, Dad and Denis still out there, waiting.

The public gallery was packed. They'd queued round the block hoping to get in. They said touts were selling seats at £30 a ticket. I could see them both in the dock. Craig was in a wheelchair, his back was still bad after his dive from the roof. Derek was standing.

They usually allow prisoners to sit during a long trial. But not Goddard. Not Derek. He'd been made to stand through it all. He was wearing a new grey pin-striped suit that Dad had bought him and a new grey tie. He looked very pale.

I arrived just in time to hear the clerk asking the jury whether they found Christopher Craig guilty or not guilty of murder.

'Guilty.'

Then came Derek William Bentley.

'Guilty with a recommendation for mercy.'

Then a court official took what looked like a small piece of black material and put it on Lord Goddard's head. I remember thinking: What's that judge doing with a black headscarf? It's not raining inside here. I didn't understand. I thought I'd better ask Dad so I got up and went back to the corridor.

'Dad, the judge has put this black scarf on top of his wig. What does it mean?'

Within seconds we were back in the court, just in time to hear Goddard say, 'Take him down.' Derek was in floods of tears as the warder led him away.

Craig was next.

Christopher Craig, you are under nineteen, but in my judgement, and evidently in the judgement of the jury, you are the more guilty of the two. Your heart was filled with hate, and you murdered a policeman without thought of his wife, his family or himself; and never once have you expressed a word of sorrow for what you have done. I can only sentence you to be detained until Her Majesty's pleasure be known. I shall tell the Secretary of State when forwarding the recommendation of the jury in Bentley's case that in my opinion you are one of the most dangerous criminals who has ever stood in that dock.

While the jury were out considering their verdict in this case I had to deal with another boy whom you led into it in holding up an elderly couple at the point of revolvers and stealing from them; and it is quite obvious that the people in this country will not be safe if you are out of prison. I shall recommend the time which I suggest to the Secretary of State that you shall be kept in confinement. The sentence upon you is that you be kept in strict custody until the pleasure of Her Majesty be known. Take him down.

Craig looked towards his family and smiled.

Dad took hold of my arm and we went back to Mum, who was still sitting with Denis in the corridor. Our faces said it all. I suppose Dad must have said the word, guilty. But I can't remember. I can't even remember Mum's face. I just remember Denis saying, 'Will it be all right, Dad?' Nobody came up to us. Not the solicitor, not Frank Cassels. Just a journalist.

'Well, it could be worse. The jury have recommended mercy, so with any luck he'll get a reprieve.'

With any luck. Derek's life was down to luck.

The next ordeal was to go down and see Derek again. I didn't cry. I had to be strong. I had Mum to take care of, there was Denis to be looked after and Dad was near collapsing. When we were shown in I noticed Derek's eyes were red, but he wasn't crying, perhaps for Denis's sake, perhaps for Mum's. I remember feeling really proud of him.

'What does it mean?' was all Derek kept saying, and Dad kept saying that he didn't know.

'I think they are doing it to frighten you so that you don't mix with that type again.'

This seemed to cheer Derek up. What else could we say?

'And don't forget they did make a recommendation for mercy.'

Derek asked what that meant and Dad explained that it meant he'd get a reprieve.

'Because you didn't kill anyone, you gave yourself up, you didn't have a gun.'

Dad told him we would appeal against the sentence and that we would never give up. As we left he put his arm round Derek's shoulder.

'Chin up, Son. Don't forget, they've just done it to frighten you.'

Then Derek ruffled Denis's hair and hugged Mum.

'Chin up.'

The case had lasted only two days. Just ten hours, start to finish, that's all. Like a dose of salts. It would never happen like that now. Nowadays they'd take at least a few months to put together all the evidence for a murder trial, and that's not even when anybody's life is at stake. It was only five weeks since the shooting. The trial would have started even earlier if Craig's barrister John Parris hadn't asked for a few more days. He'd only got given the brief *two days before* the original date for the trial. It was only put back a couple of days because he complained. It was all done in such a hurry. They said Goddard wanted to get it all over and done with before Christmas.

After twenty minutes of trying to be cheerful with Derek, we came up from the cells not saying a word. Dad with his arm around Mum. Mum holding Denis's hand. I walked alone, my thoughts still with Derek. We had no idea what was about to hit us.

As we stepped outside there was a sudden clicking and flashing and shouting that for a moment had us rooted to the spot. Denis burst into tears. Everyone was just pushing and shoving and I was grabbed by someone, a man who I'd never seen before who pulled me through the crowds and into a car. I kept looking back, trying to see what had happened to Mum and Dad and Denis but it was all madness. About four minutes later, it might have been less but it felt like an age, the door opened and Mum, Dad and Denis were shoe-horned in. Our kidnapper was Len Cotton of the *Sunday Dispatch*.

As I said, no one had been much interested in the Bentleys before, so Dad decided to talk to them and tell them some of the things that hadn't come out at the trial, particularly about Dad's having asked for police protection from Craig for Derek a week before the shooting, and about his epilepsy.

That afternoon we took a wreath to Mrs Miles. Before we left Derek, he had asked us to take her some flowers, to say how sorry

125

he was about what had happened. Dad wasn't sure it was the right thing to do, but we did it because Derek asked us to. We got the wreath from Rogersons on the corner and took the bus up to where she lived. It took a lot of nerve, I can tell you, going up and knocking on her front door. Somebody else answered. They took the wreath but Mrs Miles didn't see us herself. Well, you can understand. But she did tell the newspapers that she didn't think Derek should be hanged.

After the verdict Derek was moved to Wandsworth Prison. The next day was the first visiting time since the trial, but I didn't go with Mum and Dad. 'Uncle Len' of the *Sunday Dispatch* went instead. Dad wasn't happy about the false pretences. He was worried it would go badly for Derek if they found out. But they didn't. Dad said Derek was quite taken aback when he found he had a strange uncle. He didn't click at first. Dad said to him, 'This is your Uncle Len, Derek.'

'I didn't know we had an Uncle Len, Dad.'

Dad just winked and they carried on with the visit as usual. Len didn't say much, according to Dad. But the article was going to be done as if Dad had written it, so Len Cotton wanted to capture just what it felt like, going to the condemned cell, from the dad's point of view. Journalists were like that in those days. Harry Proctor wrote the same kind of thing about Craig's dad. He even tried to get John Parris to take him in to see Craig when he was in Brixton, saying he could pretend to be Parris's clerk.

The *Sunday Dispatch* paid £200. Dad didn't feel bad about taking it. If we were going to fight we needed money, if only for stamps. But because they'd paid us, until the story was printed that Sunday we weren't allowed to talk to any other reporters. It was very difficult and we never did it again. But having that little bit did mean we didn't have to go everywhere by bus. Going with reporters meant them always being there, and sometimes we just wanted to be on our own. So for the appeal, for example, we went by hired car, from Rickshaws of Norbury.

It was coming up to Christmas. Christmas.

Christmas at our house had always been special. But this year there were no Christmas parties. But I did go to one Christmas party, backstage at the Astoria. All the girls had been very kind. Rita even visited Derek in the condemned cell. But that might have been later. Anyway, I thought I would go. And Mum and Dad thought it was a good idea, to show that the Bentleys weren't beaten. But at the party I did something which I know must seem strange. I got engaged.

Laurie worked for a carpet company in Croydon as a salesman. We'd been walking out since the autumn. My engagement with Maurice hadn't lasted long. He'd begun to play around with the daughter of one of the cleaners at the Astoria. A right docherty. And I couldn't be doing with that.

I'd met Laurie at the Assembly Club in Norbury on amateur night. He'd not long come out of the navy after National Service. He was nice looking, slim build, nice fair hair, fair complexion. I always went for the boys in uniform and he was sitting with a group of his old service friends.

How could you get engaged, people say, with Derek under sentence of death? But that just shows how sure we were it wouldn't come to that. And there were lots of good reasons. First, he asked me. He wasn't the first. But he was the first to have the ring with him. Maurice hadn't given me one. It was a diamond hoop, with five stones set in gold. But saying 'Yes' to Laurie was also down to a bit of bravado. Craig's sister got married two days after the trial. Looking back there might have been a bit of 'if she can do it so can I'. And anyway, all our emotions were running high. Perhaps I thought Laurie would comfort me. It was also a sign to the world that Derek must be innocent as no one would want to marry a murderer's sister.

Now that Derek was a condemned prisoner, we were allowed to visit him every afternoon for half an hour sometime betwen 1.30 and 3.30, except Christmas and Boxing Day. Every morning a written permission form would arrive by post with the names of who could visit that afternoon. So, if Mr Hutchings wanted to see

Derek (which he did, at least once) then Mum and Dad would tell the warders when they went what names to put on the form for the next day. You could rely on the post in those days and the form always arrived the next morning.

The warders were kind to him, Derek said. But only as kind as they were allowed to be. We brought in a bowl of fruit for Christmas, but they said he couldn't have it. So we took it home to wait for his release. It was still on the sideboard on the day he died. Then Dad threw it out.

But we were still hopeful. The appeal was set for 12 January. In the meantime, someone called Sid had telephoned Dad and said we shouldn't wait for the appeal but start a petition for Derek straight away. We didn't know anyone called Sid, in fact I don't think Dad ever met him, but he said he'd had dealings with this kind of thing before.

It was lucky Dad took his advice. Until the verdict it had always been the 'Craig' case. Then with Craig just going to prison and Derek being sentenced to death, everything changed. Overnight it became the 'Bentley' case. But what happened was nothing to do with the newspapers. They weren't on Derek's side. After all the high drama of the trial was over, it was old news and they stopped writing about it. The newspapers might have forgotten about it but the people didn't. In those days people followed murder trials like they do now with *Eastenders*, knowing every little twist and turn, and everyone with an opinion. And when the verdict was announced, ordinary people knew it was wrong. For the first few days it was just a trickle but by Christmas they were pouring in. Letters saying how sorry they were, letters asking what could they do, letters sending money – postal orders, five-pound notes, to help in the fight. I even remember a half-crown stuck to some children's writing paper with a sticking plaster sent by a little girl, aged twelve.

By then we were prepared. With Uncle Bert being a printer, petition forms were already ready. Sid had told Dad we needed 1,000 names to present to the Home Secretary. I don't know how many we sent out but in the end they say there were over 150,000 names. At the beginning, Dad wrote his own letters to say thank you. But he couldn't do that for long. We're talking about hundreds, even thousands of letters a day, so Uncle Bert had to print up a letter which Dad would sign, saying thank you for your support and asking people to write to their MP or the Home Secretary. I don't know how many thousands of those we sent off.

The next thing was a telephone. Although there was a waiting list, the GPO installed one the day after Dad asked for it, and no charge. We didn't have time to get down-hearted. There was too much to do. Pollard 7733 never stopped ringing. Mum and Dad and I would answer the phone. Everyone else was doing letters. I don't know what we'd have done without the billiard table. Letters and telegrams asking to help were on one side, letters with cheques and postal orders at the back. In the middle were the petitions, on the right were the thank-you letters signed by Dad. Everybody who came through the door found themselves helping, old friends like Lillian, Laurie of course, journalists, strangers, anyone who turned up. Philip and Denis folded. Other people wrote the names and addresses. Mum and Lillian were out in the kitchen brewing cups of tea and making sandwiches.

One man turned up and offered his services full time. Dad seemed quite pleased to have him until he found out that this man had been charging journalists to come in the house and what's worse, pocketing the money himself. So that was the end of him.

Soon we had to have our own postman who did nothing else but deliver our post. He needed a van. Letters that hadn't been opened were put in the bath then, when there was space, they'd be opened, read and put into the system on the billiard table for being answered.

Suddenly the name Bentley was everywhere, on cars there were stickers saying 'Bentley must not die'. Little old ladies sat under umbrellas at street corners collecting signatures. And this wasn't the summer, remember. It was winter, midwinter. The cast of a Christmas show *Red Riding Hood on Ice* had a whip-round and sent us a cheque for £200 to help us get a new solicitor. Like us, everyone thought Derek had been badly let down by his lawyers. But you couldn't change mid-stream. There were so many offers of help, so many kind people. Some were anonymous even then. But they gave us faith in human nature and even if their names are lost for ever, they know who they are, just like the people who lied to send Derek to his death know who they are. There was an old man who came to the door and asked us to give his rosary to Derek. He had seen Derek's picture in the paper and recognized him as the boy who had bought him a cup of tea when he didn't have the money, one afternoon in the café at Reeve's Corner, next to where Mr Hutchings' warehouse was.

Like I said, because Derek was in the condemned cell we could visit him every day. For the first few days it was a bit sticky. We used to tell him how things were going. How the animals were. I took in a photograph of me with Judy in the garden. I showed it to him through the glass but we weren't allowed to give it to him because it was cut from a newspaper. But they did let him have the rosary.

I don't rise to anger easily but a year later when Christie, the murderer of 10 Rillington Place, was in the condemned cell, in Wandsworth just the same as Derek, there were photographs in the papers of food being brought in for him from outside. That was a man who not only killed five women in the most horrible ways, but who in cold blood let Timothy Evans go to the gallows for the murder of his wife and baby, murders that Christie himself had done. All Derek had asked for was apples.

The condemned cell wasn't like Brixton. It was like two rooms. We couldn't touch him. It was as if they were taking him away from us in stages. We were separated by this great thick piece of plate glass. Our voices went through a grill thing at the bottom. I never got used to it. You could hear what he said, but his voice was always far away, muffled, like you might hear it in a dream. And in dreams it's always that glass that I see.

CHAPTER TWELVE

The appeal was held on 13 January. Derek would get a reprieve. It was only a question of when. And it wasn't only us who thought so. Years later we found out that Derek's barrister Frank Cassels bumped into Lord Goddard a few days before the appeal. Goddard told Cassels he didn't doubt Derek would be reprieved in the end, either at the appeal or by the Home Secretary. But six days before the appeal, something happened which should have been a warning bell. They announced that Fairfax, Harrison, McDonald and Jaggs were being awarded medals for bravery. It was in the newspapers. Fairfax got the George Cross – Britain's highest peacetime medal for gallantry, Harrison and McDonald got the George Medal and Jaggs the British Empire Medal.

Mum said for us not to take any notice. 'They're ten-a-penny medals. They mean nothing. What about those heroes lying in their graves abroad? They got nothing. They give medals for another sort of lying now.'

In England an appeal against conviction can only be made on points of law, technicalities, not just that the jury got it wrong. In Derek's case there were two main points of law. First, and the one with the best chance, was that he was under arrest on the other side of the roof, and had been under arrest for a good quarter of an hour before PC Miles was killed and so the 'joint adventure' with Craig was over. That was it really. There was no new evidence that anyone was aware of.

The second thing was that Lord Goddard's summing-up was unfair, that he hadn't gone over Derek's defence properly, hadn't spelled out just what Derek said happened compared to what the police said, everything that summing-up is supposed to be about. The judge isn't *judging* when he's summing up. It's not up to him to tell the jury how to vote, which way to go. He's supposed to be reminding them of the various arguments, all the important evidence and telling them what the law says about it, because common sense and the law are not always the same thing. Reminding the jury of the arguments was particularly important in Derek's case because the jury wasn't sent out until the day *after* they heard the final speeches, because Lord Goddard wanted to get home early. And in those days they weren't allowed to take any kind of notes.

Now, as I've said, Lord Goddard was the Lord Chief Justice of England and I don't know if that had an effect on how the appeal judges looked at it, but it wouldn't have done their careers any good if they'd had a go at Lord Goddard, would it?

There were three appeal judges: Mr Justice Croom-Johnson, Mr Justice Ormerod and Mr Justice Pearson. It wasn't at the Old Bailey it was in the Court of Appeal, at the Strand end of Fleet Street, not half a mile from where Derek and I were born. We drove there in a hired car from Rickshaws of Norbury. The courtroom was on the first floor. There was no appeal for Craig, so it was only Derek in the dock this time. He was bearing up well. It was cold that morning and under his jacket Derek had on a grey cardigan, like a knitted waistcoat with buttons.

We didn't make the same mistake as last time and sat where he could see us, so we heard everything, but that morning most of it was lost on me. I don't think Derek understood a single word. All he said when we saw him in the cells afterwards was, 'Why was it so short?'

The appeal judges are supposed to have read the trial transcript, to know what the appeal is all about before they begin. But unless they were putting it on for the benefit of the public gallery (which like at the Old Bailey was bursting), they didn't know the ins and outs of it at all. For example, about the business of Derek saying 'I knew he had a gun but I didn't think he'd use it,' in the back of the police car. Lord Goddard had said in his summing-up that *three* policemen had heard him. But only two gave evidence in court about it. Constable Alderson, the one sitting in the back with

Derek, wasn't called and didn't give anything in writing either. The appeal judges said Goddard's mistake didn't matter as Alderson's written evidence was available in court if anyone had wanted to see it. Not true. Nothing from Alderson was ever filed in the court. To this day nobody has seen the notes Alderson made that night.

In his summing-up which lasted forty-five minutes, Goddard only said two sentences about Derek's defence. When Cassels read out those two sentences to the judges, Justice Croom-Johnson just said: 'Doesn't that cover it? I agree it's short.'

Cassels said that because there was such a difference in the police's version of events and what Derek said happened, all the differences should have been pointed out to the jury. Croom-Johnson would have none of that either.

> Surely it is for the learned judge to decide what he is going to lay
> before the jury, and so long as it is done, I will use an expression
> of my own that you won't find in the books, fairly and squarely,
> that is sufficient.

Fairly and squarely. Fairly and squarely.

The business about Derek being under arrest they had more time for. Here was an interesting point of law they could all squabble about. But once again Derek's not understanding added another nail in his coffin. Because he knew he was staying with Fairfax, siding with the police of his own free will, because he didn't want to be involved with Craig any more, Derek said he wasn't under arrest. Under arrest to Derek meant being stopped from getting away. Derek didn't want to get away. But of course he was under arrest. The prosecution at the trial had said so. Even in Derek's statement he said he had been arrested. Everyone knew he was. Everyone, prosecution and defence, accepted that from the moment Derek left Craig and went with Fairfax to the other side of the roof, he was under arrest. But because Derek had said in court that he wasn't under arrest, the appeal judges used that as an excuse to throw out the appeal.

It is a little difficult for Mr Cassels because his own client was asked specifically at the hearing whether he was under arrest at the time when this shot which killed Miles was fired. He would not have it. He said that he had not been arrested, that he was not under arrest, that the police officer had not detained him, and all the rest of it. In the face of that it seems to us that it is idle to suggest that this point, if it be the point, about the arrest is one which the jury could take into consideration and about which the Chief Justice ought to have directed the jury. The answers given in cross-examination by an individual on trial do sometimes have the result of destroying the possibility of a good point of law being persisted in, which the learned counsel has endeavoured to get on its feet before a jury, and it seems to us that there is nothing in this point on either of the two grounds.

Funny that. For the first time they decided to accept Derek's version of events. But only because it suited them.

The idea that there was a failure on the part of the Lord Chief Justice to say anything short of what was required in putting that sort of case to the jury is entirely wrong.

We were so confident that the appeal would go Derek's way that it quite shook the stuffing out of us when the leader of the appeal judges Justice Croom-Johnson spelled it out. It was, he said, 'nothing more than an ordinary appeal in a murder trial, an ordinary appeal which is, in our judgement, without foundation and which is accordingly dismissed.'

So there it was. Derek was right. It was over so quickly. You'd think the judges would go away after they'd heard everything and talk it over somewhere else. But they didn't leave the Bench. They just sat there with their heads together.

As we went back to see Derek, we didn't talk about it. Luckily we had Denis with us. Like on the last day of the trial, he came to see Derek. No one thought then that this was the last time he would ever see his brother, but it was. And it was good Denis never had to go through that, knowing he was seeing his brother for the last time. As it was, both of them were so pleased to see each other. And we did have a little stroke of luck. The warder with Derek was someone I'd been out dancing with a couple of times. I'd met him at one of the dances at Caterham barracks when he was a Coldstream Guard. He was just a friend. But that morning he was great. Talk about a 'friend in court', and when I told him Denis hadn't seen Derek since the trial a month since, he gave us a bit of extra time.

It was Denis who did all the talking. You couldn't stop him. Telling Derek about the car Mum and Dad had bought him for Christmas that worked with a battery. Telling Derek how the lawn was just starting to grow through the wire Dad had put over it to stop the chickens turning it into a mud patch. Telling Derek how Judy missed him and how every time the front door went she rushed down, thinking it was him and how she still slept on his bed whenever Uncle Bert forgot to shut the door. Telling Derek what fun they would have when he got back home.

We went straight to the car, Dad pushing his way through the photographers and press. Mum held Denis tight by his hand as she shouted out through her tears, 'The real culprits are getting away with it.'

Right after the trial the *Daily Mirror* had a front-page article saying WILL BENTLEY HANG? They talked about the jury's recommendation for mercy, they said that sometimes in spite of a jury's guilty verdict, the Home Secretary would reprieve if there was a shadow of doubt. And in Derek's case there was more than a shadow. It was more like a blackout. So even though the appeal was dismissed, we hadn't given up hope. But a few days later the date of the execution was set. It was only two weeks away, 28 January 1953.

The next step was to appeal to the House of Lords. This is only allowed when there is a point of law of public importance. There is no book of English law, like the Ten Commandments. English law is common law, it works on precedent, on similar cases that have been decided before. In Derek's case, the business of when the 'joint adventure' had come to an end was make or break. If the court accepted that it ended when he was arrested, then he had nothing to do with what happened later. This question had never been settled in an English court, so it was a genuine reason to take the case to the Lords.

But, just like after ordinary trials, not everyone is entitled to appeal. It stands to reason, otherwise everyone who was found guilty would do it. You have to get permission, 'leave' to appeal, based on whether they think you have grounds. But who from? Someone without an axe to grind? Someone who doesn't have a career to think of? For the House of Lords, you have to get leave to appeal from the Attorney-General, who, like the Home Secretary, is always a politician. Since October 1951 the Government had been Conservative. Labour's post-war reforms had bitten too hard on people's purses so the Tories were back with Winston Churchill as Prime Minister. The Attorney-General was Sir Lionel Heald. The Home Secretary was Sir David Maxwell-Fyfe.

When Derek's appeal was dismissed, what had been a snow-storm of letters and telegrams became an avalanche. The newspapers were still sitting on the fence, but for the people, from the highest in the land to the lowest, it was now as clear as the nose on your face. Derek Bentley must not hang. At Fairview Road we could hardly cope even working around the clock. Mum and Denis went to bed. Denis usually slept on a put-u-up settee in the front room but for those last few weeks he took to sleeping in my bed. No one slept on Derek's bed. Apart from tidying up the mess the police made, Mum just left it ready for him to come back to. Every week when she changed the sheets, she changed his just as if he was still there. Sometimes when you couldn't find her, we knew that's where she was. Just sitting on Derek's bed. Crying.

Dad and I didn't go to bed. Mostly we just carried on, reading more letters, reading law books people had brought, Dad in his chair, me on the floor. The front room looked like a hurricane had hit it, with newspapers, letters, telegrams and books everywhere. And there were all the flowers. They'd arrive in boxes from Holland and France. They'd arrive in posh delivery vans. They'd arrive brought by people themselves. We soon used up all the vases and for the rest we just stood them up in the sink in the kitchen. People sent presents for Derek too, lots of them. Boxes of chocolates, a bracelet from a girl, her own I think, that she wanted him to wear for luck. A box of hankies, a tie, a tie-pin. He wasn't allowed them, of course, but he was very touched.

After the business of the *Sunday Dispatch* Dad decided he wasn't doing with any more of that. No more exclusives. The more publicity we got the better. I learnt that then and I have never forgotten it. And it wasn't just English papers that were interested. They came from all over to watch the world-famous British justice at work. Although we kept our spirits up as best we could, it wasn't easy. We knew time was running out. Journalists would order in food from the café at the corner. They all had healthy appetites. In would come plates of roast lamb, roast chicken. They always bought for us too, but we just picked. We didn't really want food. What we lived on was cups of tea. It was the Englishman's cup of tea that kept us going.

After the appeal was dismissed, the phone never stopped ringing. It was continuous. No sooner did you put it down than it rang again. And not just during the day. It was ringing through the night. It was plugged into the front room so it didn't disturb Mum and Denis, and Dad and I just snatched half-hours of sleep on the settee when we could. Sometimes when I was lying there in the dark looking at the shapes on the ceiling where the light from the streetlamps sneaked in, I thought of Derek looking at those same shapes in the days when he slept on the settee when we first moved to Fairview Road, when the Jenningses were still there.

Of course, it wasn't just the Bentleys people contacted. Thousands wrote to their MPs and to the Prime Minister, Churchill and wrote to the Home Secretary, for it was Maxwell-Fyfe and only

Maxwell-Fyfe who could grant a reprieve. They still say that Derek's case is the greatest public protest ever in the history of British justice.

One of the first things we'd done after the trial was to contact our own Member of Parliament, Mr Harris, Conservative MP for Croydon. I've forgotten the rest of his name because it doesn't seem worth remembering. We arranged to see him at the town hall. All he said was Derek must be guilty or they wouldn't have sentenced him. Then he walked away. Just walked away. Until then Mum and Dad had always voted Tory, even in 1945. Because they were loyal, loyal to Winston Churchill who had won the war. But they never voted Tory again and neither did I.

Sydney Silverman, the Labour back-bench MP whose amendment to abolish capital punishment was voted in by the House of Commons in 1947, was the first MP to contact us. He phoned soon after the appeal was dismissed and we met him at the House of Commons the next afternoon. I waited in the Members' Lobby, where I'd taken Lillian just a year or so before, while Dad went off to talk to Mr Silverman alone. When they came back Dad looked much more cheerful. Sydney Silverman had told him he would do all he could to get Derek's case debated in the House. But time was running out.

On 20 January we got a letter from the shadow Home Secretary Aneurin Bevan. We went to see him at the House of Commons the same afternoon, after visiting Derek. Mum wasn't up to it, so it was just Dad and me. Mr Bevan was very kind. After he and Dad had finished, he came over to talk to me. Asked me how I was coping and how Mum was and I told him, not good at all. He said how tired I looked.

'But we've still got fight left in us.'

'I don't doubt that for a moment.'

Then, with less than a week to go, on 22 January came the news from the solicitors that leave to appeal to the House of Lords had been refused. According to the records the application for appeal to the House of Lords was lodged and refused on the same day. As

I've said, the point about when a 'joint adventure' ends had never been decided in English law. If it was lodged and refused in the course of one day, how long did it take the Attorney-General to decide? It was the end of the legal road. All we had left now was the Home Secretary. We were devastated. It was as if suddenly we felt the truth of what was going to happen. For the first and only time Dad took the phone off the hook.

And if anyone thinks we still had our heads in the sand, something worse brought it home to us the next day. A parcel arrived addressed to Mum. With it was a note saying, 'Your son will need this'. Inside, carefully wrapped up in tissue paper, was a piece of rope tied into a noose.

Now it was MPs who rang with their support. Whenever Dad wanted advice all he had to do was ring. He thought they were wonderful. I couldn't help thinking we could have done with it earlier. I can't remember their names now. But there were over 200 of them, all pushing for a debate.

On 23 January it was time to take the petition to the Home Secretary and with it Dad was sending a personal letter to Maxwell-Fyfe of his own, a father pleading for his son's life. Mum was still in no state to go. She wasn't sleeping and the half-hour daily visits to Derek wiped her out because she had to keep strong for him. So Dad and I and two parcels of signatures got into a taxi and drove to Whitehall. Two parcels was nothing compared with what we had. It was only 11,000 names. By the end we had 150,000. But we'd been told two parcels would be enough.

We didn't get to see Maxwell-Fyfe himself. A Home Office official took the petitions from us. Dad thought he seemed distressed. I think it was Philip Allen, the Permanent Under-Secretary. We told him we had more signatures and he said if we wanted to bring them in they would be 'received and considered'. It took five minutes. I don't know how many times I've been to the Home Office over the years. Governments and Home Secretaries have come and gone. But nothing changes. It's always the same. I hand in the petition, or whatever it is. Somebody comes through a door to see me. We exchange sentences. And that's it. It takes five minutes. It always takes five minutes.

As we left the reporters crowded round us. But this time we needed them. Dad read out the 'official' letter he had handed in with the signatures which went through the reasons that everybody knew so well. Then he said to them: 'Remember, a boy's life is in the balance. No amount of legal arguments or books written afterwards will bring him back to life. We his family feel sure that we can leave the fair-minded British public to make up their minds and to take every action within their rights to save my son.'

As we were leaving a man came forward and spoke to Dad. He was not optimistic for Derek.

'Don't forget, Mr Bentley, a policeman has been killed. Craig can't be touched so they've only got Derek to balance the books.'

The police had always been our friends. Ever since I was a little girl and Dad would tell the local copper to keep an eye out for me. That was when we were living in Blackfriars; I used to like swinging from a lamppost just across from us in Priory Buildings. It was gaslights then and there was this arm sticking out for the lamplighters to lean their ladders on when they had to change the mantle, which was about every two months. To light it they just needed a long stick with a flame on the end. What I did was throw a rope over this 'arm', tie a fat knot in the bottom of it, twist the rope, then sit on the rope and go spinning round. You had to stick your feet out otherwise you'd bang into the lamppost. We all did it. But because of Derek's accident, Dad was worried stiff I'd bash my head. So he told me not to and asked this copper to keep an eye out for me. But after a weekend of not swinging, I thought I'd risk it. So, it was up and over with the rope and the next thing I knew, there's this copper holding me by the ear and leading me home.

The police were everybody's friend in those days. Dad even knew Constable Miles, the officer who was killed. He'd mended a radio for him. Ordinary law-abiding people, like the members of the jury, really did think of them as the friendly bobby on the beat, like Dixon of Dock Green. Nobody could have imagined they would lie and kick people in the head. When PC Miles was killed one of the reasons public opinion was all for the police was because of how badly police widows were treated. They only got £2 16s a week. (Later in 1953 the pianist Winifred Atwell did a piano marathon to raise money for Mrs Miles. Luckily they had no children.) Police pay wasn't much better. The police made no secret of how they felt. They only got £5 a week. And remember Derek as a dustbin man was getting £6.

Although there was terrible unemployment after the war, with all the servicemen returning to Civvy Street and munitions factories being closed down, it's not surprising that the police were under strength if they couldn't pay them a decent wage. The Government claimed they didn't have the money to pay them more. But they should have done. It's the same old story. The police felt angry at how they were being treated, especially as not only were their numbers down but crime was up. Lots of people had made a fortune during the war, in the black market. And they got away with it. After the war things were even shorter and, with so much money at stake, gangs had sprung up organizing black-market rackets. Also they say there were 25,000 deserters roaming around the country. Without papers, without coupons, they were having to steal to keep alive. Although people like me never saw them, the police were worried about guns. Servicemen returning from the war brought back 'souvenirs' and no one had any idea how many were around. All the guns in Craig's collection were like that.

On 24 January Dr Denis Hill, who had done Derek's epilepsy test at the Maudsley Psychiatric Hospital before the trial, wrote to the Home Office. He knew that nobody had taken into account Derek's illness, in spite of what he had written in his report. He didn't know that Dr Matheson, the prison doctor at Brixton who wrote Derek's medical report for the trial, had played down Dr Hill's findings. He wrote that Derek Bentley should not hang. He was the leading expert. But nobody listened.

On the same day as Dr Hill wrote to the Home Office, a telegram arrived at Fairview Road that just said 'See me at once'. It came from Mrs Sarah Bartley of Southend. Dad hadn't heard of her. Neither had anyone. But with less than three days to go we were clutching at straws.

So Dad hired a car. This time he went on his own. Mum couldn't be left alone for so long. So I stayed to look after her. When Dad came back he was full of it. Mrs Bartley was very smart, a widow in her early sixties and very intelligent, he said. She knew all about Derek's case and she had given him hope. David Maxwell-Fyfe, the Home Secretary, was her brother, she said.

'I have written to him asking him to spare your son's life. Have no fear, Mr Bentley, Derek will not die.'

Dad stayed talking to her for over an hour. Dad went to his grave believing that she really was Maxwell-Fyfe's sister. But I know now that she was not. David Maxwell-Fyfe was an only child. Now, even after forty years, cranks still write to me, even knock at my door. What do they do it for? What can Mrs Bartley have thought she was doing, taking Dad away on that wild-goose chase with Derek's life just three days to run?

CHAPTER THIRTEEN

Although the Home Secretary was the one to recommend the reprieve, it was always done in the name of the Crown. So Mum decided to write to the Queen herself. Usually we wrote letters with the help of people who knew about the law, but Mum wrote this one on her own. There was no fancy language, no legal points, just one mother writing to another.

This time Mum had to go herself. So she and Dad went to Buckingham Palace to hand it in. When they got there the policeman on duty told Mum that the Queen was at Sandringham and she would just have to post it there. So that's what she did.

A reply came by return. A letter of acknowledgement from one of the Queen's private secretaries. It wasn't much but it gave Mum some hope. As I said, we were grasping at straws.

The weekend had come and gone and still there was no word from the Home Office. But no news was good news, or so we thought. Then on Monday, 26 January, around lunchtime, another reporter was at the door. Mum asked him in for a cup of tea, like she did to everyone. But he said no thank you, he just stood on the doorstep and said was it true that the Home Secretary had refused a reprieve.

It wasn't anyone we'd seen before. Dad was in the kitchen. Mum called him to come.

'Will, this young man says the reprieve's been refused. I told him it's not true. We'd have heard.'

This reporter was only young, not much older than me. He looked so embarrassed. He was sorry to trouble us. He said the newspaper, I think it was the *Express*, had got the news that morning.

'I hope it's not true.'

All the other important decisions in Derek's case we knew about either because we were there, or they came through the solicitor.

None had come direct from the Home Office. But we should have had an answer before this. There was only forty-eight hours to go to the time set for Derek's execution.

Then I thought about the bath, still full of letters, because we had so many.

'They wouldn't have just posted it, would they, Dad?'

And I turned and ran upstairs. Dad followed and we began to rummage through the envelopes. Most of them were white or blue in those days, small and square-shaped, paper rationing I suppose, so finding it didn't take long. A long brown envelope with OHMS on it, addressed to Dad. He tore it open. As he read it tears filled his eyes. Then he walked out of the bathroom towards the bedroom where Mum was lying down. And he read it aloud, or tried to, but it was more like a mumble and I could hardly hear, especially when Mum began screaming over and over again. 'No, no, no, no, no.'

> *Sir*
>
> *I am directed by the Secretary of State to inform you that he has given careful consideration to the petition submitted by you on behalf of your son Derek Bentley, and I am to express to you his deep regret that after considering all the circumstances of the case he has failed to discover any sufficient ground to justify him in advising Her Majesty to interfere with the due course of law.*
>
> *I am, Sir, Your obedient servant, [signed] F. Newsom.*

The Home Office had sent the letter by post. Not by messenger, not by telegram. Their decision on Derek's life came in an envelope that looked like something from the Inland Revenue, no more important than a tax return. It was posted on Saturday. Two days lost. But it was more than that. It shows what the Bentleys were fighting. Fighting something that didn't care about people. We were asking for compassion for Derek. What chance had he, someone they thought was a criminal, when they didn't even have compassion for his family who had never done anything wrong.

We didn't have to tell Derek the news ourselves. The Governor had already done it. At 9.20 that morning he told him that the reprieve had been refused so the sentence would be carried out at 9 a.m. on 28 January as arranged.

Derek wasn't there when we arrived that afternoon. We had to wait about twenty minutes before he came.

'Sorry I'm late. There was a nice man who wanted to shake my hand.'

The nice man was Albert Pierrepoint, the hangman. We had seen him on our way in. Not that we knew who he was. He was just a man. But after it was all over I recognized him from his picture in the paper. Shaking hands was the way he had of checking up that the measurements he had been given by the prison were right. I've got those measurements now in documents from Wandsworth Prison. Derek William Bentley, height in shoes 5 foot 10 7/8 inches. Weight in shoes 173 pounds. They hang them in their shoes, without their shoe-laces of course. Why no shoe-laces? To stop them hanging themselves with them.

Everything in those prison documents is so cold. The original date for the execution, set straight after the trial and before Derek's lawyers lodged the appeal, was 30 December. But Mr Pierrepoint informed the Under-Sheriff of Surrey that the 30th was not convenient, but he could manage 31 December. Then after the appeal, it was moved to 28 January. There had always to be three Sundays between the sentence (or failed appeal) and the date of execution. That wasn't changed, so it must have been convenient.

People often ask me if Derek knew what was going to happen. I don't know. That afternoon, Monday, the 26th, I think he did know.

'I'm not afraid to die, because I never hurt anyone, Mum. Everyone knows I didn't kill Mr Miles and God knows I didn't.'

Although we'd always gone to church, for Derek it didn't mean much, just something we did on Sundays. But about a year before the shooting he met a Jehovah's Witness in the street and began talking. Sister Lane her name was. Derek always had a soft spot for the elderly. When he saw them on their own in the street, he felt sorry for them, said that nobody loved them. He had this thing about people not being loved. We used to go for walks in cemeteries and he would pick flowers for graves that didn't have any. He said they were people whose families didn't love them. My job was to clean out the vase and fill it with fresh water and Derek would pick flowers, dandelions or that pink weed you find on bomb-sites, willow herb. In the winter he would even buy flowers with roots and plant them. Pansies usually. It started in Edgware but in Norbury going for a walk with Derek often meant going to Croydon cemetery. Strange to think of him there now. I try to keep fresh flowers there all the time, otherwise he might think that he was one of those people whose family didn't love him.

Sister Lane lived not far from us at Fairview Road and she invited Derek round to listen to Bible stories. He'd always loved Bible stories ever since he was a boy. Mum and Dad didn't mind. Mum said it didn't matter if she was a Jehovah's Witness. It was the same God. What was good was that Sister Lane had the Bible stories on records, which she lent him. Derek had a Bible which Nan gave him, I think, when he was little. But, not being able to read, it wasn't much use. With the records all he had to do was put them on. He used to come back and tell me what she'd told him, things like we'll all come back again after we're dead. The stories were just the old gospel stories, but she made them easy for him to understand. And the Bible itself, even if it's read out loud, takes a lot of understanding.

I think those things that Sister Lane told him helped him over those last few days. But whether he knew it would really happen I will never know. We never talked about it. Just the opposite. We kept telling him not to give up, that we were still fighting for him, to give him some hope.

To keep his spirits up, and ours too, we just kept talking about the usual things, the animals of course, always the animals, his friends Geoffrey Rogerson from the flower shop on the corner and Philip, about how dreadful it was Robert being killed in Korea. Philip never came to see Derek in Wandsworth, although he was on the list. He said he didn't want to, that he'd rather wait till he got home.

I remember that afternoon Mum saying that his face had healed up well. He told us the warders had been telling him jokes. But he couldn't remember any of them. It didn't surprise me. Knowing Derek he wouldn't have understood them in the first place. He asked if Dad had planted any flowers yet. Dad said no, it was still too cold. He asked me how Laurie was. How plans for the wedding were getting on. He liked Laurie. Laurie used to take him up to the pie shop in Thornton Heath for a pie or a sausage sandwich. Sausage sandwich was Derek's favourite. He never thought of it as meat. It was just sausage. That was Derek all over. He just didn't understand.

As those last days ticked by, Mum and Dad felt so inadequate. They never said as much to Derek, they had to keep his spirits up. But it was terrible to see. Terrible. All his life we'd looked after him and now, in his hour of need, we could do nothing.

'I'm not afraid to die, because I know I didn't kill anyone.'

His blue eyes were looking at Mum. His mum who he idolized.

'I know, Derek, I know you've never done anything really bad.' And tears were spilling down her face.

Then for the only time Derek broke down and said in a quiet voice that seemed too far away, 'Help me. Please help me.'

We'd been there half an hour and I don't think I ever stopped trembling. Gooseflesh one minute then feeling so hot. Shaking as if it would never stop. I felt so helpless. What could we do? Dad told him that we weren't giving up, that his case was going to be debated in the House of Commons the next day. That he had thousands of friends. But how could Derek understand any of it?

Soon after we got back to Fairview Road, Harry Proctor, the journalist from the *Sunday Pictorial* that had been dealing with the Craigs, told us that Mrs Craig wanted to see Mum and Dad. That she had new evidence that might help Derek.

Just the mention of the name Craig was enough to make Mum ill. 'You go, Will,' she said. 'But I can't.' But Dad said she must go with him. He was so gentle with her, so understanding, as he always was, that finally she agreed. The Craigs only lived a few streets away so, with Dad holding Mum's arm and Harry Proctor beside them, I watched them walk away towards Derek's final hope, the mother of the boy who had started it all.

I didn't go. I just stayed at home, answering the phone. Dad came back very impressed with Mrs Craig. They'd been there about an hour going over what Craig had told her, things which she felt could help Derek. Mum and Dad arranged to go with her to the Home Office the next morning. Looking back now Mrs Craig's new evidence didn't have a chance – the evidence of a convicted murderer, because that's what it was, things Christopher Craig had told her during visits. He had told her that Derek had never said 'Let him have it, Chris'. He told her that anyway Derek never called him Chris, just Kid or Kiddo. But he had also said that the words that had been so damaging for Derek in claiming that he knew Craig had a gun, 'It's a .45 Colt and plenty of bloody ammunition,' *were* spoken on the roof that night, but not by Derek, by Craig himself.

So the next morning, Tuesday, 27 January, Dad and I met Mrs Craig outside the Home Office to present this 'new evidence'. Mum was too ill to go. She stayed at home looked after by Lillian and I went with Dad. After Mrs Craig left Dad talked to Sir Frank Newsom the Permanent Secretary at the Home Office about all the things that hadn't come up in the trial, his epilepsy, his being so slow, the war. Sir Frank listened but didn't say anything much, except that he would present the new evidence to Sir David Maxwell-Fyfe within the hour. It took five minutes.

Although we didn't know it then, Dr Denis Hill, who had examined Derek at the Maudsley, telephoned the Home Office at about the same time as Dad and Mrs Craig were there. He still hadn't had a reply from his letter and asked for permission to publish the EEG tests he had done on Derek. Permission was refused. To make this information on Derek's mental condition available to the public, said the Home Office, 'was not in the public interest'.

Our next stop was the House of Commons. Inside it was packed and outside there was already a large crowd. They were there for Derek. Sydney Silverman was there to meet us. He had put a Motion on the Order Paper the night before for Derek's case to be debated this afternoon. He said he was confident that in open debate there would be a massive vote for a reprieve. Fifty MPs had signed the Motion, many more had signed it afterwards and hundreds of others had pledged their support. But the Motion wasn't on the Order Paper. So he was going to raise it with the Speaker, William Morrison. We went into the visitors' gallery. At the first opportunity Sydney Silverman spoke.

I desire your indulgence, Mr Speaker, to ask about a Motion which I sought to put on the Order Paper last night, but which, I understand, by your direction ultimately did not appear. I will endeavour to put my point as shortly as may be and, of course, without raising any of the merits either way of the subject matter of the Motion, but I hope I may have your indulgence for a minute or two in dealing with the matter, because it seems to me that this is a question which involves the whole matter of the authority of Parliament and the right of Parliament to control the Executive in any action which a Departmental Minister takes, and I would say especially in matters where the Royal Prerogative of mercy is involved.

At a few minutes past seven last night, I took into the Table office a Motion in these words:

'That this House respectfully dissents from the opinion of the Home Secretary that there were no sufficient reasons for advising the exercise of the Royal Clemency in the case of Derek Bentley; and urges him to reconsider the matter so as to give effect to the recommendation of the jury and to the expressed view of the Lord Chief Justice [who was the trial judge] that Bentley's guilt was less than that of his co-defendant Christopher Craig.'

149

There were about fifty honourable Members who supported that
Motion, not all from one side of the House, and among the fifty there
were no fewer than ten Privy Councillors, honourable Members who
have held high office under the Crown. The fifty also included the
former Solicitor-General and one of the former Under-Secretaries of
State for the Home Department.

I mention these facts as part of the claim which I would modestly
make that the Motion was by no means a frivolous Motion; that it was
a well-considered Motion, so far as one could make it so, and not a
Motion which would be regarded in any quarter of the house as one
which obviously ought not to appear upon the Order Paper.

He said that overnight the fifty had grown to over 200. He said
that the Motion had been accepted by the clerks, and he had been
in the House the night before till after 8.30 p.m. and no one had
said that there were any irregularities that would mean it couldn't
go on.

But, it was not on the Order Paper. Mr Silverman asked why it
was taken off. The Speaker referred him to the Parliamentary
procedure reference book. Silverman went on arguing. He knew
there were no reasons for withdrawing the Motion. He was a lawyer
himself. Another Labour MP, also a lawyer, Mr Paget, joined in.

I think the great condemnation which we made of the German people
was that they stood aside and did nothing when dreadful things
happened. We are a sovereign assembly. A three-quarter-witted boy of
nineteen is to be hanged for a murder he did not commit, and which
was committed fifteen minutes after he was arrested. Can we be made
to keep silent when a thing as horrible and as shocking as this is to
happen? I ask your guidance because I feel that the great mass of
honourable members here feel with me that we ought to be provided
with an opportunity to try to prevent this dreadful thing happening.

Then another Labour MP, Leslie Hale, joined in. His argument
was broader. In not letting MPs challenge the Home Secretary's

decision, the Speaker was taking away from MPs the one way they had of challenging anything. Then it was Aneurin Bevan. He tried another tack. He said what worried him was the removal of Sydney Silverman's Motion from the Order Paper for no good reason. Then Silverman got to his feet. He asked that the Motion to challenge the Home Secretary's decision be adjourned. Moving an adjournment would mean a debate. He had written this new Motion out by hand and it was passed up to the Speaker. But it did no good. Then another Labour MP, Desmond Donnelly, stood up. Another Motion, this time to challenge the Speaker's actions.

Had the Speaker decided all this on his own? He was a Tory. He denied it, of course. But then, he would, wouldn't he?

Sir David Maxwell-Fyfe had been sitting there throughout it all. He didn't move a muscle. Neither did the rest of the Government front bench. This was the Speaker's decision:

A motion can be put down on this subject when the sentence has been executed . . . After the sentence of death has been executed, the Minister responsible may be criticised on the relevant vote of supply, or on the adjournment. I have stated that this is the practice of the House, and I cannot alter the practice of the House!

Telegrams by the bagful were being brought into the Chamber while he spoke, telegrams sent by ordinary people to their MPs that piled up in front of Maxwell-Fyfe. From people who could not believe that something like this could really happen in England. England that won the war against Hitler. England that was at the start of a new and wondrous Elizabethan age.

What was Parliament about, said Mr Silverman, if it couldn't challenge ministerial action? But, until Derek had been hanged, there had been no ministerial action to be challenged. That was the logic of Parliament.

*

151

We had to leave. It was time for Derek's visit. As always the visiting order had dropped on to the mat that morning. 'January 27th, 1953, William Bentley, Lillian Bentley, Iris Bentley.' Our last visit.

We went back to Fairview Road to get Mum. Dad began to tell her what had happened and said we would soon hear. Silently she handed him a letter that had just been delivered by messenger from the Home Office.

I am directed to inform you that the Secretary of State has given the fullest consideration to your representations, but very much regrets that he has been unable to find any grounds for modifying the decision previously communicated to you.

As we set off for Wandsworth, we were still hopeful. Mr Silverman had said he had organized a deputation of six MPs, led by Aneurin Bevan, the shadow Home Secretary, to press for a reprieve on the grounds of public opinion which had grown over the last two days since news of the refusal of the reprieve was known.

But, as everybody knows, there was no reprieve. At nine o'clock the next morning, while we stood in the front room in Fairview Road, holding each other, praying silently, praying for poor, poor Derek, waiting for the chimes of Big Ben on the radio, a large empty cupboard in the condemned cell was pushed back to reveal a door into the execution chamber. Albert Pierrepoint walked through. He shook hands with Derek. A hospital orderly then handed Derek a large cup of brandy which he drank. They say Derek was crying. They say his last words were, 'I didn't say it. I didn't tell Chris to shoot that policeman.'

Then they tied his hands together and put a white hood over his head that Albert Pierrepoint took from his breast pocket where it looked like a handkerchief, and marched my brother through the door to the execution chamber and his death.

Outside Wandsworth Prison the crowd waited. At nine o'clock

the men all removed their hats. There was one minute of silence and then the crowd sang 'Abide with Me' and the 23rd Psalm, 'The Lord is My Shepherd'. A warder came out to fix two notices. One that the execution of Derek William Bentley had been carried out and the other signed by the prison doctor saying he was dead.

The crowds went mad. The frame for the notices was smashed. The police were pelted with coins, police helmets were wrenched off, some people even got into the prison itself. But it was all over.

It was over for them. But it would never be over for us. The next day Derek's last letter arrived. It was Harry Proctor's idea. Derek had dictated it to a warder. The words might have been a bit tidied up. But not much. It's Derek all the same.

Dear Mum and Dad

I was glad to see you on my visit today but I was a little disappointed that Rita could not come. I got the rosary and the letter and I saw the photo of the dogs. Iris looked quite nice surrounded with all those animals. I couldn't keep the photo because it was a newspaper cutting.

I told you Mum it would be very difficult to write this letter, I can't think of anything to say except that you have all been wonderful the way you have worked for me. Thank Rita for writing to me, tell her I'm thinking of her. Don't forget what I told you today. 'Always keep your chin up', and tell Pop not to grind his teeth. Oh! I mustn't forget to thank Lil and Bert for writing and coming to see me. Give my love to them both and to everybody else that we know. Tell Ronnie to keep away from the boys and to stay on his own.

I hope Dad has some more televisions in. I forgot to ask him how things were on the visit. Dad and I used to have some fun on that one of Leslie's, he certainly had some spare parts for it.

Oh Dad! Don't let my cycle frames get rusty they might come in handy one day 'cause old Sally [Derek's name for his bike] *has got a cracked frame and I want you to change it before something happens to you, and dad, keep a strict eye on Denis if he does anything wrong, though I don't think he will but you never know how little things can get you into trouble, if he does, wallop him so he won't be able to sit for three weeks. I am trying to give you good advice because of my experience.*

I'll tell you what Mum, the truth of this story has got to come out one day, and as I said in the visiting box that one day a lot of people are going to get into trouble and I think you know who those people are. What do you think Mum? This letter may sound a bit solemn but I am still keeping my chin up as I want all the family to do.

Don't let anything happen to the dogs and the cats and look after them as you always have.

I hope Laurie and Iris get married all right. I'd like to give them my blessing, it would be nice to have a brother-in-law like him, we could have some fun together. We could have gone to the club and drunk ourselves to a standstill on the great occasion of them being married, tell him to lob out my flower, tell him to keep my mac clean and my ties. Laurie and I used to have some fun up at the pond till four o'clock in the morning, by the café. I always caught Laurie to pay for the pies, he never caught me once. That will be all for now. I will sign this myself.

Lots of love,

Derek.

My sister Joan not long before she died. She was only twelve but she had brains to burn.

Nan and Aunt Rose at Folkestone, where they always went on holiday because that was the place to be seen.

On the roof at Priory Mansions: Derek with the butcher's dog, me with my itchy green swimming costume.

Spring 1941, up on the roof, Derek and me wearing our 'black'. I had three dresses the same, and we wore black for eighteen months, six months each for Nan, Joan and Aunt Rose; that's how Mum worked it out.

Derek, aged about ten, at the end of the war when we were living in Hillingdon Street. I carried this round with me for years which is why it is so battered.

Above: Derek took this of me just before my twenty-first in the garden of Fairview Road.

Left: Uncle Bert, Mum and Denis with Derek in front holding Blanko, one of his cats. I suppose Derek must have been about sixteen. Dad was taking the picture.

The foyer at the Streatham Astoria, the only picture I've got of me in usherette's uniform. The deputy manager was leaving and they gave him a barometer.

Me and Maurice in the lounge at Fairview Road just after we got engaged. We broke it off after a silly tiff but he was always the one for me. I don't know that I ever got over him.

Derek in front of Lady Casson's Hillman. It was kept in the garage next to our house and Derek kept it polished. In return she'd let him take it out for a bit of a run.

This was Mum's favourite picture of Derek – and mine too. I took it on his nineteenth birthday, the last one he ever had.

Craig being carried into Croydon Magistrates Court for the commital in November 1952. You can see Claud Pain behind him, wearing an overcoat and trilby, all set to give evidence.

There was a riot outside Wandsworth prison when they posted up the notices saying Derek had been hanged. The crowd who'd been there all night keeping vigil threw anything they could lay their hands on and broke the glass.

Derek's funeral at Croydon Cemetery. Although it was fifteen years after Derek was hanged, a proper Christian burial meant a lot to Mum. Both Dad and Uncle Bert had to keep hold of her, she was so overcome.

Mum, Dad and me outside Wandsworth prison with Derek's wreath. Mum looks so old and tired but it was Dad who died first, less than a year after this picture was taken.

Maria and me on holiday at Hastings in 1966. We couldn't pass by without feeding this horse. Like all the Bentleys, Maria loves animals.

Maria and me after the premiere of *Let Him Have It* in Leicester Square Odeon with Tom Courteney who played my dad in the film.

Until Derek is proved innocent, the fight goes on.

CHAPTER FOURTEEN

I don't know how we got through those first few days. Even though it was Derek we were fighting for, it was like we had been fighting for our own lives too. We were like survivors from a shipwreck that after days of hopeless swimming had just managed to reach shore. We were exhausted. Although Derek had been gone from Fairview Road for three months, right up till the end we never lost hope that he'd be coming home. Like Dad told him, we knew he would have to go to prison because of being up on the roof, but as long as you know when something's going to end, you can cope. We didn't talk about it, just carried on as normal as possible. But that was just on the outside. Inside we felt as empty and useless as an old cigarette packet.

All the Speaker's talk about letting the House of Commons debate Maxwell-Fyfe's decision not to reprieve Derek *after* the sentence was carried out, was just part of a game. A game with rules only one side seems to know. On Monday, 2 February, Sydney Silverman tried to get it talked about. He did it by moving the rejection of the Consolidated Fund Bill and for some reason that I don't understand he hoped this would let him talk about Derek's case. It didn't work. Although Derek's name has been mentioned time and time again in the House of Commons, in all these years there has never been a debate.

On 3 February Dad went to Wandsworth Prison to collect Derek's things. Only when he got back did he realize they hadn't given him Derek's new clothes, the ones Mum had got him for the trial. He hadn't realized because it was all parcelled up in brown paper. Derek's overcoat was there, plus his old socks, a hankie, some letters, a tie and his comb. But no suit, no shirt, no shoes. Dad began to boil with anger.

'It's not the clothes, it's the principle that matters.'

Later of course I realized that they must have buried him in them. Because, if you think about it, people do get buried in their clothes. But we weren't thinking. It was the clothes that tipped Dad over. Only then, after all those weeks of torture, did Dad break. Not that he hadn't cried before. He'd been red-eyed day after day, night after sleepless night. But not out loud, not in front of us. Once, in the dark, in the back of a car, when we were coming back from the House of Commons, I'd heard him crying, but this was different. To see your dad, that tower of strength, just bent over and sobbing and sobbing was something terrible. I thought he was going to have a heart attack. I remember making him a cup of tea and trying to calm him down.

'Look what you've done, Dad, you've made my mascara run.'

But it was terrible, he cried like the earth was opening up in front of him. I will never forget it till the day I die.

After I went back to work, I would still find myself looking out for Derek, to see if he was waiting for me. It was from habit. Because that's what my brother would do, come over to Streatham, wait for me to finish, then walk me home. It was about two miles there and two miles back. He'd walk four miles just so I wouldn't have to walk back on my own in the dark. At the trial the prosecution barrister made out Derek was lying when he said he took the bus to Croydon with Craig just to have a bit of a walk around. I don't know about that night. I wasn't there. But that's just what Derek used to do and it wouldn't surprise me if that's what Craig had said to him that night, to get him to go with him. 'What about us going for a bit of a walk, Del.' I can just hear him say it. It's what we all used to do. Up the cemetery, up Streatham Common. Or get the bus, a threepenny ride up to Croydon like Derek and Craig and the others did that night, and a wander around the shops, just looking. In the winter when it was too cold or wet for a walk, we would sit in the waiting room at Norbury station because they had a big open fire. Lillian and I would take our knitting and just chat. It was somewhere we could talk on our own, without Denis or Mum or Dad listening in. It wasn't that we had secrets. It was just when you're young you want to be on your own.

For me the worst time was always coming home, opening the front door and somehow expecting Derek to be there. As soon as she heard the key in the latch, Judy would be up, tail going like mad, but when she saw it wasn't him she just turned round and went back to where she'd been lying. Until the next time. You could go the whole day bottling it all up, then something like Judy not knowing Derek would never come back was enough to break your heart.

If I felt bad, it must have been ten times worse for Mum and Dad. Derek was their first-born son. Mum had brought him into the world. Dad had helped deliver him and saved his life though the blood transfusions when he was just a day old. But they hadn't been able to save his life when he was grown. Over and over they kept thinking wasn't there something more they could have done. If only they hadn't been impressed by Norman Parsley that night, Derek would never have taken the bus to Croydon. If only, if only. They didn't say as much, but you could just feel the words hovering above their heads like those balloons in comics. If only.

Derek was so beautiful as a baby, with his smile and his blue eyes and his blonde curls. I know he was slow, but that only made you love him the more. Mum idolized him. Out of all of us, he'd always been the one for her. I think boys do go to the mother like girls go to the father. Like Dad and me, we were always close. She'd already had so much to bear, first Joan, then Roger, now Derek. Not to mention Nan and Aunt Rose. She kept his room just as it was, like he left it, his toys put away, his comics tidied in piles in the cabinet by his bed. We still called it Derek's room, even though Uncle Bert slept in there on his own now. I went back to sleeping in my own bed. Denis went back to sleeping on the bed-settee in the lounge. Nobody ever slept in Derek's bed.

But not everything stayed the same at Fairview Road. The coat Mum wore to the court was big green checks and from then on she would never have green in the house. Having red hair, until then green had been her favourite. It was all over. The settee and the two chairs were green, they went. The green carpet in the lounge, that went. Plus a green cloth on the mantelpiece under the ornaments, so did two green vases and a bone-china tea service, not to mention the hat and coat. The settee and chairs got put out on the pavement for the council to collect, the rest Mum threw on to the carpet, then she and Dad rolled the whole thing up and dumped it. A new furniture shop had opened up on the High Street, so they bought a new settee and chairs in their opening sale. Not expensive, just covered in brown Rexine, a kind of fake leather cloth. We couldn't afford a new carpet, but Dad had a square of lino which he nailed down and then varnished round the edges. The only carpet was a runner in front of the fire.

It did her good, doing something. There was no such thing as counselling then. The only counselling Mum got was cups of tea over with Mrs Leppard or Mrs Ruhe.

'Come on, Lily, the kettle's boiling.'

Everyone around us, all the neighbours, was very kind. And Ken Allen of the *Evening News*, one of the reporters who'd been with us all through, his mother would come over and see Mum.

She wasn't on her own. Dad didn't go back to work for six months. Not only because of not wanting to leave Mum, but his arthritis had started playing up badly. Although he was getting on, he'd always been so youthful, full of life and fun but now his bones ached like an old man's and his hair was grey.

I went back to work two weeks after Derek was hanged. I nearly didn't have a job to go back to. The day after the trial Mr Smith the manager of the Astoria telephoned to say that I wasn't wanted back. Some reporters had turned up asking questions, claiming they were looking for me. It wasn't good for business, he said, and he was sending on my cards. Dad went mad. Luckily he knew someone who worked in Rank's head office who had been a bouncer at the Astoria years before. So strings were pulled and Mr Smith was told he had to keep me on.

I didn't tell them when I'd be back at work, I didn't know. It was only that morning, Monday, 10 February, that I decided it was no good sitting around moping, so I just got a clean dicky front out of the airing cupboard, took the 109 bus and turned up at 1.30 p.m., ready for the usherettes' parade, back to ordinary life. Nothing had changed. Everything was still there in my locker. The girls were so kind, gave me a real welcome. There was one who said, you know how I feel, Iris, but I can't say anything because my dad's a policeman.

I never told the girls what happened to the necklace they gave me for my twenty-first. It was a beautiful three-row pearl choker. But they couldn't have known about the pearls. Even I didn't know. It was Mum who told me. 'Pearls mean tears,' she said. She was never happy about me wearing them but I could hardly give them back. But after that terrible night on the roof, it began to worry me, having them in the house.

Anyone else would have stayed indoors that 5 November, three nights after Derek was arrested. But not Dad. He wouldn't let anything spoil things for a child. Denis was only nine, after all. The bonfire was in the alley beside our house. Everyone at our end of the street shared it and Dad was in charge, as usual, lighting the blue touch paper on the fireworks, Catherine wheels, Roman candles and rockets, and telling all the youngsters to stand well back. It was when I was staring at the flames in the bonfire that I decided the pearls had to go. First I thought of putting them in the bonfire but decided no; they would still be there when it had died down. But my mind was made up. The next day I waited till it was dark, then I walked up to the allotments at Thornton Heath. I tore the strands apart. They didn't just fall off. Each one was separated by a knot. I had to pull off each pearl and threw it as hard as I could into the field next to the allotments. Mum was right. Pearls mean tears.

Being back with my friends at the Astoria was like a defence, a comfort. But sometimes it was all too much and I'd just be standing at the cash desk or at my post and the tears would just come and I couldn't stop them. A few weeks after I'd been back there was a film called *The Tall Headlines*. It was all about how a family was affected when the eldest son was hanged for murder. It starred Michael Denison. There was no way I could stay for that.

Although the interest in Derek's case had died down, it hadn't gone away. When Fairfax, Jaggs, McDonald and Harrison were given their medals a newspaper wrote that Mum had phoned DC Fairfax (Sergeant Fairfax as he was now) and threatened him. It was rubbish. We didn't even know where Fairfax lived, let alone his telephone number. As if Mum would do something like that anyway. As she said, 'I'm too full of grief to waste my time on a liar.' It was just trouble-making. She believed that there was only one judge, God in heaven, and that those policemen who lied would get their punishment when the time came and in the meantime they'd have to live with Derek's life on their consciences.

After Derek was killed, all we wanted to do was to close the door to journalists and newspapers. They'd never really been on our side. They were just reporters wanting a story, the more sensational the better. They were only interested in Derek to sell their newspapers. The Bentleys, the Craigs, it was all the same to them. But it was one of those first reporters, Ken Allen, who explained to us that publicity through newspapers was the only way we were going to keep Derek's name from being swept under the carpet. Mum wasn't convinced. All she wanted was to be left in peace. 'You mark my words, if we don't shut the door now it will go on for years,' she said. She was right. But so was Ken Allen. It has been keeping the publicity going in the press that has kept people reading about it. All those letters to the Home Secretaries that have come and gone over the past forty years. Where did they get us?

Not that the press believed in what we were doing until very recently. For them it was just a story. But it was our only way of keeping Derek's name alive. I'm explaining this now because people often ask why we let the press enter into our grief, into our lives. First it was because they would tell us things, news, things they'd heard on Fleet Street. Usually it was because they thought it would make a good story for them. But sometimes it was just something they thought might help us. Where else would we get that kind of help, that kind of information? People who criticize forget that these journalists were far more worldly-wise than Dad or Mum and they would come up with ideas. Even to this day, if capital punishment is being discussed on the media, they give me a call. I'm useful to them and they've been useful to me, to Derek. But that doesn't say the Bentleys always liked what they wrote, or even what they wanted us to do. But we did it because it was the only way.

It was about a month after Derek was killed that a journalist told us that Maxwell-Fyfe was the chief speaker at a conference on crime and punishment, organized by the Conservative party at Church House, Westminster on 28 February. Someone told Dad people would be allowed to ask questions, so he had his, all written out in advance, on a bit of paper. We got there early and sat in the front row. And then there he was, Sir David Maxwell-Fyfe, the man who could have saved my brother, the man who turned down the pleas of everyone, including it later turned out, his Permanent Secretary Sir Frank Newsom. I know you shouldn't judge a bird by his feathers, but Maxwell-Fyfe was a vile-looking man, small and puffed up. With his bald head and hooked nose he looked like a vulture.

Juvenile crime, he said, was the fault of family upbringing. I couldn't stand it. My heart was beating loud in my ears. How dare he say that about us. Because that's what he was doing. If you bring your children up like that, he said, what do you expect. Well, they weren't going to say that about our family. As if to prove him wrong I didn't shout out or anything like that. I'd been brought up properly, I knew how to behave. I waited till question time, shaking like I had done when I last saw Derek, then I stood up and spoke. My voice seemed to be coming from someone else.

'You say delinquency starts in the home, I don't believe that. There's no way my brother was brought up badly.'

It was Maxwell-Fyfe I was speaking to, and it was for him to reply. But he didn't have the nerve. He just looked at another man on the platform, a Dr Spencer from the London School of Economics who'd been saying much the same thing. So this Dr Spencer answered, saying that research said they were right, that criminality started in the home.

'It is your word against mine,' he said. 'Your word against mine.' That's what it always boiled down to, words. But it was always their words that won. The police's word against Derek's and Craig's. Dr Matheson's word against Dr Hill's. Maxwell-Fyfe's word against Parliament's. But there were to be no more words from Maxwell-Fyfe that night and soon after my speaking up detectives hustled him out the back way like a criminal. They knew who we were all right. Dad never got to ask his question. But it didn't matter. The Bentleys were not going to be silenced. As we left the hall Dad squeezed my hand.

'We must keep it up. We must never let them forget, never let them push Derek's name under the carpet.'

It was just what we needed to get us going again. Over the next few days Dad was out in the shed banging away with the hammer. By the weekend everything was ready. It was a platform made out of a tea-chest. The top which you stood on was hinged and there was a padlock. There were two high steps to climb on to it at the back which were were covered with brown lino to protect the wood. The top was the same. The front extended up and hid our legs and ended in a shelf for the leaflets. It looked like a do-it-yourself pulpit, which in a way it was. Painted on the front bit in big letters was BILL BENTLEY. All we had to do now was get it to Marble Arch.

At Speakers' Corner, as it is called, people are allowed to talk about anything they want, provided it's not obscene or blasphemous and does not constitute an incitement to a breach of the peace. Before the war Joan and I used to go past on our Sunday walks. Little did I think then that one day I'd be one of those mad-looking spouters. Every weekend the place would be crowded with people sounding off about religion, communism, politics, the Bomb, all the things you're not allowed to discuss at the dinner table. On a busy Saturday or Sunday, there are hundreds of people so you had to stand on something, or else you wouldn't be seen. That's what the tea-chest was for.

There were no set places at 'Spouters' Corner', as we used to call it. First come first served and no argy-bargy. The best place was in the middle, so once we knew how it worked, Dad would try and get there by 8.30 a.m. sharp.

That first morning when we set up the platform it was cold but dry. But the weather didn't matter to Dad. He never went anywhere without his umbrella. When it was really sheeting down, the one not talking would stand on the top step at the back and hold it over the other. It was one of those big black gents' umbrellas so it covered the both of us. When Dad was up there talking, it worked fine. But as I was taller than him, when he was holding the umbrella and I was talking, I could barely see out from under, and the spikes at the end of the spokes were always snagging at my hair.

It took nerve standing up there and spouting. You never knew how the people crowding round would react. Even when we were used to it, there was always that fear that something would happen, that someone would throw a rotten tomato at you. It did happen, but never to us. Dad was a bit shaky at first, he had never spoken in public in his life. The most public thing he'd ever done was being a choirboy at Southwark Cathedral. I'd done nothing, except my question to Maxwell-Fyfe and all those shows in the tree-house and in the front garden in Edgware. But we had to do it for Derek, and the family firm of Bentley & Daughter set out their stall at Spouters' Corner, come rain or shine, summer and winter, hell or high water as Dad would say, most Saturdays and Sundays for the next three years. At the end of every day we hid our 'soap-box' in a patch of shrubby trees. Nobody ever touched it or even tried to force the padlock. Not that they'd have found much, only Uncle Bert's leaflets.

Our aim was the same then as it is now. In fact, we always had two aims, first to tell Derek's story, to keep Derek's name alive until we could prove his innocence, and second to campaign against capital punishment. 'How do you expect to have law and order if you don't execute?' they'd say. We'd say that most murders are done by members of the family or other people the murderer knows. That they'd probably do it anyway. Then they'd say, 'Murderers are just junk, they're not fit to be on the earth.' We'd say, 'If they're junk, so are you. If you have got it in your heart to hang, then you're no better.' They'd be firing questions at us and sometimes there'd be hostile voices shouting that we should have been hanged too. But whatever they fired at us, I always tried to keep a civil tongue in my head. If we went hammer and tongs they would think we were violent and what we were trying to put over was that violence breeds violence. Nowadays that's not so unusual an idea. But it was then.

And we told them about Derek. We told them about Derek's epilepsy: it had never come out in public, not at the trial, not afterwards. We told how the police refused to let Dad be with Derek while he was being interviewed. We told them how Derek was beaten up in the police station, how his eyes were so swollen he couldn't see. There were no camcorders in those days, no video of Rodney King being beaten up in broad daylight in the streets of Los Angeles by the police. People thought the police were all like George Dixon of Dock Green. We weren't only fighting for Derek, of course, a lot of what we said about what happened when Derek was arrested, was the same for anyone who was illiterate or not up to dealing with the police. If the police needed to make arrests, to get convictions, how much easier to find someone who couldn't speak up for themselves, who couldn't explain what had really happened, and just pin it on them. You got medals for that. Of course, we had to be careful about running down the police. We never said straight out that the police lied, you never knew who might be listening, but we went as far as we dared to make it obvious.

The first thing that helped us was Christie being arrested. It happened not long after we had started campaigning at Spouters' Corner. John Reginald Christie was arrested on 31 March 1953 for the murder of five women. He was tried in June and hanged in Wandsworth Prison on 15 July. Christie's name was already well known. He had been the chief witness for the prosecution at the trial of Timothy Evans three years before. Evans, who lived at the top of 10 Rillington Place in west London, where Christie also lived, was hanged in 1949 for murdering his wife and his baby daughter.

Timothy Evans was completely innocent. It was Christie who had killed Mrs Evans and baby Geraldine. Christie lived on the ground floor of the house and, although this was not discovered until his confession, he had already killed two other women who were buried in the back garden by the time Timothy Evans, his wife Beryl and the baby moved into the same house. They were sexual murders. Christie then took a fancy to Evans's wife. By this time she was pregnant again. The Evanses were hard up and Beryl couldn't face having another baby so soon, and Christie offered to do an abortion for her. He had been a policeman for a few years and said he had medical knowledge and had done them before. Of course it was a lie, but it gave him an opportunity to give her some gas. That was how he killed his victims. He gassed them before having sex with their dead bodies. Beryl, like the other victims, would have thought it was the kind of 'gas' dentists give you, an anaesthetic, but it was just ordinary killer gas from the mains.

Timothy Evans, like Derek, was a bit slow and, again like Derek, he couldn't read or write. So when Christie told him his wife had died having the abortion, instead of going to the police, he was so bewildered, he just pretended nothing had happened, said his wife had gone away to stay with friends, and went back to his home town in Wales. But after a few days, because he was so troubled – after all, his wife who he loved had just died – he went to the police in Wales, but instead of telling them the truth, he 'confessed', said that he had killed her himself. He had lied because he didn't want to get Christie into trouble (doing an abortion was against the law and he still thought Christie had been helping and Beryl's death was just a terrible accident and also Christie had organized to look after the baby) and because, like I said, he wasn't clever enough to understand that Christie was setting him up.

Then when he was charged with murder, Evans saw the light and changed his story and told them the truth about Christie. But because he had lied, the police didn't believe this 'new' story. There was plenty of evidence that Evans could not have done the murders, evidence given by council workmen, but the police were so convinced that they were right, that Evans *had* murdered his wife and baby, that they made these witnesses *change* their evidence about dates and times, just so it would fit in with their story of Evans being the murderer and not Christie.

I already knew a lot about Timothy Evans because, like a lot of other people, I followed the trial in the newspapers when it happened in 1949. I was eighteen and I had been against capital punishment ever since I was nine. It happened not long after we arrived at Edgware. There was a game they played at Camrose Avenue school called Hangman. You drew bits of the gallows and the body. It was the same idea as noughts and crosses. The one who finished drawing the body was the winner.

It was Donald the boy I shared a desk with who was doing it. 'What's that?' I said. And he told me it was someone being hanged till he was dead. Then he made a horrible face and pretended to choke. It really upset me and this boy just laughed all the more. That afternoon when I got back from school I asked Mum what it all meant. Did they really hang people?

'Yes. When somebody kills someone, they get killed themselves.'

'But who kills the hangman? Who kills the hangman?'

This question was never answered, not then, not now.

It wasn't that I thought Timothy Evans was innocent. The evidence the court was presented with was so strong. Nobody knew then that the police had changed the evidence to suit their case and Christie was, after all, a policeman, and the chief witness and, as I said, no one believed a policeman would lie, let alone murder anyone. But I was so strongly against capital punishment that I started up a petition. I just stood outside Norbury railway station every morning at rush hour and at weekends and collected signatures. Then I posted them off to Timothy Evans's mother. I marked the envelope 'Mrs Evans, mother of Timothy Evans, Cambridge Gardens, Notting Hill'. I don't know whether it got there, but I expect it did. When people wrote to us about Derek that's what they used to write. In those days they always gave out the name of the road in the newspaper reports.

Now, with Christie arrested, it was all out in the open. Although the police said at first there was no connection between Christie's victims and Mrs Evans and her baby, everyone knew that was rubbish. It was just an attempt to cover themselves. Even people who still believed in British justice knew that was stretching coincidence too far. By the end of Christie's trial in June, every normal person knew that Timothy Evans was completely innocent. An innocent man had been hanged, hanged by the evidence of the man who had done it. If there hadn't been capital punishment, if Evans had just been in prison, the courts would have been able to right the wrong and set him free. As it was, there was nothing anyone could do. Except say sorry, and they took long enough to do that.

Sir David Maxwell-Fyfe, still the Home Secretary, ordered an inquiry. It was supposed to be carried out in ten days before Christie was to be hanged. Rush to judgement once again. The Scott-Henderson Report as it was called came to the conclusion that there had been no miscarriage of justice on Timothy Evans. Their main reason was that although Christie admitted all the other murders, he never admitted to killing the baby Geraldine, and it was the murder of the baby that Timothy Evans was hanged for. But then a pervert like Christie was probably quite proud of his 'sex' murders. Murdering a baby is different.

But no one believed the Scott-Henderson Report. In his book about it, *10 Rillington Place*, Ludovic Kennedy shows how it was another 'spot the difference' whitewash, like Derek's medical report.

But anyone with any brain knew that an innocent man had been hanged and everyone was shocked. It was as if everyone in England took on some of the guilt of his death. But his death helped Dad and me in our campaign to abolish capital punishment.

'Derek was innocent too. One day we will prove it but, like Timothy Evans, it will be too late.'

The Scott-Henderson Report also helped, because people began to see that the Government were quite capable of doing a white-wash. Also they began to see that the police *do* lie when it suits them, that just being in a policeman's uniform (as Christie had been) was no proof of honesty.

But then, of course, there was the other question. Shouldn't such an evil monster die for what he had done? Christie must hang. But our answer was always the same. No. Wasn't it a better punishment for him to repent his sins in prison over the years left to him? Mum may not have come with us to Spouters' Corner but she was as strong as a rock in her faith. She never had any hunger for revenge. So we used to tell them, like Mum said, 'There's only one judge, and we'll all meet him in the end.'

CHAPTER FIFTEEN

On 30 July I went to Wandsworth Prison. It was Derek's birthday, he would have been twenty. I just wanted to put some flowers, red carnations, on his grave. I knocked on the gate but they wouldn't let me in. He had been buried in an unmarked grave somewhere out the back. It made me so angry that the next day I wrote to the Queen and asked for permission for Derek's body to be buried with the rest of his family in Nunhead cemetery. Derek was dead now, I said. What difference did it make where he was buried. Why shouldn't he have a grave where his family could put flowers like anyone else? What had we done to deserve this cruelty?

Mum didn't want me to write to the Queen. It hadn't done Derek any good when she had written, mother to mother, pleading for the life of her son. Mum wanted nothing to do with her. The coronation of Elizabeth II had been on 2 June. It was the first time something like that had been on television and not many people had televisions. We did. But it stayed off. It was probably the only one in England. The Queen, who could have used her Royal Prerogative to save Derek, wasn't welcome in 1 Fairview Road.

Getting Derek's body released became the first battle in the fight to clear Derek's name. It took thirteen years, but we did it in the end. As the prison authorities wouldn't let me in, I left the flowers by the gate. It was the first time, but not the last. Every year since 1953, on 28 January, we have laid a wreath at the gate of Wandsworth Prison. While Mum was alive, she wrote the message on it LEST WE FORGET. Now it's down to me.

The 2nd of August 1953, two days after I wrote to the Queen, began as a normal Sunday. In the morning I went with Dad to Spouters' Corner. We finished at two o'clock, went back home, had a sandwich and I was on duty at the Astoria at half-past four. My post that day was in the back stalls. At about nine o'clock the deputy supervisor Judy Dalleas told me to collect a teapot from the manager's office, they needed it in the canteen, she said. The stairs going up to the canteen were very badly lit and on my way back I slipped, my leg gave way and I fell down to the bottom. I tried to get up but my knee wouldn't take the strain. I took off the chiffon scarf I had round my neck and bandaged it round as best I could. I pulled myself back up the stairs where the internal telephone was to try and tell Judy what had happened. But it wasn't working. By now my knee was throbbing like hell. I went down the stairs again, hanging on to the banister and using the side wall for support and walked to where Judy was at the back of the stalls. As luck would have it Uncle Bert was in that afternoon. It was a Robert Mitchum film and he'd come in on my pass. As I limped past he saw me and came and asked me what was up. I told him and he said he'd take me home. I said I'd have to ask permission first. Judy said no, that it was nothing and that we were too short-staffed. She told me to sit down next to her and rest it. By now it was really swollen. When the programme was over she made me check the seats as usual. By this time I was in tears. I was in agony. Uncle got a cab and took me home. Dad took one look at it and called Dr Reynolds. She bandaged it up but said I'd need to go to the hospital for an X-ray. I was in such terrible pain that the next morning she sent for an ambulance to take me to the hospital.

That afternoon I phoned Mr Crossley to say the hospital had said it would be six weeks before the plaster came off. Well, that was it. He said I needn't bother coming back. That they couldn't be short of an usherette for that long and they would have to employ someone else. My cards would be sent on to me, he said.

That was all I needed. Ever since Derek's case they had wanted to get rid of me. Having a 'murderer's' sister working there didn't fit in with their image. This must have seemed like the perfect excuse. But I had learnt about fighting now. I liked being an usherette. It was what I wanted to do. And I was not giving up. The new solicitors we had got after Derek died agreed to take it on. But the first hurdle was getting Legal Aid. The Bentleys had no money. Legal Aid was refused. They don't have to give you reasons. Then my solicitors said it would be worth reapplying if I got an engineer's report on the condition of the stairs. But all this cost money.

I tried not to let it get me down, but it did. Being indoors the whole time wasn't like me. No dancing, no going for walks, no work. When I got used to the plaster it wasn't so bad. It took much longer to get anywhere, but I could do it. But there was something wrong about how they put on the plaster. It was too tight and stopped the blood getting to the muscles. But I didn't know that then, not having had one before. Near the time it was supposed to come off, Lillian and I went to the Brixton Empire to the music hall. Top of the bill were the comedians Jimmy Jewel and Ben Wariss, the Bentleys' favourites. At the interval I stood up, and my leg was completely numb and I keeled over and broke the plaster cast. We never saw the end of the show. The St John Ambulance put us in an ambulance and it was back to Mayday Hospital in Norbury. Whether the fall at Brixton had made things worse I don't know, but they decided my knee hadn't mended properly and put another plaster cast on for another six weeks.

Things were made a bit better by having Maurice in the house. When Maurice got out of the RAF he had nowhere to live. His father had moved to America with Maurice's sister and so Mum and Dad had said he could sleep on the bed-settee in the back dining-room. We pushed the billiard table to one side, but even so it was a squeeze.

Maurice was always the one. He still is. We'd got engaged at my twenty-first but split up not long after. Just some silly row, as you do when you're that age. Then I'd met Laurie. But Laurie wasn't Maurice. Laurie liked his drink too much, and I hadn't seen him since the night I'd told him the wedding was off. Now with Maurice there all the time, it wasn't long before we were courting again. He moved out three months later when he found his own place. These days everyone would imagine that, being in the same house, there would have been some hanky-panky going on. Not with Mum and

Dad upstairs and not the way we'd been brought up, no way. In those days the most we got up to was a kiss and a cuddle in the back alley. Nothing more. Dad was very strict about that sort of thing.

At about this time, Denis got scarlet fever. He moved into my room and I slept down in the front lounge. At least looking after him was something for me to do. As I'd had scarlet fever it was safe for me to be with him and I would spend hours just reading to him and dousing him with calamine lotion. Since Derek's case, Denis had lost all his usual spark. At school he was bullied and got at. And that didn't really get better until he left his primary school. Maurice being there really lifted Denis. Maurice would play with him, take him out and try and be the older brother he didn't have any more. I wouldn't be surprised if that's why Dad suggested Maurice come and stay with us, though he never said so.

It was about October, when the phone rang late one evening. Dad took it. It was a man's voice.

'Fancy you doing that.'

'Doing what?'

'Selling your son's suit to Madame Tussaud's for five thousand pounds.'

'I don't know what you're talking about, I haven't even got the suit.'

Of course Dad didn't sell the suit. Now, as I said, I know Derek was buried in it, because they hang you in your own clothes, not the prison ones you wear every other day in the condemned cell. It's grotesque. But Dad was convinced they'd burned it and was so angry that he wanted to sue the Home Secretary for the cost of the suit, which was about £30. A lot of money in those days. They'd bought the best suit they could afford for Derek's trial. You got a return flight to Paris for £9 10s. It wasn't the money, it was the principle that counted and it was a way of keeping the name of Bentley alive. In the end it came to nothing because suing is expensive and, as I said, we just didn't have the money. But when the matter was raised by an MP in a letter, Maxwell-Fyfe replied to him that the rules were changed that July and that from then on clothes would be handed back to the next of kin with the rest of their belongings. After that I suppose they hanged them in prison clothes.

As for this call about Madame Tussaud's, Dad said, 'It's nothing but a cruel hoax.' No money in the world would make Dad sell anything of Derek's. But the idea of Derek being an exhibit in Madame Tussaud's got him rattled. The man had said that it was in the Blackpool Madame Tussaud's. We had read that waxworks of Christie were on show in both London and Blackpool, so he decided we should go and see for ourselves. We didn't tell a soul. We didn't want any publicity. Mum wasn't up to the journey, so it was just me, Dad and Denis. Denis came because the father of a friend of mine from the component workshop had shares in Blackpool Tower. With Denis having been so ill and with having lost his brother in such a terrible way, Dad decided he would do anything to make things up for him.

We took the Friday night sleeper. Going to Blackpool wasn't like going by Intercity. It was still steam trains then, and took for ever. We were jam-packed, eight to a compartment. Denis went to sleep leaning against me. I remember how excited he was. He'd never been on such a long journey. Neither had I come to that, but I didn't like the flashes as we went over the points and I was worried for Dad about what we might find at Madame Tussaud's.

It was drizzling with rain when we got out at Blackpool early next morning. We knew that Madame Tussaud's was near the front but what with not knowing our way around and me with my leg in plaster, it took us a long time to find. Dad didn't say who we were, he just bought the tickets and we went straight to the section on murders. It was gloomy and horrible. But luckily there was no sign of Derek, just Dr Crippen, who poisoned his wife; and Haigh, who did the acid-bath murders; Edith Thompson, whose lover killed her husband; and Jack the Ripper. Not that anyone knows who Jack the Ripper was, it was just a masked man, dressed in toff's clothes of the time, because everyone knew he was an aristocrat. Then we found an alcove curtained off and you could see a mark on the floor. Was that where Derek had been? Denis and I stayed while Dad went off to find someone to ask. Remember, no one knew who we were. But when Dad asked if they had a waxwork of Derek Bentley and they said no, they only had waxworks of people who were guilty, Dad told them. The man shook our hands.

'Your son was innocent, Mr Bentley. Have no fear, we will never have an effigy of him.'

It was such a weight off our shoulders and we still had the whole day in front of us. This was to be Denis's day, a happy day for him to remember. First we went up the Blackpool Tower. It was so high. You could see for miles. The beaches were all sand, not like at Brighton which is pebbles. Then we went to the Tower Ballroom and were introduced to Reginald Dixon the organist who was very famous. It was the first time I'd met anyone like that. He was very kind and said he'd play a request on the radio the next week. He was as good as his word and he played 'Wheel of Fortune' for Iris Bentley the next week. It was Derek's favourite song.

Next we went to Blackpool fun fair which was huge, far bigger than Battersea. The man who took us spoke to someone there and arranged for us to have all the rides free. We didn't go on the big dipper because of my leg. But somehow I managed to get into the bumper car and went bobbing round on the merry-go-round with the beautiful carved horses that went up and down, with my leg hanging straight down. When it got dark the Blackpool illuminations came on. They are lights like the Oxford Street Christmas lights, only bigger and longer. They stretched all the way from the fun fair right down to Cleveleys at the other end of Blackpool. There were no more trams in London, but there were here and the tramline ran right along the front. We went on the pier. Denis wanted to play the slot machines but Dad drew the line at that. Denis had the time of his life. The train back to London didn't leave until two in the morning so, after having a fish-and-chip supper at a café there was nothing for it but to wait in the station waiting-room and we just dozed.

Then these prostitutes came up, though I didn't know that's what they were at first. I don't know why they bothered with Dad. Denis had gone to sleep next to me so perhaps they thought he was on his own. But these wouldn't leave him alone. I was really shocked and went off Blackpool after that. But everyone else we had met there was very kind and the people we met that day never forgot the Bentleys. Every year since then there have always been flowers from Blackpool on the anniversary of Derek's death.

When people in quiz shows look back at 1953, they always make it sound like a golden year; the Coronation, the conquest of Everest, the four-minute mile. But for British justice 1953 was a black year. First there was Derek and then, with Christie's arrest and trial, the truth about Timothy Evans.

In the autumn, Reginald Paget and Sydney Silverman, the MPs who had fought so hard for Derek in the House of Commons, brought out their book *Hanged and Innocent*. It was the first time anyone had written about the Croydon Rooftop murder, as it was called. It was published by Victor Gollancz, a well-known left-wing publisher. The chapter about Derek was written by Paget and it set out the reasons why Derek should have been given a reprieve. Paget was a lawyer.

1 It was traditional for those near the age of eighteen to be reprieved.
2 If Craig wasn't to die, who was the 'leading actor', then Derek shouldn't.
3 Derek's medical condition and intelligence put him very close to the McNaghten Rules.
4 Two parliamentary commissions in 1839 and 1878 had said that death caused without malice needed to be reviewed.
5 Where there was a 'scintilla' of doubt, the Home Secretary should reprieve.

Just one of those points should have tipped the scales in favour of a reprieve. All five applied to Derek. So Paget decided what had tipped the scales of justice for Maxwell-Fyfe was something else, heavier than all those five reasons. It was that a policeman had been killed so somebody had to hang. Paget said that Derek's execution 'was a supreme indecency'.

Not long after we got back from Blackpool came the trial called the Clapham Common murder. There had been a fight on Clapham Common between some boys on the evening of 2 July. I say boys, but I suppose they were late teens and early twenties. One of them, called John Beckley, died from being stabbed. It happened near the bandstand on Clapham Common. Six of them were on trial the first time, in September, but the jury couldn't reach a verdict so the charge of murder was dropped against all of them except one, Michael Davies. On 22 October came the second attempt, the trial of Regina v. Davies. It looked bad for him. He'd been identified by a girl on top of a bus who'd seen him running, two of the other boys involved said they'd seen him with a knife. But he said he'd never had a knife. Unlike the other boys who kept changing their stories, Michael Davies never changed his tune. He had been in the fight, he even admitted punching John Beckley, but he never knifed him. He didn't even own a knife. Although he'd never been to prison, he had a previous conviction for handling stolen goods, nothing much, but he was on probation. Like in Derek's case, the defence weren't allowed to call witnesses other than the accused, if they wanted to have the last word before the summing up.

Michael Davies was found guilty of murder and sentenced to death. Like Derek he was sent to the condemned cell in Wandsworth Prison.

As I said, in those days, with no soaps on the television to get steamed up about, newspapers were full of trials, especially murder trials. From now on until the day the death penalty was abolished, Dad read anything and everything about murder trials. As soon as we read about Michael Davies's death sentence, Dad got in touch with Mrs Davies, Michael's mother and offered his help and said they should set about doing a petition.

Mrs Davies was in a terrible state. She lived off the north-east corner of Clapham Common, in a small street called Turret Grove.

Her daughter Joyce, Michael's sister, was keeping everyone calm. Mickey, as his family called him, was completely innocent. The other boys had been picked up by the police within hours of the fight, but they didn't think of Mickey, who they knew because he was on probation, because he wasn't like that. They didn't come rushing in to arrest him, they just had a word with his mother and asked her to get him to come down to the police station when he got back.

Of all of them, he was the most unlikely. John Beckley had been stabbed nine times. The wounds were all over, front, back, head. Probably more than one person did it and they weren't about to give themselves away. What better than pinning it on someone who didn't have the nous to lie a bit? Because hardly anyone had seen him there at all. He was the one who said he punched Beckley, he was the one who said he punched another boy who had a small stab wound, Ryan. Nobody else did, not even Ryan.

Dad felt very positive that Michael Davies would be reprieved. His theory was that although the jury had not recommended mercy, as they had done with Derek, the difference was that Michael Davies had just been found guilty of killing another boy like him, not a policeman. If Davies was reprieved, it would be proof to Dad that Derek's death was a political decision and nothing to do with either the law or natural justice.

Michael Davies was given leave to appeal. Not, as I explained before, because the jury got it wrong, but on a point of law and the judge's summing-up. Michael's judge had been about as impartial as Lord Goddard had been in Derek's case. The point of law they were relying on was that a jury must be warned about not relying on evidence coming from someone who could be considered an accomplice, unless it is corroborated by somebody else, but the judge had forgotten to say the words to the jury, the words warning them. And that made all the difference in law. The appeal was on 1 December 1953. The leader of the appeal judges was Lord Goddard. It was thrown out.

As soon as we heard we went straight round to see them. Mrs Davies was very tensed up. She was under the doctor and her daughter had taken over running the campaign. Helping them was Lord Longford. I'm not sure how he got involved. Unlike how we felt about Derek's lawyers having let him down, everyone felt Mickey's lawyers were doing everything they could and their barrister, a labour MP called David Weitzman, was the best. Like with Derek, the next stage was trying to get it to the House of Lords. Because of all the trials and retrials, Mickey had already been in prison for nearly six months. Dad told Mrs Davies that she mustn't let anything go by.

'You must work hard, harder than you've ever worked in your life, otherwise you'll never forgive yourself.'

But unlike Derek's case where the Attorney-General decided that there was no point of law that would interest the House of Lords, Michael Davies was granted leave to appeal to the highest court in the land and on 12 January, Dad and I went to the House of Lords and sat with the Davieses.

Mum didn't get involved in any of this. She was still too frail to cope and would burst into tears at the slightest thing, which wouldn't have helped the Davies family or Mum.

There were about ten of us. The House of Lords was different from the Commons. It had lots of red plush, rich hangings on the walls. The seats had cushions. There were lots of barristers rushing around that were there to fetch and carry and take notes, I suppose. Judges in long wigs and red cloaks with white fur. All of a sudden a shout went up from someone near us in the public gallery.

'That's not British justice.'

I felt myself tense up, felt my throat go tight. But Dad could read my mind.

'Pam, don't you dare.'

And of course I didn't. But I was tempted. Very tempted. Somebody in uniform came through the door at the back and gave the man who had called out a warning.

'If you do that again you'll be removed.'

The man got up, gave us all a grin, and went out anyway. He'd said what he wanted to say.

The hearing went on and on. They talked about the first trial, the second trial and the appeal. You couldn't tell how it was going at all. Then it was all over, and you still didn't know. This time they were going to have to think about it. That seemed much better to me and much more hopeful. We all left together and had a cup of tea in the tea-shop across the road by Westminster underground station. It was like we were all balancing, walking a tightrope. One false move and we'd fall. Then we went home. Dad phoned Mrs Davies as soon as we got in just to check she had got back all right, but they'd told us it would be a while before she heard.

Several days went by and then we did hear. It had been turned down. Now it was all down to a reprieve and the Home Secretary, still Maxwell-Fyfe. In fact everyone was so pleased with him he'd been made a lord, Lord Kilmuir. (Or Kill-more as he was called by those who knew.) The date of Michael Davies's execution was now set for 2 February. The days ticked by and Dad and I went down to take Mrs Davies the next batch of petitions we'd collected. We were just having a cup of tea and talking about what to say in the letter that Mrs Davies and Joyce would write to Maxwell-Fyfe. I remember how Dad kept on saying, it'll be all right, you see. The man who died wasn't a policeman.

Then there was a knock on the door. Mrs Davies went to answer it and Dad and I carried on talking. When Mrs Davies came back she had a telegram in her hand, held out toward us. She was crying. It was from the Home Secretary. Michael Davies would live. We all cried. Mrs Davies cried for relief. Dad and I did too but also for the pain of knowing that Derek would never come back to us. Mickey Davies ended up serving seven years of life imprisonment. He was released in 1960. He is still fighting for a free pardon. Books have been written and nobody now believes it was him, but no one has ever come forward and confessed that they were the ones that did it, and unless something like that happens, he'll always be branded a murderer.

CHAPTER SIXTEEN

Mrs Davies had gone through seven months of hell. Three separate trials, then two appeals. We hadn't been involved at the beginning but that Christmas was Mick Davies's twenty-first birthday and we thought of him and his sister and mother as we sat down to our Christmas dinner. Maurice was with us, although he had got a place of his own now. He had a job with the Mayfair cinema in Tooting as projectionist, but he was always around. We were definitely back together again.

At Christmas you always think back to other Christmases and we found it hard to be merry. Last year Derek in the condemned cell, this year Mick Davies. I had never met him but being with his mother so much and her talking about him all the time, I felt I had. And we knew just what they were going through. But Dad was determined Fairview Road would not be a place of gloom, because of Denis. We had a wonderful tree which Dad and Denis decorated, complete with fairy lights and paper chains and bunting.

My leg was still in plaster. Every time I went back to Mayday Hospital they ended up putting another one on, like it wasn't quite cooked. Soon after the New Year I was due for another visit. This time Dad came with me. When he saw the state of my leg he went mad. They said it still wasn't mended and were all for plastering it up again. But my leg was so thin, Dad put his foot down and said he was taking me to Guy's for a second opinion.

Guy's sent me straight down to their orthopaedic department in Orpington, Kent for physiotherapy and injections. The muscles in my right leg were quite wasted away and after five months in plaster my right leg was shorter than the other. I went every day for a week, and afterwards once a week. There were two problems, first the weakness caused by the plaster being on so long, and second the fact that it wasn't mending properly. I don't remember when they discovered what was wrong, but it turned out my kneecap was crumbling because of some disease that had got in. They did the operation, removed the kneecap and pinned the joint in January 1955. But until that happened I was just told to do as little as possible. With the plaster off, and one leg shorter than the other, I limped. Denis and his friends called me Hopalong Cassidy. *Hopalong Cassidy* was an American television programme about a cowboy. But Hopalong was the hero, so I didn't mind. But it wasn't only the limp. I had carried on helping Dad at Spouters' Corner and the meetings we held at libraries sometimes, and because I was walking lopsided, my back decided to play up.

There seemed no end to it. I began to get what I now know were panic attacks. Once I was in Woolworth's in Streatham. For no reason that I knew of my heart started racing and my head swimming. I felt I was going to black out. I was terrified, terrified that I was going to die, terrified I wouldn't be able to get back home. I felt completely out of control. It got so bad that I was fearful of leaving the house, in case it happened again. At night it was worse. I would go to sleep, then wake up at one or two in the morning and not sleep again. It was always that glass. Always that glass between Derek and me. My fists would beat against it, making no noise, but it wouldn't break and I would wake up crying and crying. I thought I had a tumour on the brain. After a while Dad said I should go and see Dr Reynolds. She gave me some tablets. I don't know what they were, but they made me feel dreadful, so slow and woozy, like I'd had too much to drink. I couldn't think straight. She also decided I should go and see a psychiatrist. As I was already going to Guy's for my leg, she sent me there.

It's the only time I have ever seen a psychiatrist. I went once a week for about three months. Mum always came with me but I saw the doctor on my own. One of the first things he asked Mum was did I swear. Mum was very surprised.

'Oh no, Doctor. Iris doesn't swear. She was brought up properly. There's no "language" in our house.'

'Well, I think she should start learning.'

And there and then he made me say after him 'Bloody' and

181

'Bugger'. I'd never been one for swearing. In fact, my friends used to offer me money to swear, but I never did.

Every night, he said, I had to shout 'bloody' and 'bugger' as loud as I could into my pillow before I went to sleep. It all sounded very strange. But Mum said he was the doctor so I should do as he said. So I did. I didn't say anything to Dad. Not for any particular reason, just didn't think to. So that first night, there I was shouting 'Bloody, bloody, bloody' and 'Bugger, bugger, bugger' into my pillow and in comes Dad. He heard me through the door and the pillow and wondered what on earth had happened hearing 'language' like that at Fairview Road. Luckily Mum told him what the doctor said. Dad just looked bewildered.

'Well, if it helps you get better, Pam, you can swear as much as you like.'

At the time I didn't like the psychiatrist and didn't like going to see him. After that first visit I didn't want to go back, but Mum made me. My leg was now so weak that she used to come with me but, like I said, I saw the doctor on my own. To me he seemed very hostile. But I realize now that that's what he was trying to do, rile me, trying to make me angry. He taught me to scream into my pillow. I'd had to hold it all in because of not wanting to upset Mum and Dad. All the anger had gone inside and that's what was making me ill. And it wasn't only anger at the outside world. If Mum and Dad were thinking 'if only' they hadn't let Derek go out with Norman Parsley that night, my 'if only' was far more terrible.

In dreams it came out as *if only* I had broken the glass. I felt hatred for myself. *If only* I had shut the door that Saturday afternoon at Priory Buildings when Derek was four. *If only* he hadn't fallen. Before then he was just a normal little boy, after then he wasn't. If he hadn't fallen he would have had his wits, he would have learnt to read. If he'd had his wits none of it would have happened. But I didn't tell the psychiatrist about that. They say when something terrible like that happens, people always feel guilty, even if it's nothing to do with them. They say that what with epilepsy being in the family (an aunt of Mum's died having a fit) he would have got it some time anyway. But it didn't stop me feeling responsible, feeling guilty.

It wasn't that we never talked about it at home. Mum especially was always talking about Derek. She wanted to talk about Derek all the time.

'We must never stop talking about him.'

I just put my arms around her as she cried, just saying over and over again, 'My boy, my boy.'

'I'll look after you. I'll never let anything else happen in this family.'

I wanted to cry, but I had to show that I was strong, that I could look after her. It was the same with my dad. Until that day when he came back from Wandsworth Prison with what was left of Derek's things, he had never cried. But after that, he did break down quite often. And to see your dad cry hurts you inside. What could I do to help him?

'Come on, Dad, he's watching us, he knows we're still carrying on.'

'I know, Pam, but I just want to see him there sitting in his chair.'

I suppose for the first few months I was the strong one. But you can't go on under that strain and it not take its toll.

It was what was called in those days a nervous breakdown. It was like an illness. But tablets can't help you. You have to do it yourself, from the inside. Gradually with the swearing and screaming into the pillow and the visits to Guy's, I came out of it and within about three months I was my old self again. Well, nearly. Before, it had got to the point where I couldn't enjoy myself because of feeling bad about Derek. I would always be thinking whatever I was doing, Derek should be doing this, Derek would have been doing that. But once you've been down that road, you never forget. It's no good bottling feelings up inside. You've got to talk about them. Now, if there's no one around I talk to myself. When things are getting me down, I just look in the bathroom mirror and talk back to myself.

'Come on, Iris. This isn't you. Pull yourself together. You've got to get cracking.'

It's no good other people saying 'pull yourself together', that never works. It's *you* that's got to be determined you want to get better. Nobody can tell you. And I never forget that nothing I can go through can be compared with what Derek went through.

For people who've never been down that road it's very difficult to understand. It's like you've missed the turning and got separated from everyone else. Like Uncle Bert did one night in the smog when he, Dad and I were coming back from the Astoria. You know it's still there, that straight road that you somehow left, but you can't get back on it. But once it's happened to you, you know you've been there and I think it helps you recognize what other people are going through.

It was about then, when I was coming out of the nervous breakdown, that I got to hear about Caryl Chessman. He had been on death row in San Quentin, California for six years. He was thirty-three and had seen fifty other men walk past his cell which was on the way to the electric chair, which was how they did it in America. He had started stealing when he was fifteen, to get money for his mother who was crippled from a car crash. He was famous for having stolen a police car and used it to go on the rampage, stealing and shooting all over California while using the police radio to have a go at the police who were chasing him and the other man with him. I decided to write to him, to tell him about my brother and to tell him about what Dad and I were doing in our fight against capital punishment. I never heard back from him directly, but I got a letter from his lawyer who told me that he had got my letters and that they had given him hope for the future. NBC, an American radio station, heard about me writing to him and arranged for me to do an interview over the telephone about what people in England thought. It was done through the BBC, who have special rooms with telephones in so that it sounds just like you were there, not like being on the phone at all. It was the first time I had ever done anything like this. It's one thing having a chat to a journalist sitting in your own lounge, it's quite another to be sitting in an underground room, having to answer questions very carefully, knowing you're being heard by millions of people. It was nerve-racking then and nerve-racking even when I do it now, forty years after that first time.

In June 1954 Ken Allen told us that there was a play about Derek's case about to come to London. It had its first performance in Aldershot but then it moved up to the Cambridge Theatre in London. *Murder Story* was written by Ludovic Kennedy and Derek's case was, he says, the reason he first became involved in miscarriages of justice. It's because of Ludovic Kennedy that Timothy Evans finally got his free pardon and it's because of Ludovic Kennedy that the convictions against the Birmingham Six, Guildford Four, and Maguire Seven were also shown to be wrong. *Murder Story* is not about a shooting on a rooftop. It doesn't have any characters called Derek Bentley or Christopher Craig in it. But to me saying it's not about Derek's case is like saying you can't tell margarine from butter.

Lots of journalists called and said we should go and see what we thought. So I phoned up, said my name was Iris Bentley and asked for ten seats on 22 July. The girl said she would have to check the bookings, then she said she was very sorry, but they were sold out. It was a lie. I called again about twenty minutes later, this time using my mother's maiden name, Cooper, and got the tickets. It didn't surprise anyone. In fact, the journalists had expected it. You had to live through those times with me and my parents to realize what we were up against.

Our seats were in the dress circle. The name of the young man condemned to death in the play may have been Jim Tanner, but it was Derek down on that stage. Donald Bradley, the actor who played him, deserved an Oscar.

Everything about him, the way he looked, talked, moved, was Derek. Over the years I've seen my brother played by so many actors, but no one ever got as close as this. He was Derek to the life.

As for it not being Derek's case, it most certainly was, except in the details. 'Jim' had a cosh which he said he had never used and wouldn't know how to use, like Derek said about Craig's knuckle-duster. Being in that theatre it seemed like we were reliving everything. I don't know now how Dad and I managed to sit through it all, but we did, we knew we had to. At the end, in the condemned cell, a warder and the chaplain talked about the hanging itself. You didn't see it, they just talked about it but that bit I couldn't take, and I closed my eyes and put my hands over my ears.

Murder Story wasn't about the police lying, or the police beating up people they've arrested. It was about the evil of capital punishment, which Ludovic Kennedy calls 'legal killing'. But there was one thing that was wrong. The thing that makes the hanging worse in the play was that 'Jim' learns to read in the condemned cell, giving the impression that all he needed was a bit of encouragement from his family. For the play it made killing him seem that much worse but in Derek's case that's just not true. His brain was damaged. He couldn't read no matter how you tried. I know. I did try.

That was what really got to Dad, all the stuff about the family being too easygoing. It wasn't true. We never got away with anything, except on our birthdays. When Dad said no, he meant no. At dinnertime, he didn't dish up until we were all sitting. If you put your elbows on the table he'd say, 'Didn't you sleep last night?' Ludovic Kennedy had no idea what we were like as a family. He had written the play based on what Lord Goddard had said about the Bentleys.

'If he'd come to see us,' said Dad, 'he'd have seen we weren't like that.'

And the father drank. Dad never drank. He was practically teetotal. But although he was cross, Dad wasn't really angry. He knew it could only help with Derek's case.

Now that I was feeling better in myself, I set about getting a job. I had a 30 per cent disability allowance provided by the Ministry of Labour but it was hardly anything and I didn't like living off Mum and Dad. I'd always paid my way, plus I was bored just being at home. During the day was worst. Maurice would come around most nights after finishing at the cinema, and at weekends. I couldn't dance with my leg but it didn't stop me going out. There was still Spouters' Corner. When my leg was really playing up Dad would do it on his own. But the Bentleys were a team now, and I didn't like to let him down.

Towards the end of my time at the Astoria, I had done shifts as relief cashier. Being a cashier, you don't move around much, so I thought it wouldn't be too hard to find something. Nothing. Relief cashier didn't count as experience, they said. I tried to go back to coil winding. Nothing. The component workshop where I'd worked before becoming an usherette had gone bankrupt. Winding coils for radar, which is what I was doing when I left, was skilled work, but it was the same story everywhere. No vacancies. Whether it was to do with what had happened with Derek or whether it was just the sight of me dragging my leg around, I don't know. But there was no work for Iris Bentley. The psychiatrist at Guy's had said it wasn't good for me to be on my own, so I would spend afternoons helping a friend who had an outworking job painting toys from her home. She was very badly paid, just a few pence for each one, so I couldn't take anything off her. It was just something to do, someone to chat with. Eventually I got a part-time job doing the books for a friend of Dad's who lived at Thornton Heath. I'd always liked working with figures. And it was interesting, but I didn't get to meet people as it meant working at home.

I still hadn't got Legal Aid for my case. Dad was now thinking about suing Mayday Hospital for negligence as well as the cinema. But in the end the solicitors said that suing hospitals was a waste of time. That doctors never split on each other.

The operation on my leg was done on 23 January 1955, eighteen months after I fell down the stairs. My surgeon was Mr Stamm and it was a success, he said. It was done in the hospital out at Orpington and I stayed there for just over two weeks. For the first time since Derek's death I missed going to Wandsworth Prison on 28 January.

Although Mr Stamm said the operation was successful, it didn't mean I could walk normally again. I still couldn't bend my knee and the right leg seemed even shorter. Guy's gave me a built-up shoe but I hated wearing them, they made me feel like a cripple, so I hardly ever did. Now I realize that can't have done my back any good, not having my weight evenly distributed. But I was young and didn't think like that.

But by 10 February I was out. It was a day I was determined not to miss, the first debate on capital punishment since Derek's execution. Dad and I queued up with everyone else to go into the public gallery.

It was supposed to be a free vote, meaning MPs could vote with their consciences, not following party lines as they usually do. But there were party lines just the same. The Tory party (the government) were for keeping hanging, the Labour party for suspending it for five years. Chuter Ede, an old man now, was the Labour Home Secretary that had refused Timothy Evans a reprieve. So it caused a big stir when he got up and began to talk about why he hadn't felt able to, about how overwhelming the evidence had been against Evans. But then he said, 'Evans was not guilty as charged.' That was quite something, remember the Scott-Henderson Report rushed through by Maxwell-Fyfe after Christie was convicted but before he was hanged, said that Evans *was* still guilty. Whether that persuaded a few to change sides I don't know. But the vote was very close, 245 to 214. It was an exact change around from the vote for Sydney Silverman's amendment to the Criminal Justice Bill in 1947 when 245 had voted to abolish capital punishment against 222 who wanted to keep it. Although the House of Commons was packed that night, 160 MPs didn't vote at all. Enoch Powell was among the Tory MPs who voted to abolish it. Strange when you think of the other things he's stood for that he's been against capital punishment all his life.

The next thing that helped us in the campaign against capital punishment was Ruth Ellis. She was young and glamorous. She ran a club in Soho. At lunchtime on Easter Sunday in 1955 she waited outside a pub in Hampstead, near where she lived, and shot her lover David Blakely as he came out. She didn't try to get away. Just waited to be arrested. She'd recently had a miscarriage and she'd found out he was involved with another woman. The trial was straightforward. She was found guilty of murder and hanged on 15 July. She was only twenty-eight. Somewhere there was an ex-husband and two children.

After the case Dad and I had organized petitions around Norbury and sent them straight to the Home Secretary, who was then Gwilym Lloyd George. There was no appeal. Some people thought she was shielding someone else, that the gun she used had been given to her by this person. But no one came forward. The night before the hanging they said that evidence about who owned the gun had been given to the Home Office. But if there was, it was too late.

There had always been this tradition in England that far more women than men were reprieved. Not based on anything else than English gentlemen who ran the legal system feeling it 'wasn't cricket' to hang one of the 'fairer sex'. After Ruth Ellis the atmosphere changed. At Spouters' Corner people who didn't worry about hanging young men suddenly were anti-hanging.

No one could use the excuse that Ruth Ellis was a menace to public safety. No one could say that capital punishment was a deterrent. She knew what she was doing, she knew what would happen and she did it anyway. Public opinion was shocked and Sydney Silverman took the opportunity to try again.

In November 1955 the Government rejected all the major recommendations of the Royal Commission on Capital Punishment, which Clement Attlee had got going in 1948. The Commission's report was published at the end of 1953.

But on Thursday, 16 February 1956, we were back in the public gallery in the House of Commons. Once again it was packed. Once again all the old arguments for keeping hanging were trotted out and once again it was a free vote. Again, the Government line was no. The Home Secretary Gwilym Lloyd George said the Government proposed to retain hanging but change the rules for murder, so that more cases where people were killed were turned into manslaughter, which would mean imprisonment, not execution. But Labour wasn't going to be soft-soaped from the main issue. The Labour MP who had been Solicitor-General in the last Labour Government interrupted.

'The country has been profoundly disturbed at the recent case of Evans, the case of Bentley, the case of Ruth Ellis. Would any of your proposals affect any of these cases at all?

'No, I should not have thought so.'

Then Chuter Ede got up. He said that the changes would not have stopped the hanging of any of the cases he'd had to deal with when he was Home Secretary.

The Home Secretary said the only real thing against capital punishment was hanging someone who was innocent. But he went on to say how unlikely it was to happen.

'The police, the judge, the jury, the Court of Criminal Appeal – all of them anxiously searching for the truth, falling into error.'

Oh yes. Dad and I remembered all those people searching anxiously for the truth.

'I do not believe that in recent times there is any case in which an innocent man has been hanged. I say that advisedly, and after full consideration of the cases of Rowlands and Evans.'

Rowlands was hanged in 1948. He was accused of murdering a woman. He had an alibi. He was completely innocent.

Then he went on with the same old story about hanging being a deterrent. And, anyway, he finished by saying, for a final safety net there is always the Royal Prerogative of Mercy.

There were times when I felt like screaming.

Perhaps the worst was when William Reid, a Labour MP, told of an execution he had been at when he was a young man in Glasgow. He described everything that happened in detail. I put my hands over my ears, I didn't make a noise but my eyes streamed with tears. He told how the Prison Governor was the most upset by it all. Mr Reid had asked the doctor why the body was not taken straight down after the hanging. He was told that Home Office rules say it must hang for an hour, that death was sometimes not instantaneous but that after an hour the person would be dead by being strangled, definitely. Some time after this execution, said Mr Reid, the Prison Governor committed suicide by lying down on a railway track.

'It is more than twenty years since I attended that execution. The picture of that hanging will never be effaced from my memory as long as God gives me breath.'

The Motion was: 'The death penalty for murder no longer accords with the needs or the true interests of a civilised society,' and said the Government should 'introduce forthwith legislation for its abolition or for its suspension for an experimental period'.

When all the speaking had finished, you could feel the tension. Still nobody knew how it would turn out. We kept peering down as people came out of the division lobby, trying to work out how it was going. But you couldn't tell. Dad was not optimistic. In May 1954 the Tories had got back with an even higher majority, and Sydney Silverman had told Dad and me that his hopes of getting his Private Member's Bill through (which he'd introduced in November 1954 under the Ten Minutes Rule) were not high.

But, like I said, since the hanging of Ruth Ellis, something had changed. At ten minutes past ten the teller came in with the numbers. The motion was carried by 293 to 262, a majority of thirty-one. Exactly the same majority that last year had been for *keeping* capital punishment. That time only seventeen Tory MPs had voted to abolish it, this time there were thirty-seven. Young MPs who had come in at the election in May had voted against, and done the trick. When the result was announced, there was a great cheer and it was like looking at schoolboys who had just won at football. I had never seen anything like it. They were flinging their order papers in the air. Anthony Eden the Prime Minister and the rest of the Conservative front bench sat there like statues.

But it did no good. The Conservative MPs may have changed, but the House of Lords was still stuffed full of the same people who had been there in 1947 when Lord Goddard had made sure Sydney Silverman's amendment didn't get through.

It wasn't thrown out by the Lords until the autumn. Until then people under sentence of death were given reprieves as well as any other convictions for murder until it was decided by the Lords. Leading the rejection was Maxwell-Fyfe. Because he was now Lord Kilmuir he had been made Lord Chancellor. Although Home Secretary after Home Secretary was now converted to abolition (including Lord Templewood, who moved the debate in the Lords), Maxwell-Fyfe said the Silverman Bill was 'an unwise and dangerous measure, the presence of which on the Statute Book would be a disaster for the country and a menace to its people'. He knew best, in spite of the fact that the House of Commons had now voted twice (in 1948 and 1956) for the abolition of the death penalty on a free vote. The future Archbishop of Canterbury, Ramsey, made his maiden speech for abolition. When it came to the vote, both archbishops (York and Canterbury) and eight of the nine bishops in the House of Lords voted for abolition. But even with God on Silverman's side, it made no difference.

CHAPTER SEVENTEEN

I can't remember when we began to notice things moving in Derek's room. There was a wooden ball on top of the newel post at the top of the stairs. It was a bit loose and Derek and I would put our hands on it together when we came down from the loft. I never liked coming down from the loft in the dark; I always thought my feet would miss the last rung. Putting our hands on it was like the Pope kissing the earth. It meant we were safe.

Ever since Derek died, I'd always had a funny feeling when I put my hand on the post. But that was only me. The other things affected everyone. We didn't realize what it was at first. If I saw Derek's pillow had a dent in it where his head used to go, then I thought Mum had been there, crying. When she saw it, she probably thought that it was me. Then sometimes the bedclothes would be folded back, as if someone had got out of bed, and there'd be the hollow left in the mattress where someone's been sleeping. It didn't happen every day, just sometimes.

Even though Derek's bed wasn't slept in, Mum still washed his sheets and pillowcases once a week. It was hard work in those days. There were no washing-machines or launderettes. Sheets got washed in the bath. First she'd get them wet and then tread them down with her bare feet into the soapy water, soap which she grated off a hard block (there was no soap powder then), then she'd have a scrub with a rubbing board. They'd be hung out on the line till damp dry, then it was out with the ironing board. No drip-dry nonsense. My mother used to iron every one. It wasn't anythng special to do with Derek. Mum was always like that, even in Priory Buildings. Cleanliness was next to godliness. The only time she didn't do it herself was in Hillingdon Street when we used the laundry and in Edgware when she was in hospital just before having Denis, when I did it.

Then one evening in early 1956 my friend Lillian went upstairs to use the toilet. When she came down she said, 'Who's that in Derek's room, Uncle Bill?'

'No one, why?'

The only person who could have been there was Uncle Bert, but he was downstairs with Mum and Dad watching television. Anyway, he never spent any time up there during the day.

'But I saw the door handle move.'

So Dad and I went up to have a look and, of course, there was no one there. But there was ash in the ashtray, Derek's ashtray on his bedside cabinet, which like everything else Mum kept spick and span.

It had to be Derek. Like I said, it was the only way he could come back. And the ash was his way of telling us it was him. There was nothing frightening about it. Even Uncle Bert who still slept there wasn't bothered. You could even say it was comforting, knowing that he'd come back.

But it was different for outsiders, even close friends like Lillian. She was terrified and said she wasn't going up there again. If she wanted to go to the toilet she'd go home, she said. And she did. She only lived in the next street so that wasn't a hardship, but it made us think. In the end we decided we had to do something about it.

It was Harry Proctor of the *Sunday Pictorial* who said a spiritualist might be the answer. Journalists were still in touch with us. They telephoned Dad every so often to see how things were going. Although the interest in Derek's case had died down, it hadn't gone away.

So one day in about March we all went to this house in Pimlico, Mum, Dad, me and Harry Proctor. It was in one of those big terraces near Victoria station that are now all bed and breakfasts. A woman dressed in black opened the door. She was the only human being we saw from beginning to end. The lights were very dim and there was solemn music, like the death march, which was unusual in those days when they didn't have music in shops or lifts. Then we went into a big room with a very high ceiling, red velvet curtains and a few easy chairs around. Nothing else. We kept expecting someone to come in, but no one did. Then the lights changed to red and a voice said, 'Hold your heads down.' So we did as we were told. Then the voice changed.

'Dad, Dad.'

That wasn't Derek. I knew straight away. It was all wrong. Everything about the place was phoney. The voice came from nowhere, like it was coming through the wall. I realize now it must have been a tape recorder but ordinary people only had gramophones then, tape recorders were just for the BBC. This voice went on saying things like 'Thank you for trying, but you've done enough. Don't do any more, it's making you ill. Tell Iris, thank you and tell her to look after Mum.' My brother never called me Iris, he called me Sis. It was all a con.

We left feeling like anyone would if they knew they'd been had. We didn't blame Harry Proctor. When we were safely back on the underground he said, 'Well, that was a load of old bunkum.' And it was. I'd read books on the spirit world long before. I'd always had a feeling there was something there. I know there's a life hereafter. We don't just get born, get married, have children and then die for nothing. There must be more to it than that.

We didn't give up. It wasn't that we wanted to exorcize Derek's spirit from number 1, Fairview Road. Just the opposite. They say when you've 'gone over' your physical problems disappear. Derek's 'feeble-mindedness' was physical and we thought now he was on the other side he would have his full intelligence and he might be able to tell us things that would help us in the fight to clear his name.

What we needed was a medium who would come to our house. We had heard of a spiritualist newspaper called *Two Worlds*. Dad called them and asked if they could find us a medium, one who didn't know about the Bentleys. They said they would try. They called back and recommended someone called John Lovette, who lived in Battersea, and had just come back from Africa, they said.

The night John Lovette came, Denis stayed with a friend. No

sooner had Mr Lovette sat down in the lounge when he grabbed his throat and made noises as if he was going to choke.

'Something terrible's happened. It's like somebody's been hanged. Or am I on the wrong wavelength?'

Dad told him to go on. The medium's neck was all red.

'If you've been involved with this as a family, it's terrible.'

Then he began rubbing his finger. His voice seemed to change but it was what he said that made me shiver.

'Sis, the ring.'

There was no 'Iris' this time.

'Yes, the ring my brother gave me.'

'You haven't got it on. Why haven't you got it on? Put it on. It's in your purse.'

He was right. It was in my purse. I took it out and put it on and it's been there ever since. Derek gave it to me not long after my twenty-first. That ring had a long history. It started off as Philip Stevens's. He'd bought it when he got engaged, but the girl dropped him and gave him back the ring. Philip didn't want it any more and gave it to Derek, and Derek gave it to me. It's gold, studded with tiny diamonds. And since that night it's never been off my finger.

Then, still speaking with this other voice, the medium went on.

'Where's my camera, Dad, the one you bought me? I can't see it.'

'I've got it here, son. Don't worry, I won't throw it away.'

While this was going on, I began to shiver. I had on this sleeveless ice-blue velvet A-line dress. I remember thinking I must go and get a cardigan because I felt so cold. Then all of a sudden I was gone, like I'd fainted. Everything sounded far away. I didn't know it then but I was in a trance and Derek started to speak through me. Mum and Dad said afterwards that my voice changed. I've always had more of a cockney accent than anyone else in the family. In Edgware they even sent me to elocution lessons to get rid of it. Derek sounded quite different. Plus his voice was deeper. I can't remember any of what I/Derek said. I wasn't really there. But Mum and Dad told me that this time there was nothing about giving up. Quite the reverse. I/Derek said that he wanted us to carry on because 'there's a lot of guilty people'. He/I also talked about his dogs and cats and Sally, his bike. Then he/I started crying and the tears dripped on to my dress, making a terrible mess of it. They were Derek's tears, channelled through me, the medium said. They never came out even though we tried washing. In 1972 I lent it to the BBC for their drama documentary on Derek's case. I never got it back.

When I came out of the trance I was in a right state and said I never wanted that experience again. But the medium said I should feel lucky to have been able to be a channel for Derek.

John Ralph, the reporter from the *Sunday Dispatch* who had sat through it with us, wrote it up the next week.

'It was a formidable, nerve-testing experience. I report what occurred. I cannot say I am convinced, but no one could fail to have been impressed.'

We didn't care if he was convinced or not. We were. It was as if a great cloud was lifted. It might seem strange but that's just how it was. You'd think it would have been upsetting but it was just the opposite. At the end of the seance Mum said, 'Now I know you're with me, Derek, I don't worry any more.'

John Lovette had noticed my bad leg (well, it was difficult not to notice it, sticking out like an old soldier's) and had asked about it. I told him all the ins and outs and he said had I thought of going to see a healer. Well, I hadn't. It wasn't the sort of thing people did in Norbury. John Lovette had arranged to come back the next week for another seance, this time in Derek's bedroom. In the meantime, he said, why don't you go and see Harry Edwards about your leg.

Harry Edwards was a famous faith healer. They even said he'd helped Queen Mary. So the next week Mum and I went down with a journalist from *Two Worlds*, Mr Neech, to see him. He lived about fifteen miles further out of London, near Cobham, Surrey. He looked just like Jesus, and people didn't look like that in the fifties. He had long hair, whiskers and he wore sandals. The sanctuary where he did the healing was built on at the back of his house. It was beautiful, with doves flying around. I shouldn't be surprised if

197

heaven isn't like that. It was the most peaceful place I think I have ever been to. Harry Edwards had an assistant, Mr Burton. Mr Edwards put his hands on my knee and Mr Burton stood behind me and put his hands on my head. It felt lovely and warm, like a hot-water bottle. I felt so peaceful. Then, when I stood up (I was sitting down when the healing was being done, my leg stuck out in front), I found I could bend it. I could walk nearly normally. When I got home, Dad and Denis couldn't believe it. At the same time Harry Edwards had a go at Mum's back. It did seem to straighten out a bit, but it only lasted a month or so. But my leg never went back to how it was before. With being able to bend it properly, the muscle tone could start building up again.

The next week John Lovette came again. This time we went into Derek's bedroom, and the voice only came through Lovette.

'Hello, Mum, is that you?'

As soon as Mum heard it, she took hold of John Lovette's hands as if they were Derek's.

'Pleased to see you, son. Mother's here, don't worry. Everything's forgiven, Derek.'

This time Derek talked about the hanging.

'I was strong then. Did they tell you I was strong, Dad? My last thoughts were all for you. Dear old Dad, I won't bother you any more. Give my love to Denis the Menace. They've given me a second chance. I'll try to make it up to you, I'll work hard.'

He said he was happy where he was.

'Don't keep crying. I'm not going to go away, I'll stay.'

Mr Lovette said that the things that had been happening would stop now.

'Derek was only trying to attract your attention.'

And he was right. The stair carpet stayed where it was, the bed stayed made, there was no ash in the ashtray. But when Mum was very depressed, things started happening again. But it didn't worry us. In fact it was a help. It was as if Derek, was saying don't worry, I'm here with you, Mum.

Not long after the case, John Parris, Craig's solicitor, had written to me and asked if I would consider doing a book about it with him. The person writing it was going to be Leonard Parkin. It was when I was still working at the Astoria, before my accident. I remember we went for a walk on Streatham Common and talked about it, but it never came to anything. In September 1955 the publishers W. H. Allen wrote to Dad and said would he be interested in doing a book. Dad decided that we were running out of steam at Spouters' Corner and that a book would reach far more people. So he said yes. Mr Roberts the writer they got in to help would sit with Dad and go through the story. But we never got to know him well. Sometimes I would be asked about things, sometimes Mum would be, but only when Dad's memory was a bit hazy. The advance for the book was £125. It doesn't sound much, but £100 was a lot of money in 1955. If it had been a bestseller then there would have been more, but it wasn't. *My Son's Execution* by William George Bentley was published in June 1957. When I read it now, I know there's things wrong about it, but maybe that was just down to the writer. Perhaps like Ludovic Kennedy getting 'Jim' to learn to read in the condemned cell, he wanted to make things more dramatic. What still comes through after all these years is Dad's dignity and the terrible pain of being crushed by a machine that no one could stop.

On 12 December 1956 the case about my leg was finally listed to be heard in the High Court. I had only had one day's notice. A telegram arrived the day before saying 'Appear in court tomorrow.'

It still seems unbelievable but, out of all the judges in the world that could have done my case, it turned out to be Lord Goddard. What was Lord Goddard, the Lord Chief Justice of England, doing with a little case like mine? Newspaper reports said Goddard asked whether I wanted a different judge. Newspaper reports say that I said no. But I can't remember any of that. If I did, it must have been because I was so shocked. Imagine. There was the man who had hanged my brother. Perhaps it was that Neil Taylor, my barrister, thought Goddard would be more for me, given what he'd done to my brother. Anyway, Goddard it was.

When it was my turn to give evidence, I got up from my seat at the back of the court and was just making my way to the witness box when Goddard shouted across the court, 'Hurry up, Miss Bentley, I haven't got all day.'

I was livid. That's why I was there, because my leg was bad. Even though I could bend it now, it was still as thin as a stick of celery and walking was painful and slow.

I told him all about the accident, about the slippery stair, about the bad lighting, about the operation. My barrister had already said that my recovery was slow because of the Bentleys' 'terrible tragedy' in January 1953.

Judy Dalleas told about how we were watching Robert Mitchum and Lord Goddard said one of those things that judges are famous for.

'What's that? Mitcham. You were watching a film in Mitcham?'

'No. The film was starring an American actor called Robert Mitchum.'

Lord Goddard had never heard of him. The press made quite a meal of that.

The learned judge said he wanted to see the stairs for himself and arranged to go to the Astoria the next morning. I made sure I went too. It was a joke. He arrived in his Bentley, all gracious waving of hands. We were back in court in the afternoon. He said there was nothing wrong with the stairs. The lighting was sufficient. He said that to call them dangerous was fantastic. If my claim was so fantastic how come I'd got Legal Aid? They don't throw their money around and it was after seeing the engineer's report on the stairs that they'd granted it. I hadn't been backstage at the Astoria since I'd left. When I'd had the accident the steps had been painted dark red. Now they were white. After three years you wouldn't expect the same bulb to be there but the bulbs had all been changed for brighter ones. The case of I. P. Bentley v. Circuits Management was dismissed. I tried to appeal but Legal Aid was refused. There was nothing more I could do.

In March 1957 we were back in the House of Commons again.

This time the Government put forward their own bill, which was passed. It was called the Homicide Act. It didn't abolish hanging, but it divided murder into capital and non-capital homicide. The death penalty was still kept for five categories of capital murder, including policemen.

Back in Norbury things weren't going well with Maurice. He was still fooling around with other girls. It didn't help that the newspapers carried on inventing stories about me. In September 1957 the *Sunday People* said I was getting engaged to someone who was in the choir at St Phillip's where I used to teach Sunday school. It was rubbish, but Maurice and I had another of our rows. He said, well, you know where to find me. I said, well, you know where to find me. But we were both so proud that we never did.

But I didn't mope. There was plenty going on at Fairview Road. Denis was now a teenager and Dad was determined that Denis and his friends would always have somewhere to go. That somewhere would be Fairview Road.

The first year or so after Derek died, it was hard on Denis. Mum and Dad took the decision not to involve him in the campaign. Dad said he had lost his brother, he wasn't going to let him lose his youth. And there's no denying it, I spoiled him. He was all I had. By the time he was at his secondary school it seemed to affect him hardly at all. He was very good looking and was never short of girlfriends even when he was only fourteen. He was tall, over six foot, even taller than Derek. His hair was reddish while Derek's was more of a dull gold.

In 1958 Denis was sixteen. Things were better than when Derek and I had been that age. At least now the choice wasn't just the pub or the street, by the late fifties we had coffee bars. The coffee bar in Norbury was called The Cactus and in Streatham it was The Tarantella. How they made any money I don't know. Although everybody went there, all we did was have a coffee, put money in the juke-box and sit and talk for hours. I was much older than Denis's friends, but it didn't matter. I felt very protective towards him. I wanted to know them all. No Craig would ever get near

Denis. I still wasn't up to doing much real dancing. But every Saturday night there was rock 'n' roll at the Bentleys.

It was all very formal. No drainpipes allowed. The girls wore full skirts over petticoats as stiff as greaseproof paper, which we did by rinsing them in sugar. Tops were clingy and our waists were cinched in with wide elastic belts which fastened like nurses' belts. Even though it didn't do my back any good, I wore high heels like all the rest, three inches at least with cut-out sides or sling-backs. My face was hidden under make-up, Max Factor Pan Cake, false eyelashes, mascara in a little box you spat in. I'd always had curly hair and then, how I longed for it to be straight. So I had it high in the front and backcombed to get rid of the curls.

Friday was Locarno night, down in Streatham. Boys would always say, 'See you next Friday. Meet you inside.' It meant they didn't have to pay. Girls were on one side, boys on the other. On the stage there would be a live band, either rock and roll or skiffle. Girls usually just danced together. Girls danced so much better than boys. They were all left feet.

'Dancing?'

'No, not at the moment.'

Denis and I had our own skiffle group. Denis plonked away on his guitar while I had a tea-chest with an old broom handle and a piece of string. But for the Saturday parties we played records. The old wind-up was up in the loft and we had a new radiogram with a silver stick in the middle where you piled up the records and they dropped down one by one. People brought their own and marked them with initials so they wouldn't lose them. They'd be sorted out at the end.

It wasn't just Denis's friends that came every night to 'Denis's Den' which was what we called the back room. Dad was on a crusade to keep people off the streets. Everyone was welcome. The house was open all the time. There'd always be a sandwich and a drink of Cydrax, Tizer or orange squash.

Dad had begun to live again through Denis. He was the life and soul of the party, he even bought a jacket with 'Rock Around the

Clock' written on it. Everybody loved Uncle Bill. He didn't stop the party at eleven like other parents might have. Where would the boys and girls go? So the dancing went on until Dad said, right, that's enough. People who lived not too far away Dad would see home himself. Anyone left would bed down, sometimes there were as many as eight or nine. Girls slept in the lounge, boys in the back room. The girls in the lounge did best. They had the cushions from the two settees. I can't think now what the boys slept on. Mum would get out the hangers and the girls' dresses would be hung up on the picture rail in the hall. Walking to the front door was like an obstacle race with all these petticoats sticking out.

To make sure there was no hanky-panky, Dad would take a kitchen chair to the bottom of the stairs and sit there until he thought everyone was asleep. They thought he stayed there all night. But he didn't. He just went up to bed when he thought everyone was asleep. But he was down in the morning before they were awake saying things like, 'That's better, Paula. Now I can see you without all that make-up.'

He was strict, but not fierce. If anyone needed somewhere to stay for a few days they only had to ask. I remember one afternoon coming back and finding a girl called Barbara who I'd never met before. She was pregnant. Her family had thrown her out. She had nowhere to live, so Mum and Dad said she could live with us until the baby was born. Mum and Dad were more generous than any other people I've ever met.

Uncle Bert was still up in Derek's room. But nobody ever slept in Derek's bed.

For his sixteenth birthday, Dad bought Denis a racer bike. It was expensive and he bought it on the HP from a shop in Croydon. Not long after, the handlebars just snapped. Dad telephoned the shop, told them what happened, said that it was dangerous and that he would be bringing it in to swap it for a new one. They said that it was nothing to do with them. That there was nothing wrong with it when it had left the shop. So Dad told them he wasn't paying any more instalments. And he didn't. The bike was unridable and sat taking up space in the shed.

On the evening of 22 January 1959 there was a knock at the door. It was the bailiffs. They wanted £35. It was for the bike. Dad wasn't in so I said they should come back later. But they said no, that they were going to wait. I phoned Dad at work to see what he wanted me to do. He told me to tell them he would be back as soon as he could and that he would get the money by tomorrow. He was back about half an hour later. He said that he would get the money by the next day. But they weren't interested.

'We have come here to get the money or the body.'

'Don't you listen? I told you I'd have it by tomorrow. If you want something to take away tonight, take the bike.'

What we didn't know then was that they had police cars waiting around the corner.

Next thing was the place was crawling with police. At least ten, possibly more, all in uniform. They pushed their way into the house with bits of wood they pulled out of the fence around the front, and they had Dad up against the wall of the kitchen. Mum was in tears, then Kathy, Denis's girlfriend at the time, booted one of the policemen up the bum and that was it. They grabbed Dad and bundled him into a Black Maria which was conveniently pulled up outside and took him to Norbury police station. The next morning he was taken to Brixton Prison. He wouldn't be let out, they said, until the debt was paid.

The next day it was all over the papers. What could I do? Thirty-five pounds was a lot of money in those days, about £300 in today's money. We hadn't got anything like that, and I didn't know how Dad was planning to pay for it. The next day a telegram came addressed 'Priority Mrs William Bentley'.

'AM PAYING MONEY FOR YOUR HUSBAND'S RELEASE COULD YOU COME AND SEE ME AT ONCE. VAN DER ELST'

Mrs Van der Elst was a very rich campaigner against capital punishment. She'd always turn up in her Rolls-Royce outside the

prison on the morning of a hanging. Mum accepted her offer and
Dad came home that afternoon. But he was bruised from where
he'd been hit by a piece of the front fence. It didn't help his arthritis.
He was off work for a month. He was fifty-five. We went to see
Mrs Van der Elst. She offered to pay the legal costs to stand up and
fight the bicycle shop. But Dad said no. With the name of Bentley,
he said, we didn't stand a chance.

CHAPTER EIGHTEEN

Nineteen sixty was very tense. First, on 7 August, a reporter on the *Daily Express* telephoned and told us that Craig was about to be released. We couldn't believe our ears. He had been in prison for only seven and a half years. Mum was in a terrible state. I was fuming. For some time now I'd managed not to think about Craig at all. The Craigs had moved away around 1958. I can only remember seeing Mrs Craig once after the case. I can't remember now how long after. I was with Mum. We saw her outside the flower shop, Rogersons.

'You shouldn't concern yourself with the dead, Mrs Bentley. We must live for the living.'

It set Mum back for weeks. Then we heard they had emigrated to Australia. For some while it had been for me as if he didn't exist. But suddenly I felt anger surge up in me. But I don't know if it was anger at Craig himself, or anger that he was being let out. I think it was that really. I don't hate Craig. I've never hated Craig. But that August I felt bitter. There he was, only twenty-four, with all his life in front of him. And Derek, where was Derek? All Dad could say was, 'Where's the justice, where's the justice in that?'

A few days later another newspaper, the *Daily Sketch*, told how only ten days before, Craig had been in court for stealing a car. Stealing a car? But what about him being in prison? Had he escaped? No, as he was coming up to release he was working in real jobs, and only had to be back by eleven o'clock. He took it from outside a West End night club. He was fined £10. Craig hadn't changed. How could they think of letting him out?

Then, a few days later, another newspaper report. Craig's release was just rumours. It might even have been invention by the tabloid press for all I know. August is what they call the silly season in the press. With everyone being on holiday, they're always short of stories. So they invented one, not caring what they put us through.

It turned out Craig's release had not even been discussed by the authorities.

Then a few days later, another call. This time from Harry Proctor. Had we read John Parris's book? he said. Parris, remember, had been Craig's barrister. It was called *Most of My Murders* and there was a chapter in it about Derek's case, and a theory about a third man.

On the day after the shooting in November 1952, there was a sentence in the Stop Press column of the *Star* saying: 'Police are looking for a third youth believed to be on the roof of Messrs Barlow and Parker's premises when PC Miles was shot.'

Although it made sense, what with Norman Parsley having called for Derek, nothing more was heard of the third boy till that August 1960 when John Parris published his book. Parris was from Yorkshire and had never really fitted in with London lawyers. He had long since stopped working as a barrister. One of the things that we had never understood was that the two boys spotted outside the warehouse before they ever started climbing were both wearing trilbies. But Derek hadn't taken his hat with him. It was still at home lying on his bed.

In his book Parris says that five of them took the bus to Croydon that night, Derek, Craig, Norman Parsley, Frank Fazey and another one. He says that by the time they got to the warehouse Parsley and Fazey had left but the other one, the one with no name, was still there. When we heard this it made Dad and me think. First, it would explain the business about Mrs Ware seeing two boys with hats. Also, it would explain how Derek had got on to the roof. Remember I'd given him extra phenobarbitone earlier on that night at the cinema and he was always dizzy with heights, even coming down the steps from the loft. If someone had gone up behind him, then he might have done it. Like we did in the tree-house in Edgware. He'd only go up if someone was behind. And he would never have gone up first. Not Derek. I'm not saying he was a coward. No, it was the heights thing. So that makes three of them going up the drainpipe. Craig first, then Derek, then this other boy. Parris didn't say who it was but he said whoever it was was boasting about it and should watch his mouth otherwise he'd be up on a capital charge.

There was only one thing to do. If a third boy was there, Craig would know. We would get him to tell us. He must. He owed us that, Dad reckoned. We still weren't convinced that Craig wasn't going to be released. We'd been told the day would be 15 August. So at dawn, which is when they release prisoners, we were waiting at the gates, me, Dad and Denis. No one came out. But Dad was now sure that it was the third boy who had said the words 'Let him have it, Chris', so Dad went to the Home Office asking if we could speak to Christopher Craig. The Home Office rang Wormwood Scrubs and spoke to the Governor, Mr George Smith. He said it was all right by him, as long as he could be there as a witness. Craig refused. So then I decided to write to Craig. My letter said something like: 'Dear Christopher, I have never done you any harm. Please let me come and talk to you. Yours sincerely, Iris Bentley.' I didn't mention anything about the third boy. He never replied.

Parris's book also made Dad angry because it gave Craig's version of what had led up to the shooting. It said Derek had been involved with Craig in breaking into other houses that summer. Dad said it was all a lie. That he would have known. I still don't believe it, or about the butcher's shop Craig said they tried to break into. I don't remember any butcher's in Tamworth Road. It was all Victorian houses. The only shops were one little sweet shop, a pub and a bicycle shop at the Croydon end and a fish and chip shop this end. Bert, Lillian's husband, worked up there all his life. He said there had never been a butcher's anywhere near. But mainly I don't believe it because I don't think Derek was clever enough to keep all that secret from me. But then, he never told us about there being a third boy on the roof either.

But it wasn't only Derek's case that Dad and I worked on. The pain we had gone through ourselves meant we knew what those poor families were going through. Over the years we had done what we could. But we had no money, just our knowledge of how to organize petitions. We could put them in touch with MPs who we knew would help them. Also journalists would speak to us, because we were known and because by now we were used to speaking to reporters and on the radio and we would help in that way. Although no one knew what things went towards a Home Secretary changing his mind, petitions were still the only thing the families of condemned prisoners had to give them hope. Doing something was always better than not doing anything.

Since the Homicide Act of 1957 which separated murders into two kinds, capital (hanging) and non-capital, the number of executions had gone down. But they'd been going down anyway since the worst year of 1952, when there were twenty-five, in spite of the fact that these included three jury 'recommendations for mercy' and four 'strong recommendations for mercy'. In 1953, as well as Derek, twelve others were hanged. In 1954 fourteen people were hanged, four in spite of the jury recommending mercy, one where the jury had said 'with the strongest possible recommendation for mercy'. In 1955 there were seven, three with a recommendation for mercy (including Ruth Ellis). And, as I said, in 1956 after the Commons had said no to hanging but before the Lords had thrown it out, there were no executions. No deterrent for a whole year? Did the number of murders go up? No. The murder rate remained the same as before, around 150 a year.

After the Homicide Act the number of executions per year had gone down to two in 1957, six in 1958, four in 1959, five in 1960. The Bentleys did petitions for them all. But for murders which were clear-cut, it was hard to get people to sign. We used all the arguments which we knew so well from the days at Spouters' Corner, but often it was wasted breath. They didn't mind signing for Ruth Ellis, because she was a woman who had children. But nobody ever said she didn't do it. Just that they understood why she did it and didn't think it would do anybody any good hanging her.

The papers put in all the gory details but they didn't put in the other details, which sometimes even the juries didn't hear. They read about a brutal murder and thought, eye for an eye, the murderer should hang. I do remember one man, because his name was Derek too, Derek Adams. He had escaped from the mental home where he was a patient. The woman he killed was the mother of two young children. Three doctors at his trial said he didn't know the difference between right and wrong. That was the case where the jury gave the 'strongest possible recommendation for mercy'. It didn't make any difference. They hanged him anyway.

The cases the public did get worked up about were cases like Derek's which involved young people. In the autumn of 1960 came what was known as the Hounslow Footpath murders where four young men, boys really, attacked another man on a footpath, after they'd been drinking. Two of them hanged and two didn't. Francis Forsyth, known as 'Floss', was hanged because he was eighteen, just above the 'under eighteen' rule. Norman Harris was hanged because he was twenty-three.

Dad and I didn't get personally involved in every case because we didn't have the money to travel and not every murder happened in London. But Hounslow was in west London so we did get more involved. Not since the Clapham murder had we been so bound up with it. But this time there was no happy ending. It was dreadful. Mrs Harris, Norman's mother, had recently been widowed. The day they were hanged, I couldn't stop crying. 'Floss' Forsyth was the same age as Denis.

I had met Stewart Dingwall at a party in December 1959. My reputation for being responsible had got around and parents would go out and let their children have a party on the understanding that I was there to organize it and make sure there were no bedroom scenes. Everyone knew about the success of the Bentleys' parties. After all, I was ten years older than them. The parents would interview me and tell me what was what. I would do all the food, look after the drink, making sure no one brought anything in too alcoholic. There was no wine in those days. Just weak cider and pop. On the night, the parents would go out and I was in charge. Bedroom doors had locks in those days, so apart from the one for the coats, I would lock them all and take the keys and hide them in the kitchen. I did it with a friend of mine, Bette. It was at one of these parties that I met Stewart. The party was for Denis's age group but Stewart had come with his younger brother Peter. But even so, he was nine years younger than me. He was in the RAF, a flight mechanic in the Queen's Flight. Like I said, I always had a soft spot for a uniform.

It wasn't love at first sight. I thought of us as friends. We would just go out to the pictures, or dancing. Then, at Christmas 1960, he popped the question. He'd heard he was being posted to Tobruk at the end of January. I said yes. I'm not sure why. Laurie had proposed at Christmas and that was a mistake. I thought I was in love. But I think it was more that I was lonely and I'd recently heard that Maurice had married one of the girls he was flirting with when we were courting. Maurice was still the one for me, but I couldn't have him now. I was twenty-nine, quite old for a girl still to be single in those days, nearly on the shelf. But Stewart wasn't like Maurice. No one could be. Maurice was my ideal. He was tall, Stewart was short. Maurice was slim, Stewart could have done with losing a few pounds. But they were both RAF. Perhaps that was it.

The wedding was set for 21 January at St Philip's at Norbury. There was no time for banns. But then came the blow. Being under twenty-one Stewart needed his parents' consent. His father was in Kuwait and he said no. He did not want his son to marry into the Bentley family. He did not want him to be tainted with the family of a murderer. It was nothing to do with me, I'd not even met his dad. He was in Kuwait, an engineer working on the oil fields.

So on Tuesday, 17 January we went to Croydon Magistrates' Court. They had told us that unless Stewart's father turned up in person, they would give us permission. He didn't turn up. But he had come back from Kuwait to the house in Coulsdon which the

Dingwalls still owned, and Stewart went to see him and finally he relented. But by then we only had two days to go, so we had to get a special licence from somewhere in Westminster.

It was a cold day but at least it wasn't raining. This time I didn't buy a wedding dress, just hired one, together with the bridesmaids' dresses. I had two bridesmaids – Sandra, Denis's girlfriend and Sheila, who we had got to know through our campaign against capital punishment. But it wasn't Sheila's brother or father she and her mother were campaigning for. Sheila's sister had been murdered on Streatham Common by her boyfriend. Even though they were the victim's family, they were campaigning for her murderer not to die. It turned out she had taunted him about other men. The mother felt like we did. 'Hanging him won't bring my daughter back.' She was an extraordinary woman. When he was released, after serving his life imprisonment, she took him in and looked after him until he got on his feet.

Stewart's family didn't come to the wedding, not even his brother Peter, Denis's friend. But everyone else seemed to. There was such a crowd round the house we had to have a police escort to St Phillip's. The reception was at home. I had a wonderful two-tier, heart-shaped cake. Ken Allen and his wife managed to come, which pleased Mum and Dad.

It was a wonderful day. I had no inkling then that the marriage wouldn't work out. I was so hopeful. It was going to be just like Mum and Dad's. Give and take. But I ended up doing all the giving and he did all the taking.

Stewart was away a lot of that year and I carried on living at Fairview Road just like before. It was as if nothing had changed.

On 23 August 1961 came the A6 murder. The night before a man had hijacked a Morris Minor car with two people in it, Michael Gregsten and Valerie Storie. It was already dark when it happened, so they couldn't see what he looked like. He made them drive at gunpoint from near Slough where it happened around the outskirts of London up the A6. Near Bedford, he made them stop in a lay-by called Deadman's Hill. Then he shot the man, Michael Gregsten, and raped the woman, pushed her out of the car and then shot her. She didn't die, but she was paralysed for life. First the papers said they were looking for someone called Peter Alphon. This was quite odd, as usually they wouldn't give out a suspect's name like that. It seemed Alphon had stayed in a small hotel in London called the Vienna Hotel where they'd found two cartridge cases sitting on a bedside chair. Alphon immediately came forward and he was put in an identity parade. Valerie Storie came in on a stretcher. She identified someone else who was completely innocent. Alphon was free to go.

Then they found another man had stayed in the room of the hotel where the cartridge cases were found. He was called James Hanratty. So they began looking for him. Hanratty was well known to the police. He did house burglaries, specializing in jewellery, and stealing cars. Instead of going to see the police like Alphon did, Hanratty got scared and decided to disappear. The hunt was on. By doing that, by not coming forward, the police decided Hanratty was the one. But while he was on the run, he called the police at Scotland Yard and told them where his clothes were. He said they should test them. Right to the end he always said he was innocent of everything and if he was guilty it was an odd thing to do, to offer up his clothes for testing. But he was innocent, so he knew there could be nothing to connect him with the car. And there wasn't. Nothing ever connected him with the car. In fact, just the opposite. The murderer didn't know how to drive and had got Valerie Storie to tell him about the clutch, the lights and all that sort of thing. He even got her to start the car. And she remembers how he barely got the car moving when he left her for dead on Deadman's Hill. James Hanratty was a car thief. He was a very good driver.

The trial was one of the longest criminal trials England had ever had at the time. It lasted from 22 January 1962 until 17 February 1962. The evidence was just people identifying Hanratty as the driver of the car when it was being driven around after the crime, and Valerie Storie, who had also identified him at an identity parade. Many years later a man who was also on that same identity parade said Hanratty didn't stand a chance. When he was on the run, Hanratty had dyed his hair carrot-red. That's how he was found, in a café in Blackpool, because they recognized his carrot hair. He still had the carrot hair in the identity parade. No one else had carrot hair. Valerie Storie must have read about the carrot hair, it was everywhere. So she identified him.

The prosecution said that the business of the murderer not being able to drive was a blind, just to put everyone off the scent. But witnesses who spotted the car on its way across country from Bedfordshire to Essex, where it was found abandoned, say that it was driven very erratically even then. None of this mattered to the police. Nor the fact that Hanratty had no possible motive. An old Morris Minor wasn't the kind of flash car he would want to steal. The murderer 'stole' both of the couple's watches. But when Valerie Storie was found, both watches were fastened around her wrist. And Hanratty had no record of violence at all. I remember hearing Mr Hanratty being interviewed and him saying, 'Jim wouldn't hurt a fly.' Just the same words as Dad said to the police that terrible night, 'Derek wouldn't hurt a fly.' But a man called Peter France, another crook Hanratty had dealings with in Soho, said Hanratty told him how he used to hide 'loot' under the back seat (upstairs) of a bus. The gun that killed Michael Gregsten was found under the back seat of a London bus. (A few weeks after Hanratty was hanged, Peter France committed suicide.) Another thing was that Valerie Storie said the murderer had told her to call him 'Jim'. But at the time of the statement she said it clearly wasn't his real name. The jury didn't hear that bit.

In the trial Hanratty said he was in Wales on the night of the murder. He had another alibi, he'd been up in Liverpool 'fencing' some jewellery. The reason he'd gone on the run after his name was put out, he said, was to go up to Liverpool to persuade the 'fence' to come forward and be his alibi. But, being a 'fence', a criminal, the man refused, but the landlady in Rhyl in Wales was found and she was brought down to the trial, which was held in Bedford, near where the murder was committed. But the jury didn't believe her. She was asked whether she had spoken to any of the witnesses and she'd said no. But it was known that she had. It was the same old thing. She had lied on one thing, so they weren't going to believe her about Hanratty staying in her guest-house the night of the murder. Funny it's that way with ordinary witnesses and not with the police. The jury were out for ten hours, but in the end James Hanratty was found guilty.

When you read about the trial now, it all sounds impossible that the case was brought at all. There was no motive. Valerie Storie had hardly seen the murderer. She'd identified somebody else first. Although two people identified Hanratty as the driver of the car (seen later in Essex), the two passengers with them, who probably had a better view of the murderer (driving the car), did not identify Hanratty. Not to mention all the stuff about not knowing how to drive. It was all down to these identity parades.

When Dad heard the verdict, he got in touch with Hanratty's father. They lived in north London. Mr Hanratty was quite like Dad in many ways. Same sort of age, and not dissimilar to look at and they both had the same way of walking. Probably they'd both been in the army during the war. Although he lived in England, and was now a Londoner, you could still hear the Irish in his voice. He didn't know what had hit him. Dad helped with the petitions in the way he could do walking in his sleep. James Hanratty's appeal was held on 13 March but the judges said there were no possible grounds for an appeal. He was hanged at Bedford on 4 April 1962.

In the last letter James Hanratty wrote to his brother from the condemned cell just a few minutes before the hangman came, he said:

I am going to ask you a small favour, that is I would like you to try and clear my name, of this crime. Someone, somewhere is responsible for this crime and one day they will venture again and then the truth will come out, and then Mick that will be the

215

chance for you to step in. I feel the police will try to hush it all up if they get the chance. So Mick I am counting on you to keep your eyes on the papers. Well Mick, with that as time is drawing near, it is almost daylight, so please look after Mum and Dad for me, as you just could not wish to have better parents than the ones you have got. I only wish I could have the chance all over again. But never mind, Mick as I don't know what I have done to deserve this. But Mick, that's fate for you. Thanks for all the trouble you have been to, I can assure you that you have not been wasting your time, as it will all help to bring out the truth in the end, and Mick don't let anyone say a bad word about me. I feel I will have to say goodby [sic] for now. Give my best wishes to Mum and Dad and all the family.

Your loving brother, Jim.

PS. I hope you like the car as it is one which I am sure you will like. I wish I had paid the full amount and had given it to you as a gift before now. But please Mick remember it is a very fast car, and whatever you do take care when you drive it. With a car of this standard it is very powerful. I know you are a very good driver and know that you will take care of it, and I hope you really enjoy it for many years to come. Keep smiling Mick. Jim.

For many years, until he died, Mr Hanratty carried on fighting to clear his son's name. Dad started him off at Spouters' Corner, though they always spoke separately, and they stayed in touch over the years. He and Mrs Hanratty came to Dad's funeral.

More recently his sons (James Hanratty's brothers) have taken over the campaign. About four years after, Peter Alphon, the original suspect, made out on French television that it was him. But still nobody did anything. In those days there was no DNA testing. But there is now and Hanratty's brother believes they still have the murderer's sperm which could be checked against James Hanratty's DNA. Hanratty wasn't the last man to be hanged in England, but, even at the time, there was doubt that he had done it. And in

English law, a man is supposed to be innocent until he's proved guilty, 'beyond reasonable doubt'. In Hanratty's case doubt was written all over it.

That first year of our marriage I remember that we were very happy. When Stewart came back from abroad, we moved into a house in Kingston that his father had bought for us. It wasn't a present. It was still in Mr Dingwall's name. He had bought it on the understanding that he could stay on his trips back from Kuwait. We moved in just before Christmas 1961.

Although it had three bedrooms, the house was tiny, with rooms hardly bigger than box-rooms. If anyone came into the sitting-room, you had to stand up to let them squeeze in. Having the Dingwalls' old furniture didn't help. It came from the house in Coulsdon which they'd sold: great wing chairs and a heavy antique table and dining chairs. The rest of the stuff from their old house had been put in store. I wish this had been too. So I did my own bit of storing and just piled the chairs in the garage.

It all needed decorating and the garden, which was huge compared to the house, needed a good going over. I enjoyed that, but even with all this to do, it was a bit lonely. None of my friends lived round Kingston and all the girls my own age seemed to go out to work. But Stewart didn't believe in his wife working. He made me give up my bookkeeping job. I had enough to do at home, he said.

It seemed like we'd only been in Kingston for a few weeks and I was expecting. Dad was more excited than anyone and he started buying things for the layette right away. Every time he'd come for a visit, he'd hand over bags of nappies and matinée jackets. By the time the baby was due, I had so many baby clothes, you'd think I was expecting quads. When they came over Mum would fall asleep directly she'd had her dinner. She reckoned it was the country air.

On 8 October 1962, Maria was born. I'd hoped to have her at home but because of the trouble with my spine I had to go into hospital. I wasn't allowed to lie on my back and had to be slowly turned over and over in this hammock contraption throughout labour, just like a chicken on a spit. With me rolling around, they got confused with hearing two heartbeats and thought it was twins, which given the twins in the Bentley family didn't surprise me. But there was only one. We called her Maria after *West Side Story*.

It was only after she was born that things went really wrong. All Stewart ever wanted was a girl but when it came to it, he really wasn't that bothered. He started staying out, not coming home. And I'd find hair-grips in the car.

I think he was jealous of Maria taking up all my time. But small babies are like that. Living with them's not easy, especially in a house with no space and especially if they're bawling all the time, which Maria was. To get her off to sleep we'd put the carrycot in the car and go up and down Kingston bypass. But it rarely worked and she'd carry on bawling just the same. We'd end up with Stewart sleeping in one room and me in the other with Maria. Even so, he said he hardly slept and he had to be up at 4 a.m. to be at the base at Northolt in time.

Like I said, everyone round where we lived went out to work. There was nothing to do except walk round the shops. Sometimes I'd see someone I'd been in hospital with and have a chat about babies. Or I'd put everything in the pram and go over to Mum. But I was always back, dinner cooked, table laid, for when Stewart got home. I'd been brought up to see that when the man comes home from work his meal's ready.

Christopher Craig had been released in the summer of 1962. We didn't hear about it until later. But we didn't do anything about it. Dad had other more important things to think about. He had a grandchild.

218

CHAPTER NINETEEN

One morning in September 1964 the phone rang just as I was giving Maria her breakfast. It was Mum in tears. There was a letter from the landlords, she said, saying they had to be out of the house by the end of the month. No reason.

'It's not the rent is it, Mum?'

'It depends what you mean.'

'I mean do you owe any rent?'

'It's all here, but the old boy's not come for it.'

She told me there was three months' rent waiting to be collected in the jug on the kitchen dresser. I got Maria dressed and went straight over. It took two buses, the 152 to Mitcham, then the 115 to Norbury.

Mum had said nothing to Dad because his arthritis was playing up and she was worried something like this would set him back. If I could get it sorted, he need never know. Paying the rent was always down to Mum. Rent day was Monday. So the next Monday, I took Maria and went to Mum's and sat in the window knitting, watching out. And then, at about three o'clock, there he was, the same old boy, knocking at Mrs Leppard's door over the road. I put down my knitting, and ran across.

'You haven't collected Mum's rent.'

'Oh, hello, Iris. No. The guv'nor told me not to.'

'Why?'

'Didn't say. Just said not to collect it.'

So then I called the landlords, and asked what was going on.

'The rent's not been paid.'

I explained that it was a mistake, that Mum had the rent, just that it hadn't been collected.

'We don't want the money. We just want you out.'

It was nothing to do with the rent. It was just because of Derek.

They didn't need to spell it out but I wanted them to. I phoned up again, this time with Lillian in the phone box as a witness, and out it came.

'You Bentleys give the street a bad name.'

Dad had to be told. He went mad. We tried SSAFA, the British Legion, no one could do anything. According to the letter of the law we hadn't paid our rent. Every door was shut against us.

So that was how eight years after my leg case Dad and I ended up at the High Court again. I can't remember now who paid for it. I doubt it was Legal Aid, because Dad was working. Perhaps it was Mrs Van der Elst. I don't know. But whoever it was, it was money wasted. We should have known no one with the name of Bentley was ever going to win. Dad lost and the eviction was legal.

As soon as we got home, he was off to the shed.

'They're not going to throw me out of my own home.'

An hour later the place looked like Colditz. The front-room window was barricaded with wire netting and planks of wood nailed across, likewise the French windows in the back room. The front and back doors were bolted. Someone always had to be in, to open the door from the inside. The siege of Fairview Road had begun. Three days later workmen arrived with pickaxes and started with the front window. But with the first sound of breaking glass, a flash went off in their eyes, and they stopped. Doing a good impression of the Gestapo when no one could see was one thing, but when they saw the press was there, that was different. But three days later, they were back. This time there was no one there except Mum and what could she do on her own?

She called me from Mrs Leppard's.

'I couldn't stop them, Iris. Your dad's at work and Uncle's not back yet. All the furniture's just piled up in the garden any old how and they just threw the blankets and sheets out of Derek's window.'

I rang Stewart at base at Northolt, and he said he'd be right over. We had a Morris Traveller in those days. Mum stayed at Mrs Leppard's until he got there. Dad and Uncle still weren't back, and rather than waiting, Stewart decided to bring Mum straight over to

Kingston with the animals, six chickens, three dogs – Prince, Denis's part-Dalmatian black and white mongrel he'd got from Battersea Dogs' Home, Maurice's lurcher Bobby, who was getting old now, and Derek's dog Judy – plus whatever cats Mum could find, Omo, Scratch, Tiddles, Teardrop and Ginger.

As soon as Dad got back and saw the pile of furniture in the back garden, he phoned a storage firm. He couldn't risk leaving it so had to wait till they came. Putting it in store cost £150. We still had the money that Mum had saved up in rent, which the landlords refused to take. But it was even more than that.

As I said, the Kingston house was small. But somehow we all squeezed in. Maria moved in with Stewart and me. Mum and Dad slept in what we called the nursery, which was also where Mr Dingwall slept when he was in England, and Uncle Bert and Denis were crammed into the box-room which was mostly taken up with one single bed. We took down Maria's cot that took up the rest of it, found an old mattress in the garage and put it on the floor for Denis. You couldn't shut the door and his feet stuck out on to the landing.

Living like sardines in a tin put a strain on all of us. What was worse, we didn't know how long it was going to last. Stewart started rowing with Dad. But they were only with us till they found a place. They did their best to keep out of Stewart's way and not interfere. They stayed in one room basically and Dad did the cooking for us. It gave me a bit of a break because Dad was such a wonderful cook.

Denis was working for a builder and decorator in Mitcham and Dad was still based in Croydon, so Stewart gave both of them a lift to Mitcham every morning. After work Denis and Dad would meet up and go looking for somewhere to live. Croydon, Tooting, Mitcham, even Wimbledon, they looked in, but not Norbury. We had lived in Norbury for nearly twenty years and Fairview Road was our home, Derek's home. If they couldn't live there, then they wouldn't live in Norbury.

Dad and Denis saw the house in Colliers Wood in the window

of an estate agent's in Tooting Broadway. It was a three-bedroom house built in the twenties in a quiet road next door to a church, halfway between Tooting and Wimbledon. It had a big garden front and back, bigger than Fairview Road, and it was the garden that did it for Dad. He put down the key money, and within a week they were in. But Colliers Wood wasn't Norbury, and my mother never really made friends again because all her friends were in Norbury and after twenty years in one house, it's hard for old people to dig up their roots. But they made the best of a bad job. I'm still there today but even now, thirty years later, it doesn't feel like home, not like Fairview Road.

On Friday, 13 August 1964 Gwynne Evans and Peter Allen were hanged. They were the last people to be hanged in Britain. Because only two months later Harold Wilson won the general election for the Labour party. Although Labour only had a majority of five, he did something no one had ever done before. In the Queen's Speech for the opening of Parliament (which the Prime Minister writes) for the first time ever in the history of the House of Commons, a Private Member's Bill was included. It was Sydney Silverman's Private Member's Bill for the abolition of capital punishment.

The Bill was given its second reading just before Christmas, on 23 December 1964. Everyone knew it would get through the Commons, after all the Commons had voted to abolish hanging consistently, in 1947 and 1956. It was just a question of how much the vote had increased. But it wasn't just as expected. There was a great surprise when Henry Brooke, the ex-Conservative Home Secretary stood up. He said that ten years ago he had voted to keep hanging but he had changed his mind since becoming Home Secretary. 'I do not share the view that taking a life by the state is contrary to moral principle. But I do believe that the death penalty can only be justified on the ground that it is a unique deterrent. If it is a unique deterrent, then there is justification for it. If it is not, I do not think that the case for it can be upheld.'

Back-bench Tory MPs came out with the same old bigotry as

before. One said he did not think that anyone had 'swung' up to now who had not committed murder. Another said, 'I am perfectly happy if a mistake was made in an odd case and if one more mistake is made in the next five to ten years, if retention of the death penalty saves the life of one child.' But, just to show Tories weren't all bad, another previous Home Secretary, Sir Edward Boyle, said capital punishment for murder was a bad penalty. He said 'organized and legalized killing was a sickening and barbarous ritual and society would be better without it'.

It was May when the second reading of the Bill was passed by 355 to 170, a majority of 185. Dad and I were sitting in the public gallery, just like we always did. When the majority was announced, you could hear a great intake of breath. I felt like cheering but, like I said, I knew how to behave and so Dad and I just hugged each other.

It then had to go to the committee stage, but a few back-bench Tories still did everything they could to try and stop it getting through, which, being a Private Member's Bill, they could, by putting forward amendment after amendment. But the Government called their bluff and the committee stage was taken back to the floor of the House. We couldn't go every day, but we made sure we were there for the last day and after a fight that lasted months and months, finally, in the early hours of the morning of 26 May, the amendments were all defeated. It still had to go to the Lords. But everyone thought that if the Lords rejected it again, like they did in 1947 and 1956, they would be signing their own death warrant, because the Commons would just abolish the House of Lords completely. But they knew which side their bread was buttered and Sydney Silverman's Private Member's Bill to abolish capital punishment was finally passed by the House of Lords on 27 October, for a five-year trial period with an even greater majority than the Commons.

After his success, Sydney Silverman made a speech about what had made him so passionate and persistent about abolishing hanging.

When I was a very young man, I read in a newspaper a story about another young man. He had, in a moment of emotional despair, shot and killed the girl he was in love with and with whom he had quarrelled, so that his world had crashed about his ears. He became, naturally enough, more emotionally desperate than ever. So he shot himself.

He did not die. They took him to hospital and over many weeks carefully, patiently and devotedly nursed him back to health. But not altogether. For in attempting to destroy himself, he succeeded only in destroying his left eye. So they provided him with an artificial eye. They took a lot of care over it. They made it the right size, the right shape, the right colour, the right shade of blue. Having got it right they fitted him with it. Then they took him out and hanged him, artificial eye and all.

I thought that was horrible. It was perfectly legal. He was guilty. The judge had to sentence him to death. It was the duty of the hangman to hang him, just as much as it was the duty of the hospital to do what they could for him first. It was my first experience of the cold, remorseless, inexorable logical savagery of legal thinking and I have never forgotten it. It seemed to be hopelessly uncivilized . . .

Never again will we kill an innocent man. Never again will we kill a young man like Derek Bentley, a young mental deficient of nineteen, hanged for a murder committed by somebody else twenty minutes after Bentley had been arrested and was in police custody. Never again will we hang a Timothy Evans for a murder he certainly didn't commit and which was probably committed by the chief witness for the prosecution.

Now that capital punishment was abolished, there were a few things to put right. The first was Timothy Evans. In August 1965 an enquiry was ordered by the Home Secretary Sir Frank Soskice. A year later, on 18 October 1966, his mother's prayers of all those years were finally granted and he was given a free pardon. It was announced by Roy Jenkins, who had taken over as Home Secretary.

That it happened at all was down to Ludovic Kennedy and his book, *10 Rillington Place* (which was turned into a film starring Richard Attenborough as Christie in 1970). He had published it in 1960 and there had been a debate in the House of Commons. But the Home Secretary, R. A. Butler, had refused even an inquiry. He said it would discover nothing new. Kennedy never thought justice would be done. But now it had. Too late for Timothy Evans but not too late for his mother, Mrs Probert. But Ludovic Kennedy was still angry.

'It was not so much the fact that poor Evans was wrongfully convicted whch has kept me angry for ten years. It was the fact that successive numbers of people have been trying so hard to cover up the fact.' Just like Derek. And like Derek it would take a book to stir things up.

The fight against capital punishment was over. But the fight to clear Derek's name went on. The next thing was to get Derek's body out of his unmarked grave somewhere at the back of Wandsworth Prison. In March 1965 the body of Roger Casement, who was hanged as a traitor for fighting for Irish independence, was handed over to Ireland. So why not Derek?

People often wonder what we were able to do. What we did was pester and that's what we got other people to do who wrote to us wanting to help. We asked them to write to their MP, and to the Home Secretary asking them to press for a free pardon and asking for Derek's body to be handed over for proper Christian burial. Our hopes were first raised in 1954 when the news came of the reburial of Nazi war criminals. If they could allow families to give a Christian burial to someone called 'the Beast of Belsen', who murdered thousands of people, surely they couldn't refuse it for Derek, who never killed anybody. But they could and they did.

Nearly every week since Derek was killed, Dad and I had taken it in turns to write to the Home Office. First we just asked for permission to visit his grave, to put flowers on it. Then, after the news of the Nazi reburials, we asked for Derek's body, so we could give it a Christian burial. I don't know how many letters we had written. Sometimes they replied. Sometimes they didn't. But the answer was always the same. No. Those weren't the only letters we wrote. Every time there was a change in Home Secretary we wrote and asked to meet them to discuss Derek's case. They never replied and we never got to meet anybody.

But now, with the first Labour Government in power since Derek was hanged, things began to move.

Soon after Derek was killed we met Anne Clark. In those days she was a town councillor in the borough of Wandsworth. She had been against capital punishment ever since she could remember, she said, and was a friend of Mrs Van der Elst and John Parris, Craig's barrister. She had even gone with John Parris to see the Home Secretary David Maxwell-Fyfe the day before Derek was hanged to plead for a reprieve. A few days later she came to see Mum and Dad at Fairview Road.

Over the years she had been a real friend, from the early days of organizing meetings in libraries to later on, when she became an MP, keeping Derek's name alive in the House of Commons. In early 1965 she wrote to the Home Secretary Roy Jenkins and asked again about allowing Derek's body to be moved. She told us she was sure it would be all right but that we just had to be patient. It was so unusual, she said, that special arrangements would have to be made. The waiting was torture, especially for Mum. First they said it would be when the capital punishment bill was finally made law. But it went through the House of Lords in the summer of 1965 and still nothing happened. Then there was the question of money. Burials are expensive and the cost of a lead coffin and not just an ordinary one made of wood is out of this world. Anne did her best to get them to pay for it all, but in the end they just didn't charge for the special licence that was needed or the cost of digging Derek's body up. The rest we had to pay for. It came to over £250. A lot of money in those days when Dad was earning less than £20 a week.

There were so many conditions. There was the lead coffin, the hearse would have to go into the prison overnight, and everything had to be timed like a military exercise. The hearse with the coffin was to arrive outside Christchurch Road at 11 a.m. and at 11.02 it had to move off. We weren't allowed to wait in the street. We had to wait behind closed doors and then we had two minutes to get in the cars to follow the hearse. We were allowed a short service at the little church in the cemetery, then the burial. Just family and close friends. No press. Not even Anne (who was now called Kerr because she had married another Labour MP), who had worked so hard for us over the years was allowed. Just because she was an MP. But Anne Kerr and what she did will never be forgotten in the Bentley family. I asked her to be Maria's godmother. Sadly she died a few years later after being attacked with gas in Belgium, demonstrating against Britain going into the Common Market.

We had always thought Derek would be buried in Nunhead, with Aunt Rose and Joan, but in the end we decided on Croydon. Croydon cemetery was one of Derek's haunts for walks. It was where he would pick flowers, weeds really, to put on the graves of people who didn't have any, 'poor people who didn't have anyone to love them'. The plot we chose for the grave looked over towards Norbury, his home.

When we were finally told the date, strange to say, it took us by surprise. We got the word just after 28 January, the fifteenth anniversary of Derek's death. It was 5 March 1968, Aunt Rose's birthday.

At two minutes to eleven, the hearse pulled up in front of the house, as arranged. We had waited so long, and it was so important that everything was done just like the Home Office said.

Our own vicar, Mr Jardine, from Christchurch next door to our house, did the service at the cemetery. As he was saying the words over the grave, Maria pulled my sleeve and started laughing.

'Look, Mummy. Look at all those funny men.'

It was photographers, an army of them, popping up from behind the gravestones where they had been hiding. There must

227

have been a dozen of them. Who told them we shall never know. It wasn't us. But by then we didn't care. Derek was back with his family and would never be taken away from us again.

But although Derek was back with us, there was no headstone on his grave, not then, not now. Dad had planned the wording for so long; 'Derek William Bentley: A victim of British justice'. But Croydon Corporation, who ran the cemetery, said the words were 'offensive'. Hanging Derek was offensive. They said we could only have the headstone if the inscription was 'toned down'. So Dad offered an alternative: 'Derek William Bentley – Murdered by British Justice'. It had cost £125 to have done. But needless to say, it never moved from the stonemason's in Twickenham. In the end they had to take the words off and use it for somebody else.

It wasn't long after this that Mum had her accident. It was such a little thing but she just slipped on something as she got up from the tea table. She fell on to the arm of a chair, broke her hip and pierced her lung. Pneumonia set in right away. Dad stayed with her in the hospital but it looked hopeless from the start. She had to have a tracheotomy to enable her to breathe. Then on Sunday I got a call from the hospital.

'Get here as quickly as possible, your mother is fading fast.'

She had gone into a coma and the doctors had said there was no hope. I remember thinking, well, at least she lived to see Derek given a proper burial.

But before I went I took Maria and went into the church next door and prayed and prayed, then we went to the hospital.

Dad was as low as I've ever seen him. Only one visitor was allowed at a time and I watched through the glass as he sat with Mum, holding her hand. She seemed just like a puppet, limp and lifeless dangling from strings attached to machines.

'There's no hope,' he said when he came out.

'Oh yes, there is,' I said. And I was right. For some reason when I got home I decided to take the washing to the launderette down the road. You can go into a bit of a daze watching it go round. And that afternoon, as I sat watching it slurp and thud through the porthole, I just knew Mum was all right. This feeling was so strong there was no way I was waiting for the wash to finish, so I left it there still thudding away, and rushed back to the hospital, and there she was, sitting up in bed and eating toast just like Dad had brought her breakfast in bed on her birthday.

It was as good as a miracle the doctor said. But she was very weak. First they allowed her back for three or four hours at a time, then four weeks later, Mum was home. Although she would not always be in that wheelchair, she would never be able to do housework again.

Meanwhile things with Stewart had gone from bad to worse. It was downhill ever since Maria was born. By the time she was eighteen months old, it got so I was living on edge, not knowing what he might do. He would disappear for the night then he'd be back demanding his 'rights'. If his dinner wasn't just what he wanted, he'd fling it on the floor. If his steak wasn't tender enough he'd start throwing the pickle jars against the fireplace. I knew he was seeing somebody else but to be honest that was the least of my worries. But I think the final straw was Derek's funeral. He didn't want Maria to go, I did.

'My brother wasn't guilty. Derek was her uncle. She should go to the funeral.'

Then there was the business of his sister. She lived in Kuwait, married to a rich Arab and wanted for nothing. She lived a life of luxury and lost no time in telling Stewart about it in letters. Then came one when she accused me of stealing telegrams she'd sent him asking him to go there on holiday. There hadn't been any telegrams. And why would I have taken them if there were? It didn't make any sense. I even rang up to check with the post office. No telegrams for Dingwall from Kuwait. But that little detail didn't change anything. His sister was right and I was wrong.

On 21 July 1968 I was just taking Maria to school and as usual we walked past the local fish shop.

'I see your husband's off on holiday, then,' the fishmonger said with a wink.

'No he's not. He's at work.'

'Well, please yourself but he had enough suitcases with him for a cruise to Australia.'

The fishmonger was right. Stewart had done a bunk. The place was cleaned out. No note, nothing. He just disappeared. The next time I saw him was in court in 1975.

There was nothing for it but to move back to Mum's. Although I could probably have stuck it out in Kingston on my own, I just didn't have the stomach for any more fighting and anyway, we had no money, nothing. Even the house belonged to Stewart's father. After Maria and I moved out, Mr Dingwall came back to England and sold it.

Stewart leaving so suddenly had hit Maria hard. She was terrified I'd be the next to go. So every playtime, I would walk up to the school and just stand on the pavement outside where she could see me through the railings, just to prove I wasn't going to disappear the same way. That went on for two years. Of course I'd moved her from Kingston to a school in Colliers Wood and gradually, through Maria, through the other mothers who you'd meet in the playground, I began to make a new life for myself.

I began to enjoy life again. I didn't have Stewart bullying me. I was back with Mum and Dad. We had our own room. Dad had put in a TV. Although the rooms were smaller than Fairview Road, it worked quite well. Maria and I had 'our house' which was the front room and the box bedroom. It's only small but I like being compact and there was still room for a double bed and a dressing chest. For a wardrobe I used the one in the back bedroom, Uncle Bert's room. We shared the kitchen but otherwise we kept to our own 'house' unless we were invited. Sundays we would take it in turns to do dinner.

Over the years I'd hear things about my husband, people would tell me that they'd seen him, then we heard that he was living in Paris and had married someone there, even though he was still married to me. Dad and I even went to the French Embassy to see what we could find out. It wasn't that I wanted him back. No way.

Just that it didn't seem right him not paying anything for Maria's upkeep. Then a couple of years later he wrote from a box number asking for a divorce. But I didn't believe in divorce, and anyway, what good would a divorce do for me or Maria? My solicitor said I couldn't stop him for ever, that after seven years he could have a divorce whether I liked it or not. But I'd had seven years of unhappiness tied to him, so I decided he could have seven years more tied to me.

It was not long after that David Yallop came into our lives. It was late in 1969. One evening Dad got a call from someone called John Silver. We didn't know anyone called that. He had a friend, an author, this man Silver said, who wanted to write a book about Derek's case. Were we interested? Dad said we'd have to meet him first, so David Yallop and this Mr Silver came down to meet us one evening. David Yallop worked in television as a floor manager but he'd written scripts. He'd read Dad's book and was full of it so that smoothed his path into the Bentley household. He said he felt a great injustice had been done and he'd like to write the whole story. He also promised Mum and Dad that they'd earn some money to carry on fighting the case. So we agreed. Not only did Dad go over the story with him, but he allowed him to go through all the newspapers we'd collected, all the court documents, all the letters, everything we had, including papers that had been given to Dad by Derek's solicitor at the trial, John Stevens. For the first week or so he took over the front room. Dad was a great one for collecting newspapers. Anything about Derek's case or capital punishment, it was all there. They'd been kept in sacks out in the garage. But then David Yallop decided it would be easier to work at home. We never did get any money for it, except two years later, when a drama documentary based on the book was being shown on BBC2, David Yallop visited me in hospital and gave me a cheque for £100.

We didn't get to see any of it before the book was published and even though the book was dedicated to 'William and Lillian Bentley and their daughter Iris' we felt we had been used. Yallop had taken everything from us, but the picture he had painted of

Derek wasn't one we recognized. But by then the book was printed and there was nothing we could do. The only way of fighting Derek's case was through books and journalists. It was the only way to keep the case going. But we had no control over what they wrote. But *To Encourage the Others* did the trick, just like *10 Rillington Place* had done for Timothy Evans. Suddenly everyone was talking about Derek Bentley again. There were letters, hundreds of them, from people who read the book, and the media began to sit up and take notice. Also, although nobody knew it till years later, the Home Secretary Reginald Maudling (the Government was now Conservative again) ordered a secret inquiry. The details of the inquiry are still secret and the Home Office refuses to hand over the report of its findings.

It was now nearly twenty years since Derek had been hanged. A whole generation of people had grown up not knowing anything about the Craig/Bentley case. Unlike the other books that had mentioned it, *To Encourage the Others* was the first to put together everything. Every book about miscarriages of justice has to have a theory, and Yallop's was that it wasn't Craig that killed PC Miles at all. Yallop claimed that the rooftop that night had been surrounded by police with guns and it was one of them who had killed PC Miles by mistake. He had also found and talked to Christopher Craig.

CHAPTER TWENTY

I don't know how David Yallop got hold of Craig. It could have been through the police. It could have been through the newspapers. Life sentence doesn't mean you're in prison for life, after a few years they let you out (Craig did ten). But it's on licence, like being on probation. You're never free, you can never 'disappear'. When it came to Craig, Yallop was always cagey. He knew Dad wanted to talk to him. But he never let on where Craig lived. He said if Dad would drop Craig a letter, saying he had forgiven him, he might agree to see us. Mum blew her top.

'Isn't that the wrong way round? What about Craig writing to us and apologizing to us?'

So nobody wrote. Yallop wouldn't give us the address. He said he was worried what Dad might do. But Dad wouldn't have done anything. He told Yallop over and over again that he wouldn't and it was the truth.

'If you think I'd harm Christopher Craig you're wrong. I've never harmed anything. It's never been in my nature.'

All Dad wanted to do was talk to him. Having a go at Craig wouldn't bring Derek back. Like Mum always said, God would be his judge. Back then I'd have done anything to talk to Craig. But now, all these years later, I think it's best left the way it is, with him at a distance. I don't bear Craig any hatred or any animosity, I know vengeance is not mine. Please God we'll all meet upstairs and then I shall talk to him, when he's said sorry to Mum and Dad and Derek. I don't wish him any harm in this life. I know that he has done his best to tell people the truth. To my mind the only truly guilty people in the case were the police.

The business of Yallop not giving us a share of the money we couldn't know about till later, so where Yallop thought it would help having us along for the publicity, we went, meek as puppies. Ten Downing Street was first on the list. Edward Heath was Prime

Minister then. Of course it had been arranged in advance. You can't just turn up at number 10 and knock on the door and expect to hand in a brown paper parcel. But even though we were expected we didn't get far. I thought we'd get to see Mr Heath and I went over all the points I had to say in the car as we drove there. I knew we wouldn't have long. But we got no further than the hall. Then all we did was hand over the book to some nameless young man. Next on the list was Harold Wilson, leader of the opposition. Anne Kerr had arranged it. By now she was a junior minister. This was more like it. Not only did we get to meet him, we even had tea with him in his rooms. Maria came with us. I hadn't meant her to. But she saw I was all got up.

'Where are you going?'

'Somewhere special.'

'Please may I come. Please.'

I still said no. Then she went off to Mum and asked her where I was going. That did it. Mr Wilson was very kind, even sat Maria on his knee. He knew all about Derek and promised an enquiry as soon as he was in power. But, of course, when he did get in in 1974, it was a different story, like most things politicians promise when they're in opposition.

In spite of my mixed feelings about David Yallop I knew that *To Encourage the Others* was the breakthrough we had waited for all these years. I should have been feeling on top of the world but I was feeling terrible. I was bleeding, as we used to say 'down below'. The doctor said it was just haemorrhoids, piles. Everyone got them, he said, and gave me some suppositories. They did no good and before long I was back. Then it was more suppositories, stronger, he said, and some kind of cream. But it got far worse not better. I was bleeding more or less all the time. That Christmas I was in agony and bloated like I was pregnant. I couldn't even face Christmas dinner, my favourite meal of the year. Finally Dad saw red.

'If this was Maria you wouldn't put up with being fobbed off, don't treat yourself any different.'

So, nine months after I'd first been to the doctor, I asked for a note for the hospital. Luck was on my side and I got an appointment about three weeks later. They said they wanted me in straight away for tests. It was cancer. Cancer of the rectum. They didn't tell me then. In those days they believed in keeping you in the dark, and anyway, the idea of cancer had never crossed my mind. Nobody in our family had had cancer. But I was lucky. My surgeon, Mr Rosswick, was one of those doctors who you trust with your life, even before you realize it is your life you're trusting him with.

Even when I knew, it wasn't what might happen to me that worried me. It was Maria and what would happen to her. Mum was nearly an invalid and Dad had enough to do looking after her. Who would look after Maria? Not Uncle Bert. He couldn't even look after himself.

On 3 March 1975 I went into St George's Hospital for a biopsy. It was nearly May by the time I got out. The big operation was on 16 March. I still didn't really know what was involved until the day before when a nurse came in and explained that I would be having a colostomy. This means that instead of going to the toilet in the usual way, it all goes into a bag which you change, a bit like a disposable nappy. They cut off most of the bowel and leave the end of it sticking out just below your waist. A metal plate is fixed underneath the skin and the bag is stuck on top, held on by sticky tape. It sounds horrible and it is.

When I heard about this bag, I wept and wept. I just wanted to die. I was only forty-three. How could I bear to go on living with this horrible bag attached to me for ever.

On the cabinet by the side of the bed was a picture of Maria.

'Is this your little girl?'

'Yes.'

'How old is she?'

'Nine.'

'Don't you want to see her grow up? How do you think life for her would be without her mummy?'

And I just cried and cried. Of course I knew they were right but I don't think until then I had realized that I might really die.

The operation was a success. The cancer cells hadn't spread far so they managed to cut everything away. Everyone was very pleased. The night before the operation Maria came in to see me and Mr Rosswick had a talk with her, told her that she had to be very brave but that her mummy would be all right. A few days later he told me what she'd said. Even then Maria could be a bit of a know-all and she'd said to him:

'Of course my mummy will be all right. Didn't you know she's a fighter?'

I stayed in hospital about a month after the operation. But I was in a terrible state. It sounds ridiculous now but I was so ashamed of having the colostomy. I felt I would never be able to go anywhere, that everyone would know. Once I even tried to slash my wrists in the ladies' toilet. But luckily a nurse spotted me.

What really made me pull myself together was when the film of *To Encourage the Others* was broadcast. The night it was shown I was still in hospital.

The director was Alan Clark, one of television's famous names. It didn't mean anything to me at the time but they said we couldn't have had anyone better. He was famous for his documentaries on 'issues'. He's probably most famous for his film called *Scum*, about Borstals. They say that if he'd worked in the cinema instead of television, they'd be showing his films all the time.

Alan Clark was determined to do what he could to make it as truthful and strong as he could. And it wasn't just us that thought he was good. When he died in 1992 they did a season of his plays, including showing *To Encourage the Others* again.

It was what was called a dramatized documentary. Actors played all the parts of course, but it was as real as they could make it. Everything had to be right, even down to the size of the rooms. They couldn't get inside Fairview Road, but they came to our house and did sketches and floorplans for us to check and change if it didn't look right. They even borrowed our real furniture and ornaments. We still had most of the same bits and pieces, including the furniture in Derek's bedroom because Uncle had just taken everything over. Apart from wanting to make everything factual to help Derek's case, having as many real things as possible helped the actors. The actress who played me was called Barbara Willmott. She got really involved and came out several times to Colliers Wood to see us. It wasn't something she was told to do, just something she wanted to do. And she was very nice and even visited me in hospital.

Being acted by somebody is very strange and it was the first time I'd thought of myself as anything other than Iris, the face I saw every day in the mirror. I don't know if it made it worse or better that Barbara didn't look anything like me. She couldn't help not looking like me and anyway, to anyone else it wouldn't matter, but she made me out to be more strait-laced than I was in real life. In 1953 I was only twenty-one and a real flibbertigibbet. But as for size and shape, we were identical. I know because I lent her my red dress, yellow coat, black handbag and shoes that I'd worn at the trial, which I'd kept all those years in my wardrobe.

It wasn't just Barbara who came out to Colliers Wood. The boys who played Derek and Craig came as well. I'd never seen Barbara in anything, but the boys had both been in a series about a school called *Please Sir*, which was one of my favourites.

One day when the recording was being done, they came with a car and took us to the studios to watch. It was the first time I'd ever seen anything like that being done but even then I thought it was strange we weren't allowed on the set at all. We were told the actors would be embarrassed. But it was a lie. We were kept hidden away in a viewing room because they'd brought in Pierrepoint, the man who had hanged Derek, as an adviser and they didn't want us bumping into him. Mum and Dad never knew and I only found out years later.

The sister in the ward gave permission for a portable television to be brought in and that night about twenty-seven of us, doctors, nurses and patients, crowded around that little set. The ward was packed. They say there was never a night like it in St George's before or since. After the play finished, everyone had something to say. I was amazed. People were really angry. And I wasn't the only one who'd been crying. Books are long and not everyone has the patience for them, but a good play or film can grip you right from the beginning and explain complicated things which ordinary people wouldn't be able to grasp just from reading a book. And when people see something like that together, they can talk about it and discuss it. Although I'd talked about the case over and over again from those first Sundays at Spouters' Corner, this was the first time I didn't feel I was banging my head against a brick wall.

I was allowed home for a few hours at a time, eventually the time came when I was back for good. Everyone was so kind. I never knew I had so many friends. Every day someone would be there to walk with me up and down the road, just a few yards at a time, then a bit further, then as far as the post-box. I was like a stick and even though my parents had no money to speak of, Dad fed me up with steak dinners and milk.

By June I was strong enough to get out and about, which was just as well as on 14 June we were due in the House of Lords. It had been arranged by the Earl of Arran. But the main speech of the debate was by Lord Goodman, who had been Harold Wilson's solicitor. Although Anne Kerr had tried and tried over the years to get a debate going in the House of Commons she'd never managed it. But the House of Lords had finally agreed, thanks to David Yallop's book. The debate was about Derek and James Hanratty. Although Derek's case (and Hanratty's) had been mentioned in every capital punishment debate I'd been to, there had never been a debate specifically about Derek.

It took the form of what was called an unstarred question and the question was: 'Whether it is not desirable, in view of the social and legal implications, for an impartial review of the cases of Hanratty and Bentley.' Lord Goodman was wonderful. Neither Dad nor I had ever met him (though we did later), but he made it all so clear. What he had to say was nothing to do with the book, it was just about the trial and, in particular, Lord Goddard's summing-up.

Anyone who now, in the cold light of day and with the passage of time, reads his summing up in this case could hardly fail to arrive at the conclusion that this was not one of the most credible performances of a distinguished judge.

As for how Derek's appeal was rejected on the grounds that Derek had said he wasn't under arrest at the time when everyone had said that he was, Lord Goodman said:

This appears to me the oddest of propositions. It is equivalent to saying that if I, through some misfortune, am taken to a police station and imprisoned in a cell, I am not under arrest if the window is open by some chance and I can climb out of it.

Lord Goodman even made the House of Lords laugh when he was talking about the 'joint adventure'.

What prosecuting counsel then said, forgetting, if I may say so, the whole question of the onus of proof in criminal trials, was that there was no evidence from that moment onwards [Derek's alleged 'Let him have it, Chris'] that the boy Bentley had withdrawn his mind. Whether he was expected to write a formal letter and send it to Craig to tell him that in the circumstances he no longer wished to participate in this enterprise – what action he was supposed to take to indicate that he was resigning from the partnership – will remain one of the unsolved problems of jurisprudence for years to come. There was nothing he could do. What he did do, quite clearly, was to indicate that he had resigned from the club from the very moment of his arrest. He did not stir, he did not resist, he gave no encouragement of any kind. What he did was to remain in a state, I imagine, of absolute terror, of shaking terror while this appalling battle went on . . .

Lord Goodman went on about Lord Goddard's summing-up. Saying it was full of 'baseless speculation', how he should never

239

have mentioned the knuckleduster because it was nothing to do with what happened, let alone have it on his hand all the way through the summing-up and banging it on the table. But he kept on mentioning it over and over as if it was the murder weapon. Lord Goodman ended up by saying:

> My Lords, I believe that in the whole history of summing up in criminal trials there can hardly have been a more inappropriate and improper passage in relation to the capital trial of an unfortunate youth whose association with the crime on any account was as tenuous as one could make it. That was the summing up presented to the jury.

And as for the appeal Lord Goodman said:

> How any experienced judge, reading this summing up, could have arrived at the conclusion that there was nothing to criticise in the summing up passes my understanding and, I venture to think, passes belief.

The second speech was from Lord Arran himself. He spoke mainly about David Yallop's theory about a police gun having killed PC Miles. He also talked about the secret inquiry set up by the Home Secretary, Reginald Maudling. He asked why it was secret and said what was the point of a secret inquiry carried out by the police who were an interested party.

> I ask these eight simple questions. First, with regard to the recent secret inquiry, why was the author of the book, Mr David Yallop, not questioned? Why was Mr Christopher Craig not questioned? Why was no member of Derek Bentley's family questioned?
> Second, why for example were PCs Pain, Bugden and Alderson, who were at the scene of the crime, not questioned? Alderson, in particular, who sat next to Bentley in the car on the way to the station, was not questioned.

Third, why were Professor Sir Denis Hill, Mr Frank Cassels, Mr John Parris and many other people whose evidence has a direct bearing on Derek Bentley's conviction and execution not questioned?

Fourth, why was one item, covering a few hundred words, from a book of some 100,000 words, the only piece of evidence – according to the newspapers – subjected to the latest police investigation?

Fifth, why was evidence not taken as to the mental condition of Mr Bentley, though in fact such evidence was freely available?

Sixth, why was the manifestly biased summing-up of the late Lord Goddard totally ignored?

Seventh, why, during the latest police inquiry, was one aspect of the affair the only one taken into consideration when the other circumstances of the case were so unsatisfactory and, indeed, so horrifying?

Eighth – and this is more or less a rhetorical question – why had neither Sergeant Fairfax nor Dr Haler taken legal action against Mr Yallop who has accused them of having gone back on statements which he maintains were made? Either Mr Yallop is the biggest rogue unhanged and is guilty not only of deceiving myself – and I do not count – but of causing me to deceive the High Court of Parliament, which is your Lordships' House and the highest court in the land; or he is telling the truth, the whole truth and nothing but the truth.

He ended up by saying: 'Although we cannot bring Derek Bentley back from the dead – and when I say "we" I mean each and every one of us, for we are all responsible – we should never have put him there. As Voltaire said: "To the living we owe our respect, to the dead we owe nothing but the truth."'

But as soon as Lord Colville for the Government side stood up, it was clear truth wasn't important. Just rules. The only way Derek would get a proper inquiry would be if there was new evidence, he said. The only 'new' evidence in David Yallop's book was the ballistics evidence which was why only Fairfax and the gun witness Dr Haler had been called to the inquiry. All the things Lord Goodman had said about the conduct of the trial were irrelevant, Lord Colville said. He said the same about Hanratty, except it was made complicated by Peter Alphon still being alive. Giving Hanratty a proper inquiry would be like putting Peter Alphon on trial, he said. It all ended very noisily with Goodman and Arran and some others too butting in all the time when it was obvious Lord Colville had got his mind made up long before the debate even started.

It took another fifteen years for 'new' evidence to turn up. But of course the evidence was there all the time, it was just that no one had bothered to look for it. I blame David Yallop. Everyone thought he'd turned over every stone. He made sure that was the impression he gave. Not only to us, but to everybody else. But he hadn't. No way. All those witnesses, all those people, ordinary people who were there watching the goings-on that night, did he try to find those? No. Yallop was so sure of his police-guns theory that he didn't bother with looking for anything else. All that time wasted. It was another fifteen years before they got to tell what really happened that night. And those were the ones who were still alive. But his theory was all he really cared about. It might not clear Derek's name but it would make Yallop's and make him money into the bargain. But his precious theory was rubbish. In his book he says the bravery of the Croydon police on that fateful night 'cannot and should not be questioned'. Should not be questioned? These 'brave' policemen killed my brother. But his theory of bullets came above everything, including the truth. To me Yallop was really no better than the people he claimed to despise. Once he had the idea, he was only interested in things that fitted his theory.

But at least Mum and Dad lived to see that most people, ordinary people with no vested interests, thought Derek was innocent. That the fighting to keep his name from being swept under the carpet wasn't wasted. It was important them knowing that. Because two years later, Dad was dead.

CHAPTER TWENTY-ONE

Dad had arthritis since before Derek died. He didn't complain about it. It affected his legs mostly. But he never let it get to him. He carried on riding his bicycle even though I could see just getting on it was killing him with pain. But that bike was his freedom. He'd given up on doctors and at the end all he did was just rub in horse liniment. Other than the arthritis he was never ill, not even a cold that I can remember. But as for energy. I've never seen anyone with such energy.

That summer of 1974 he decided to organize a disco for Maria and her friends at the church hall next door on 11 July. Dad was a great favourite with Maria's friends. To them he was always Uncle Bill. Practical jokes were his speciality. The girls would be running around the garden in the summer and suddenly, whoosh, on would come the hose. Or if a group of them were staying the night, when they'd be sleeping on the floor in the front room (*our* house), the lights would go out. He'd get them all screaming and then he'd start doing the ghost noises, like chains rattling on the stairs, or he'd go outside and make tapping noises on the window. Or he'd come down the stairs with a sheet over his head and a torch underneath. It sounds strange now, but they just loved it. And he did it time and time again, so it wasn't as if they didn't know who it was. Whenever I meet any friends of Maria's from school, they still talk about him.

The party that night was just like the old days, like the rock 'n' roll parties he used to do for Denis. Maria had asked everyone in her year. She'd just discovered boys. Dad went to town. Nothing was too much trouble. He decked it all out in coloured lights that flashed in time to the music. It was great. Dad was the life and soul of the party. He even got up, his creaky legs oiled with a few drinks, and showed them how to do the black bottom. But they were only young and by nine thirty we were clearing up. By ten we were back home as Dad never missed the news if he could help it. But that night he couldn't concentrate. All he kept saying was that he wasn't feeling at all well.

'This indigestion is killing me, Pam.'

'That'll teach you. It's those chips, you know how they upset you.'

But it was nothing to do with the chips.

It was gone midnight when Dad knocked on the wall between the bedrooms.

'This pain's terrible. Can you do something?' I went down and fetched him up a drink of hot water with a spoon of brandy in it.

'Come on, get this down you.'

I rubbed his back. But nothing seemed to help. By this time the pains had gone to his hands and chest and he said he thought I should call an ambulance. I said I'd have to call the doctor first. It was nearly one by the time Dad's GP arrived. He was not best pleased about being called out. I'd already got Mum downstairs on the sofa. When the doctor had finished he told me it was probably flu. He gave Dad an injection to settle him and gave me a prescription for the morning. When he'd gone, I helped Mum upstairs back into bed next to Dad.

'How's it going? Feeling better now, Dad?'

'A bit better.'

By now it was gone two. An hour or so later, there was another knock on the wall. Mum this time.

'It's your dad, Iris. He's making this funny noise.'

I got out of bed and went into their room and gave Dad a bit of a push.

'Move over, Dad, your snoring's keeping Mum awake.'

He was on his back so I rolled him over. Dad wasn't known for his snoring but I told Mum it was probably the injection. But that noise wasn't snoring, I know that now.

The next morning I woke up same as usual, but when I got downstairs, instead of Dad clattering around the kitchen, it was quiet. He was usually up well before me. No matter how much I told him to lie in now that he'd retired, he took no notice. He didn't have it in him, he said. All those years in the army.

Perhaps the injection had made him drowsy. Good thing too, I remember thinking. I put on the kettle, made him a cup of tea and took it up.

'Come on, Dad, wakey, wakey.'

I gave him a shake. He didn't move.

'Come on, rise and shine. Don't bugger around. Get this tea down you while it's still hot.'

Then Mum said something in a very low voice that I didn't hear the first time.

'Something terrible's happened. I think I've had an accident in the bed. I think I've wet myself.'

'Don't be so stupid, Mum. You've never done that in your life, you're not going to start now.'

'Well, the bed's wet.'

As she said that, I put my hand on Dad's forehead to see if he had a temperature. I had a terrible shock. He was quite cold. As cold as a plate. I went back round the other side of the bed and took hold of Mum's hand.

'Come on, Mum. Come downstairs. I don't think you've had an accident.'

'What do you mean?'

'I think it's Dad. I think Dad's gone to Derek.'

It was the only way I could think of putting it.

'I think Dad's gone in his sleep. But that's what he would have wanted. He wouldn't have wanted to be ill, would he?'

'No.'

But I don't think it quite hit her. When we got downstairs she said, 'What were you saying?' She was more concerned that she'd wet the bed. Then suddenly there was a scream from upstairs. I'd completely forgotten about Maria. She'd gone in to see her grandad, as she did every morning. She went to give him a kiss and now she was screaming her head off at the top of the stairs.

'I want my grandad. I want my grandad.'

I left Mum and rushed upstairs two at a time. But there was nothing I could do. She was like a mad thing. Screaming and screaming. I didn't know what to do. I suppose because I was already thinking of God and heaven, I thought of Mr Jardine, our vicar next door. He came straight over. He knew Maria, not only because of church but his daughters were friends. It was just before school and of course by now all her friends had called in to pick her up, as they always did, and the whole lot of them were in tears. It was really quite frightening. Like a mass epidemic. But Mr Jardine was very good, very understanding.

'Come on, Maria. You don't have to worry about your grandad any more. The angels are looking after him now. Taking him up to heaven.'

With that she eased up. I said that she should go to school as usual, because that's what her grandad would have wanted. Because of what happened to Derek, education was very important to Dad and he'd never been too busy to help Maria with her homework and he wouldn't let her come the old soldier. She'd been the apple of his eye and her grandad was everything to her.

While we were waiting for the post-mortem van, the doctor said we should take off Dad's rings. Mum said not to bother; he never took them off so they should be buried with him. But the doctor said no, that they'd only be stolen. So he and I went upstairs to take them off. But by now his hands were quite stiff and they wouldn't shift. In the end the doctor had to break his fingers to get the rings off. I never told Mum.

He was taken to St George's. It turned out he'd had a massive heart attack. That's what the pains were. I know it was the best way to go, suddenly like that, no illness. If only I'd called an ambulance Dad might have been all right. Even twenty years ago they could do a lot for heart attacks if they got them in time. They said he'd died from hardening of the arteries, but I know he died of a broken heart.

In all this I hadn't cried. I hadn't had time and I was looking after Mum. And it still wasn't over. There was some kind of hold-up at the hospital and because his death was unexpected, they had to do a post-mortem and the funeral couldn't go ahead until that had been done. The funeral wasn't till a fortnight later, on 22 July.

I nearly missed it. The day before I had a phone call from the court.

'Mrs Dingwall?'

For a moment I thought it was Maria they were after. She'd been the only Dingwall in the house for as long as I could remember. I'd gone back to being Iris Bentley as soon as Stewart had flown the coop.

'We've picked your husband up. We'll need you in court tomorrow. The case is set for two o'clock.'

I was speechless. This was the last thing I wanted. I just didn't feel I could cope with Stewart as well as Dad. For six years not a word, then he goes and turns up now. If he had known, he couldn't have planned it better.

'I'm sorry, it's out of the question. I've just lost my father and the funeral's tomorrow. He'll just have to wait.'

They offered their condolences but said it made no difference. I had to be there. So the next morning, with only about an hour to go to the funeral, I took a taxi down to the court. I was all in black. But it did the trick. It meant they could adjourn the case till the next day and hold on to Stewart in the meantime.

There were so many cars in the cortège, so many people at the funeral, not only family and our friends but people from the highest in the land to neighbours who we hardly knew but who knew Dad because they called him the handyman of the village. There was nothing Dad couldn't mend, and he always had time for everyone. I don't think there was a person he'd helped that didn't send a wreath. The front garden was just a sea of flowers. We couldn't tread for them. You'd have thought he'd been a god on earth.

The service was at Christchurch next door. It was packed. Then the cars all moved off to Croydon cemetery. When Derek was buried, Dad had bought a family-sized plot. And he was buried next to Derek.

Dad would have enjoyed seeing all those people in the house, paying their final respects. And he was respected by so many people. Among them were Mr and Mrs Hanratty, who we'd last seen at the House of Lords debate. We'd not long had kittens. Mrs Hanratty was quite taken with a black one and asked could they have it. Mum said, of course. They called it Bill Bentley. That meant a lot to Mum.

The next day I was in court. Stewart walked straight past me, cut me dead, just like he'd never seen me before. I told the court everything and how Stewart had left Maria and me with nothing. But I found it hard to talk about being knocked about. Then it was Stewart's turn in the witness box. He didn't look at me once. When it came to the violence he just shrugged his shoulders.

'I might have blacked her eye once or twice,' he said, as if hitting a woman was no more important than a parking fine. The judge awarded Maria and me maintenance of £5 a week each.

All the times I've been in a court, everything from the Juvenile Court with Derek all those years ago, to the Old Bailey, the Court of Appeal and the High Court, I've always behaved properly, even though God knows I've had good reason not to. But when the judge said what he would have to pay his wife and daughter, Stewart went mad and began swearing and shouting out there was no way he was going to pay us a penny and that he was going to appeal.

And he did. This time it was very different. I felt so alone without Dad by my side. Mum was in no state to come so a social worker came with me, but it wasn't the same. I was put in the witness box and immediately it was like it was me in the dock. Why did I refuse to give Stewart a divorce? I told them how could I give him a divorce when I didn't know where he was. They were all firing questions at me, not just the barrister but the judge as well, just like I was a criminal. No sooner had I started on how Stewart had knocked me about when Stewart's barrister butted in.

'But, Mrs Dingwall, don't you come from a violent family?'

'No, what makes you think that?'

'Before your marriage weren't you Iris Bentley, of the Bentley and Craig case?'

With that I could feel everyone's eyes burning into me, including the judge. Even my social worker was appalled at how suddenly the atmosphere changed. Needless to say, Stewart won and justice lost and the maintenance was reduced to £3 a week for Maria and 1/- a year for me. But I never got mine. Complain? Go back to court? No point. As everyone had made very clear, with my name, I hadn't a hope.

The only person who behaved well during the breakup of the marriage was Stewart's brother-in-law, his sister's Arab husband. I wrote to him when Stewart first disappeared asking if he knew where he was and he wrote back and said he didn't know, but he enclosed a cheque for £100. But from Stewart I've never had anything. We were finally divorced in 1975.

It was in September 1975 that I first heard of Peter Murphy. He said he was putting on a play called *Example* about Derek at the Cockpit Theatre in London and would I be interested in helping. The Cockpit was a theatre just for schools. It was owned by the Inner London Education Authority. The play was written by a schools theatre group run by the Belgrade Theatre in Coventry. As well as being the director, Peter played Derek.

Example wasn't like the BBC's version of *To Encourage the Others*. Like Peter said, *Example* wasn't about the facts, it was about the truth. In it whole scenes were invented, like a classroom scene in Norbury Manor school with Derek being got at for being slow, and a scene with Craig and Norman Parsley where no one could know for sure what was really said. Dad wasn't in it at all. Neither was I. Just Mum. They even had her going down to the police station to ask for help in keeping Craig away from Derek, and guess who they had as the policeman? Fairfax. In real life Fairfax never met Derek before the night on the roof. And Mum would never have talked the way they had her talk to Derek in the play, but then she wasn't being just Mum. In the play the actress, the character, was having to be both Mum and Dad. But although it wasn't the facts, it was the truth. As Peter explained to the schoolchildren when they asked, if I was Derek's sister, why wasn't I in the play, sometimes the facts get in the way of the truth.

Because it was education the audience didn't just watch it and go home. When it was finished everyone, the actors as well, sat and talked about it, just like that night in the hospital when everyone sat around my bed watching *To Encourage the Others*. Nothing was planned. It always started with talking about the play and Derek's case but then sometimes it went on to capital punishment, sometimes it went on to how courts work, it was all down to the children. I could feel that having me there was a bit of a shock for some of them. I mean, I was the sister of someone who was hanged. Not an actor, but a real person. It was all a bit of a shock for me too at first, just being listened to.

Example was written for sixteen- and seventeen-year-olds. In the end, I knew it so well, I found myself watching the kids and thinking, they're just the same age as Craig and Derek were in 1952.

Example was like one of those cautionary tales. It didn't just tell the story on the rooftop. It showed them what can happen if you let yourself be talked into doing something you don't want to do. It showed them how important telling the truth is, but also showed them how revenge doesn't help anyone but only makes things worse. Hanging Derek was the police's revenge for PC Miles being killed. And what good did that do?

Over the years what surprises people most is how I have no bitterness against Craig. It's the police I'm bitter against, not Craig.

Having me there gave them a chance to find out how it felt when something so terrible happened to a real person. It showed that behind the headlines about someone going to prison, even if they are guilty, are a family who have done nothing wrong and how they are the ones who are punished. Derek's sentence was death. Dad and Mum's sentence was living death.

It also showed how you can't always believe what you're told, even though the people doing the telling are wearing uniforms and medals. It showed them that they should be on the look-out for what nowadays they call the hidden agenda. And all this was shown in the play, especially about Goddard and his thinking the way to stamp out violent crime was to just be more violent, flogging, birching and hanging. It showed how the reasons for Derek hanging had nothing much to do with Derek or Craig or what happened on the roof that night but were all to do with the way Britain was after the war. *Example* was more like a history lesson come to life than a play.

After Derek died, Dad gave his life not just to clearing Derek's name and ending capital punishment but doing what he could to stop the same thing happening to other people's children. Those rock 'n' roll parties we had at Fairview Road weren't just for Denis. They were to give youngsters in Norbury and round about somewhere to go on a Saturday night, to keep them out of trouble. Dad knew it wasn't much but it was at least something, something he could do. And as he said, every little helps. And now here was I, doing what I could to help the next generation keep out of trouble.

The first time it went very well and Peter asked me if I'd do it again. I gulped but said yes. Not that I'd enjoyed it, as such. I'd been shaking too much to enjoy it. But I could see how me being there made it so much more real.

I never stopped being nervous and could feel myself getting hotter and hotter as the play came to the end. It wasn't like Spouters' Corner when I always had Dad beside me for inspiration and courage. But in some strange way I could still feel him there beside me. When it came to opening my mouth, I just said, come on, Iris, if you don't know the facts, nobody does. It's just got to be done.

Schools in London would come to the Cockpit Theatre to see the play but Peter had also arranged to take it to schools in the north. What about me going too? I'd only ever been to the north once, and that was when we went to Blackpool, to Madame Tussaud's. But it was horrible weather and what with doing the play, and driving back and forwards to the different places, I didn't really see much of the countryside. An actress called Sue Jameson played Mum and, as she came from up there, she asked me to stay with her family, and everyone was very kind to me.

That tour of Lancashire began in November 1975. It wasn't only schoolchildren who saw the play, some evenings we'd be in church halls and anybody could come. It was surprising who did, even magistrates.

Although it was ten years since capital punishment had been abolished, that November the newspapers were full of bringing it back again. The reason was because of IRA bombings. The IRA had owned up to fifteen bomb attacks on mainland Britain in three months. Back-bench Conservative MPs had tried to bring back hanging for terrorists in May 1973 and again in December 1974 and lost. It all came to a head when Ross McWhirter, one of the twin brothers who had thought up the *Guinness Book of Records*, was murdered by the IRA. He was very right wing and he'd started a campaign to offer huge rewards for the capture of terrorists. Suddenly everyone was talking about bringing back hanging again, programmes on TV and in all the newspapers. It made my blood run cold. On 11 December a back-bench Tory MP, Ivan Lawrence, managed to get his Motion tabled. Again, thank goodness, they lost, but by a narrower margin than the year before. The idea that they might win and bring hanging back gave me nightmares and I realized that the work of the play was more important than ever. I take my hat off to all of them, the actors and everyone behind the scenes who night after night did that show in the freezing cold. It often wasn't much warmer inside than out.

It was when I was in Yorkshire that I did my first television show, which was on Yorkshire TV, a link-up with Ludovic Kennedy. Thank goodness for *Example*. Although I wasn't performing exactly, I'd learnt a lot just through watching and had started to learn all those things which I need now, speaking up, speaking slowly, listening carefully to the questions people ask. So by the time I did the Ludovic Kennedy link-up at least I knew what to do.

In the January of 1976 *Example* started up again in London. It was still being done at the Cockpit Theatre in Marylebone, but I didn't sit in on the performances. Instead Peter Murphy told head teachers that Iris Bentley was available to talk to the children at their schools, if they wanted. And lots of them did. I must have gone to nearly twenty. I didn't get paid or anything, they would just reimburse the train fare. The schools were just ordinary schools, and the children just ordinary children. The play was part of a social studies course. Of course these schools were nothing like the ones Derek and I went to but some things hadn't changed. Children would ask me how they could tell whether their friends were the wrong friends. I used to tell them, you soon know. Just listen to your inner self. If your inner self says you don't want to go, then don't go. I used to warn them how easy it is not to listen to your inner voice and say, oh, this time it'll be all right, I won't get into trouble. But that's just what Derek said and look what happened to him.

But what really shook them was the legal system itself. This was around about the time of the John Stonehouse trial, the MP who faked his own suicide, and I remember one girl asking me how could something so important as Derek's trial be over and done with in two days when the Stonehouse trial was dragging on for weeks. Somebody else asked whether money had anything to do with it. If Derek had come from a rich family, would it have been different? Of course these weren't questions I could really answer, and I didn't try to. They were questions nobody could answer, not the highest legal mind in the land, but the important thing was that these questions were being asked.

Going to those schools was not really about helping clear Derek's name. It was more to help keep young people out of trouble. To show them the right road. But in August, six months after *Example* had first started, the papers got hold of what I was doing and two days later, on 12 August, questions were asked in Parliament. Who by? The same back-bench Tory MP who had brought in the hanging debate the December before, the barrister Ivan Lawrence. He told Mr Mulley, Secretary of State for Education and Science, to get me banned and Norman Tebbit backed him up.

It was ridiculous. It just shows, when you know about something, how these people come out with whatever they like. It's called parliamentary privilege. They made out that I was 'lecturing', that I was being paid by the ILEA (London's labour-controlled education authority). They made out that I was poisoning children's minds.

What did they know about it? They didn't claim to have been to see the play. Had they talked to the children? No way. Their 'questions' had nothing to do with *Example*, nothing to do with the truth. It seemed to me they were just Conservative politicians who'd found a way to have a go at the Labour-controlled ILEA. If any of them had bothered to come they would have seen that all I was doing was helping to set these kids on the right road. I don't want to see children put in prison at an early age. If I have the power in me to help them, to stop them getting mixed up with things that are easier to get into than out of, even if it's only one in a class, then I will have saved two heart-breaks for mothers, for the criminal and victim. What harm is there in that?

But I didn't let it upset me. Like most politicians, it was all wind and it soon blew over. And that August, I had more important things on my mind. The sun was shining and Mum, Maria and me were off to the seaside. A week in a caravan in Winchelsea near Hastings. It's funny how holidays run in families. We only ever went to Hastings or Brighton, nowhere else. It started with Nan. 'Hastings is quality' she always used to say. Brighton was for day trips and we went by train. When we went to Hastings we took the coach. Derek loved Hastings. Even when he was at Kingswood, he was allowed out for holidays and Dad always managed to save up enough for a week at Hastings.

But this was the first time we'd got out of London since Dad had died and it was a real breath of fresh air. That year the sun shone on us day in day out. Maria, just like me, was sea mad and was in and out of the water like a dog with two tails. She always came out blue and her teeth chattering, she stayed in so long. Of course there was no swimming for me because of the colostomy. It was heart-breaking. But I was getting a bit old for showing my all on the beach anyway. So I put on an old pair of shorts and paddled with the other mums, something I never thought I'd be seen dead doing when I was young.

Mum wasn't in best health but she'd have walked the whole way rather than miss her cockles and winkles. Although she'd never see seventy again, she didn't believe in growing old gracefully and, as for her running commentary of jokes and songs, she kept us in stitches.

She still wore high heels and mini-skirts when she was up to it.

'It's only the outside that's old. The inside's young. Why should I dress old?'

But she was old. Dad's going had really hit her. She just hadn't been ready for it. There wasn't a day went by when she didn't cry for him. Her eyesight had all but gone and although she still loved her crossword, she needed help just reading the clues. But the crochet she'd done all her life she somehow managed without help. I can see her now, that hook flashing in and out with just a packet of Meredith and Drew water biscuits at her elbow and the colour TV that Denis bought her. Frankie Howerd was her favourite. But when Ken Dodd came on, she would just cry and cry. It wasn't his jokes. It was his songs that got to her.

Mum always said she never felt older than forty. It's strange how inside you don't change. I don't feel a day over twenty-one. My skin may be wrinkled and I admit that there have been times when I've looked at myself in the mirror and thought it was time to have a facelift, but then I stop and say, no. Growing old is part of life. The lines are part of it. They're like a map on my face, showing all those years of fighting, like history. Derek never had a chance to grow old. What right have I to deny my life?

Anyway, after fifty, it's like you're invisible. Nobody notices what you look like. Provided you keep your sense of humour and can have a laugh, and provided you keep your faculties, that's the only thing that matters. It's what you feel and how you feel inside. When we die is God's decision alone. God has let me grow old for a reason. To fight for Derek. To fight for justice.

But, like most people, growing old does sometimes keep me awake at night. Like most people, I don't want to be a burden. My hope is that when the time comes, I could go into a home run for entertainers. Whenever I've seen documentaries about them, they're all so cheerful and seeing the funny side, real characters. I know working in the cinema isn't like working in music halls, but perhaps they'd turn a blind eye for me. But that's what I would wish for. That's where I'd like to end my days.

But if the Home Office or the Government or anyone else who wishes Iris Bentley would just go away, thinks death might do the job for them, they've another think coming. They probably thought the part pardon they gave me in 1993 would do the trick. It didn't. They didn't know me. There's no more chance of me dying before Derek has got his full pardon than me seeing twenty-one again.

CHAPTER TWENTY-TWO

Maria's thirteenth birthday was coming up. She was growing into quite the young lady and she decided she'd had enough tea parties. This year what she wanted was a dinner party. So that's what she got. But, grown up or not, when it came to it only girls turned up. Eight of them there were, all dressed up for a night at the Ritz. I was the waitress. Mum just sat and smiled. Maria was all for having champagne. So I put out the glasses and bought some bottles of 'champagne perry' with corks and wire, just like the real thing.

It was a lovely birthday. Two nights later Denis came round for dinner and Mum said what about some fish and chips for a change. No particular reason, she said. Just fancied them. And, as Mum always used to say, a little of what you fancy does you good. After I'd been out to get them, I set to laying the table but Mum said, no, not tonight. Tonight she'd have them out of the newspaper. How we laughed, sitting around, the four of us, dousing them with vinegar and salt, eating them out of the paper just like we were at Hastings. When there wasn't a chip or a corner of batter left, Mum sat back in her chair.

'I enjoyed that better than anything else in years.'

Then off to bed she went, happier than I'd seen her in a long time.

Next morning I woke to Maria screaming. Sometime in the night, Mum had got up, had got as far as the bathroom and just dropped down dead. I couldn't believe it. The night before I'd gone in to say goodnight and however much I thought back, there was nothing, no hint, no sign that this would be the last time I'd bend over her sweet face and kiss her goodnight. But now it was Maria I had to worry about. Mum wasn't stone-cold so I wrapped her up in a blanket and pretended to Maria that she was just unconscious and phoned for the ambulance. I knew it was no use. Ever since Dad died all Mum said was she wanted to be with him. She was so tired, she said. She didn't want to go on on her own. But I never thought it would be so quick.

The first problem was money. Until you've had someone close to you die, you've no idea how expensive it is. Even without a headstone. First there was Derek's, then Dad's, now Mum's. And no insurance. It was all I could do to manage rent and food. Ordinary bills were bad enough. There was nothing left over for funeral insurance. The only money coming in was Uncle Bert's pension and my social security. The cheapest funeral I could find was £197 and the death grant that everybody gets was £30. Uncle and I worked it out between us. But we had to do it in instalments. It took a long time to pay back.

Mum was buried next to Dad and Derek in Croydon cemetery. She died on 10 October 1976 and was buried the following Thursday. All the old friends from Norbury turned up. Fred the fishmonger, Mr Peck the butcher. Mrs Ruhe was there. She was a widow now. But both Mr and Mrs Leppard had died.

I don't know how we got through. It wasn't as if I could get any work. Uncle Bert got a job selling the evening papers outside Colliers Wood underground station. I didn't like him doing it, but I couldn't stop him. He was useless in the house, and he was the first to admit it.

'I can't cook, I can't garden. Just let me do what I can do.'

If truth be known, Uncle loved it. Everyone knew Bert. He soon made friends and his great ambition was to have that board beside him saying 'Pardon for Bentley'.

And to cap it all I was ill again. This time gynaecological. Once having had cancer, they're always worried that it'll start up again, so it was back to St George's, this time at 'head office' at Hyde Park Corner. They said I had to have a hysterectomy. I said I didn't like the sound of that. Soon there'd be nothing left of me inside. They send you to different people depending on what you've got wrong with you. It wasn't that I didn't trust the gynaecologist I'd been sent to, I just didn't trust any doctor except Mr Rosswick, who'd done my first operation and saved my life. Because I'd started off with him, they said all right. Mr Rosswick is my hero. He's a doctor in a million. The way he spoke to Maria, the way he gave me confidence in myself. You don't find many doctors like that. It meant a lot.

By now the bleeding was non-stop. More investigations and this time they found some cancerous growths near the site of my cancer operation five years before and it was this that was causing the trouble.

They weren't taking any chances, so in May 1977 I went in to get them removed. But again, I was more worried about what would happen to Maria than anything else. Social Services did what they could and a cleaner came in once a week. Maria was coming up for fourteen and liked her food, so she did all the cooking for her and Uncle. Uncle Bert had never been much good at looking after himself. He could boil an egg and heat up stew, but that was his lot. Why he never learned, I'll never know, especially with his brother, my father, being such a master chef. He was five years younger than Dad, and I think he'd been the baby all his life. It suited him, being looked after, so he probably saw no reason to change. Whenever I went away, I'd cook the biggest pot of stew that would fit in the oven but he'd always complain and say it had only lasted a couple of days. Although he ate more than Maria and me put together, he never put on a pound. He was 10 stone 10 pounds all his life.

Maria didn't spend much time at home. She wouldn't leave my side. I'd be eating my hospital dinner, and there she'd be, sitting on the chair by the side of the bed with a plate of sausage and chips from Tony's café down the road which she brought in with her. If I had to have treatment she'd go to the day room to do her homework and at bedtime Uncle would come up with the dog and walk her home.

Maria was due to be confirmed in May and after all that Bible learning, it didn't seem right to put it off. So I got given special permission to be let out, just for the afternoon. But it was too soon.

Although I was in a wheelchair, no sooner had the service begun than I started haemorrhaging again and Maria had to call an ambulance. In the end everyone ended up back in the ward, cake and all.

After the operation came the radiotherapy, just to make sure that no cancerous cells were left to spread anywhere else. This was done at the Royal Marsden Hospital, which is the main cancer hospital in London. The part I went to was out in Surrey. I didn't sleep there. I was too worried about Maria. Exams were coming up and I knew there was no way she would stay at home revising with me away. So they agreed I could stay at home. So it was in every day and back every night. It made no difference. Nothing could persuade Maria to go to school. So every morning the ambulance came and we both got in. They were very kind and when they saw it was no good packing her back to school, they sorted out a teacher for her at the hospital. Uncle wasn't up to helping much, so they gave us a home help two days a week to keep the place ticking over.

We got picked up at about eight in the morning and I'd be back around five. Just weekdays, not weekends. The radiation treatment was horrible. The first time you have it, it's very frightening. They get you up on a narrow bed like a stretcher under this vast machine. Then a siren goes. It scared the life out of me. The last time I'd heard a siren like that was in the war. Of course it's just the warning that everyone must get out. So out they go and sit next door, leaving you all alone in the dark. You know they're watching you on monitors but you can't see them. It was pitch-black, like being in a shelter. Each blast of the treatment was about three minutes. Then they'd come in and reposition you. First I'd be on my back and they'd do the left side, then the right. Then I'd turn over on my front and they'd do the same the other side. I would be in that room for about twenty minutes all told. Afterwards you feel terrible. Then came the sickness and my hair began to fall out. I'd be brushing it and I'd have this brushful of hair. I thought if it keeps going on like this I'll be bald before long. They said they'd get me a wig but I said no. It sounds silly but I felt too embarrassed. So a friend cut it short, she said it would help. But I don't know if it did. It never grew back properly and now I have a really high forehead. But I quite like that as they always say it's a sign of brains.

The worst thing was the sickness which came on immediately after the treatment. They gave me tablets to stop it, but they didn't do much good. I was sick every day. I love my food but I couldn't keep anything down. I went from nine and a half stone to six and a half stone.

The radiation treatment went on for about three months. Every day except weekends. Then no more. I can't say I felt any better because I didn't. But I was back at home and they said it was just a question of building up my strength. They might have knocked out all the cancer cells, but it felt like they'd knocked out just about every other cell while they were at it. I was so weak. Maria didn't leave me for a minute. She used to sit on my bed holding my hand until I'd gone to sleep. The pain was different to anything I'd had before. It was worse than childbirth.

We'd had a holiday booked for August but it was September before we managed to have a week in Hastings. It was the same caravan site as per usual and my friend Josie and her daughter came with us. I had to take a letter to book up with a local doctor while I was there. I couldn't do a lot of running around but I did get a rest. At least Maria was getting a bit of a break.

That Christmas Maria had to do it all. If I wanted to go out to do any shopping, it had to be in the wheelchair. And being in a wheelchair people don't treat you like a normal person. Can't come in here. Can't do this, can't do that. For me it was only a few months but most people in wheelchairs are stuck there for the rest of their lives. It's bad enough not being able to walk. Having to put up with being treated as if you are sub-human shows just how 'caring' this society of ours really is.

I felt terrible having to rely on my daughter. After all she was only fifteen. But it was Maria who insisted we do everything

261

properly. By Christmas Eve we'd got the tree up and the lights were all working. The presents were wrapped and the food was all ready for the off in the morning.

I always wake early on Christmas Day. It's mainly the excitement which I still feel from the days when Christmas meant presents coming out of your ears. But also, even though there were only three of us now, Christmas wouldn't be Christmas without a turkey and all the trimmings and a turkey needs hours and hours of cooking. So it was all stuffed and ready to be put in the oven as soon as I got up.

So that morning I woke up bright and early. I didn't feel great but that was nothing new. My eyes felt funny but not so bad that I didn't fancy a cup of tea. Everything feels better after a cup of tea. So I went downstairs, put the kettle on, warmed the teapot, measured out the tea, poured on the boiling water, let it brew, poured the milk, then, when it was good and ready, poured the tea and lifted the cup all ready for the first and best cuppa of the day. Tnen it happened. My mouth wouldn't open. I tried again, lifted the cup up, tried to open my mouth, but it just stayed closed, like a miser's wallet. I thought I was going mad. Then I looked in the mirror and that was it. My face was all lopsided. At first I thought I'd had a stroke, but I could move my hands, walk. That decided it. It had to be cancer of the face. Oh no, I thought. All that radiation for nothing.

Maria was still asleep and I didn't want to wake her, particularly as it would be such a shock, but what else was I to do? When you think what I must have looked like, face all crooked, squeezing words out of the side of my mouth like a bad ventriloquist, Maria was wonderful. I can laugh about it now, but I really thought it was the end of the road. What I must have looked like with my eyes running, bending over her bed pointing at my mouth and shaking my head like a puppet. Maria found some straws left over from a birthday party and she managed to push one in the side of my mouth for me to suck through. It being Christmas Day, I didn't want to call out a doctor. Luckily we had a neighbour who was an ambulance driver. I'd got to know him because he used to take me to the Marsden. He would know what it was. I didn't have his phone number so we walked over to his house which was only a few minutes away. He said it looked like a stroke. Then, as we were walking back, who should come down the road but the vicar, Mr Whittle. Christmas or no Christmas, he said, I had to go to hospital.

In less than half an hour we were back at St George's, my second home. The casualty doctor took one look and said, 'Bell's palsy'. To check he put a spoon with something on it in my mouth.

'Now, what do you taste?'

I had no idea. I could taste nothing. Nothing at all. Like it was an empty teaspoon. It turned out to be a spoonful of salt. Imagine not being able to taste salt. So that confirmed it. I had Bell's palsy. Damaged nerves. So much for my favourite meal of the year. I had to go on to steroids immediately. But getting them down, with only a straw for the water, was like one of Dad's party games.

My face was all contorted. For the next three months I went around with a scarf round my face like an Arab. I couldn't face anyone seeing me like that. My mouth seemed halfway round my face. My left eye wouldn't shut by itself. When I went to bed I had to push the eyelid down. That eye still doesn't work properly.

Interest about Derek's case seemed to have dried up in the newspapers and it was the theatre that kept it alive. For two weeks, from 28 August until 9 September 1978, I spent every lunchtime in the back room of a pub. Not just any old pub, but the King's Head in Islington which is the most famous of the fringe-theatre pubs in London and many shows that start there end up in the West End. They called it *Lullaby for Mrs Bentley*. The music was by Nick Rowley and the words by Stephen Wyatt. It was more an opera than a play. Nobody said anything, it was all sung. It might seem strange to imagine I could enjoy a play about Derek's case, but *Lullaby for Mrs Bentley* was great. Easy to understand, funny and sad all at the same time. It ended with a candle at 9 p.m.; the clock struck and then everything blacked out.

For *Example* the audiences were mostly children, with just

occasional performances for adults when we were on tour, but this was all adults and even though it was only done at lunchtimes, the debates afterwards would go on and on, in spite of people having to get back to work.

Two years later, another play, just called *Bentley*, written by Richard Ireson, was put on at the Warehouse Theatre, Croydon. This one was more like a film the way they did it. It started with me sitting in the loft at Fairview Road, going over the newspapers about Derek, and finding things in the loft that made me remember, then in flashback came the story of the roof and the trial. The actress who played me was Carrie Lee Baker and I lent her my clothes. Although she was blonde, she still didn't really feel like me. But then perhaps no one can. Derek was played by Gary Olsen, who's now famous of course. He's the dad in *2 Point 4 Children* on the television.

It ran for three weeks in August 1980. But, although people could sign petitions on the way out, and I was there most nights, we didn't do a debate. It ended too late. *Bentley* was more political than either *Example* or *Lullaby for Mrs Bentley*. Like with all these plays there were only a few actors and they doubled up doing different parts, all except Iris and Derek. *Bentley* even included Sydney Silverman, Winston Churchill and Maxwell-Fyfe.

In May 1979, the Conservatives were back in government. The Prime Minister was Margaret Thatcher. Although she was a woman I never had high hopes of her, ever since in the early seventies when she'd been Minister for Education under Edward Heath she'd stopped the school milk. What kind of a woman was that? And her a grocer's daughter. A lot she knew about how working people had to live. How that little bottle of milk every day in the morning break would be the first thing most children would have. It kept us going during the war. And how much money did it save?

Unemployment was higher than it had ever been, but still people didn't see through her and she got voted back in, with an even larger majority in 1983. I wrote to her, of course, like I always did to new Prime Ministers. Nothing. As Mrs Thatcher's 'reign' went on, it was clear that she wasn't interested in justice for anybody, let alone someone who'd been dead for thirty years.

The eighties were difficult. There was so much else for ordinary people to worry about. Strikes, unemployment. But because everyone thought David Yallop had dug up all the skeletons, nobody bothered to do any more digging.

But I didn't give up. Education was changing. When I was at school we had English, arithmetic, geography and history and that was about it. Now it was things like 'social studies'. And for a social studies assignment, the Bentley case was just what they needed. There wasn't a month that went by without some school or group of children phoning or writing, asking me if they could come and talk to me about Derek's case. Sometimes they'd ask me to go to the school and talk to them. Sometimes children would even write their own plays. If I could I would always try and get to see them. The furthest I went was Liverpool.

It wasn't only schoolchildren that were sent to talk to me. It seems hard to credit, but I was always having police cadets turning up. I've never had any run-in with the law myself, and I have no animosity against the police as individuals. But I believe my brother is dead because policemen lied. They were as guilty of killing him as if they'd put him up against a wall and shot him at point-blank range. You've only got to look at the last few years to see that there are still plenty of policemen who haven't learnt that telling lies does you no good in the long run. All we can be grateful for is that since 1965 there's been no hanging. That at least the Guildford Four and the Birmingham Six, the Maguire Seven, Judith Ward and so many others that I've lost track of, are still alive. And I like to think a bit of that's down to Derek. If he hadn't died and got people, ordinary people, so angry, perhaps we'd still have the death penalty. I'm not saying Derek's death was worth it. I could never say that. But I like to think it was not in vain.

But, when it comes to these young cadets, I always make sure I tell them two things. The first is, for God's sake don't be a hero. You've all got a mother and a father even if you don't care about your own life. And the second is, tell the truth, then we can get a police force we can trust. Nobody trusts the police now because once you start not trusting, there's no end to it. In the old days, people believed what policemen said, which is why the jury convicted Derek. But it's got to the point now where juries are worried about convicting anyone, however strong the evidence is against them if it's only a policeman's word, not backed up by something or someone else. We know the public want criminals caught and put behind bars, but get the real villains. Get the right guy. If you don't, the wrong one will be in prison feeling angry and the one who did it will be carrying on with more of the same.

Wrongful convictions don't just hurt the innocent people locked up, but the rest of us too. And like with the Guildford Four and Birmingham Six, what chance is there now of finding who really did those bombings? If they hadn't been in such a rush to get a conviction, any conviction, the right ones would be in prison now not still out there.

I tell them, my crusade to clear Derek's name is not just for Derek, I'm doing it for them too. Until we can get back to basics, with police officers being trusted, being a policeman is going to be very hard work. The police can't work on their own. They need the general public to help them, to keep their eyes open, to give them information. But you only help people you trust.

Early one morning, sometime in 1982, a neighbour came banging at the door. The night before she'd been to the Fairfield Halls in Croydon to hear a folk-singer called Ralph McTell. He'd sung a song about Derek, she said, and by the end of it the whole of the audience was weeping. Naturally I called Fairfield Halls and asked them to get a message to him that I'd rung, that I'd like to speak to him. He called back later that day. He was on tour, so couldn't see me then but promised to send me a tape, which he did. I could hardly bear to listen to it. It was so moving, especially the last verse.

Oh you men on our behalf who sanctioned that boy's death
There's still one thing left to do

266

You can pardon Derek Bentley who never took a life
For Derek Bentley cannot pardon you
Derek Bentley cannot pardon you.

It wasn't until ten years later that I got to hear him sing it in person. It was Christmas 1992 and he was back at the Fairfield Halls. I'd gone with some friends and before he sang the song he told the audience that I was there and he was singing the song for me. You could have heard a pin drop when he began. Because in some way Derek is Croydon's shame. Everyone was crying. Afterwards we went backstage to meet him and his mother. I recognised her as soon as I saw her and that explained why Ralph McTell knew all about Derek in the first place. I recognized her from all those years ago when she used to serve behind the counter in Timothy Whites, the chemist shop in Norbury. It turned out she'd told him she knew me, but he'd never believed her.

Ever since the first days of *Example*, Maria had come with me when it didn't clash with school. Even as young as thirteen or fourteen she'd end up talking to the children too. Although she'd never met her Uncle Derek, I had always made sure she never forget him and he was as alive to her as he was to me. And Derek was alive to me. Whenever I had a problem I always talked it over with him in my mind. I still do.

Maria's never been one to hide herself away and soon she was talking to the children like she'd been doing it all her life. It was about then that she decided that she wanted to go into politics. Talking to schoolchildren and doing plays was all very well, she said, but only politicians could change anything.

She's had her heart set on becoming an MP ever since that time she'd sat on Harold Wilson's lap. I didn't take much notice. I'd never been one for politics. As far as I was concerned, Labour or Tory, once they were in power it was always a different story. Up until 1953, Mum and Dad always voted Conservative. Even in the landslide Labour victory after the war. They were patriots, all King and Country. Churchill had won the war and loyalty was always very important to Dad. Although they'd struggled, they had always had a roof over their heads and they didn't see themselves as Labour party supporters who were not much better than Communists in Dad's book. Before Derek died, Dad sent a telegram to Churchill. Churchill was on holiday in the West Indies and Dad was sure if he only knew what was happening about Derek, he'd sort it out. He would never have believed what I believe now, that Churchill was the one at the back of it all. It was Churchill who gave instructions that Maxwell-Fyfe should go to PC Miles's funeral. The Cabinet papers are still secret. We've asked and asked, but it's always the same. Seventy-five years for anything involving a capital case.

But after 1953 Dad became an out and out member of the Labour party really because the only people who'd done anything to help Derek, Sydney Silverman, Aneurin Bevan and the others, were all members of the Labour party. Although Dad never said anything, I think he felt really let down that, when it came to it, the people he and Mum had voted for over the years hadn't lifted a finger. The worst was their own MP who they'd voted for. An MP's job is to represent his constituents, whatever it's about. In papers that have recently been released, it shows that our MP did write to Maxwell-Fyfe about Derek. But face to face you could tell he thought the Bentleys were the lowest of the low. I know. I was with Dad when we went to see him at the House of Commons.

The MP we were most involved with was Anne Kerr. She'd been working for Derek since before he was hanged. She went with John Parris and Barbara Castle to see Maxwell-Fyfe the night before the execution. So over the years, as she moved up the political ladder, we would always go door-knocking and leafleting for her. Dad never had any ambitions himself in that line but there were always local councillors coming round to the house. He was interested in making things better for working people. He was always ready to help the Labour party and at election time would always go out canvassing but for himself, he stuck at what he was good at, and that was the electrical side. That's how he helped people, mending things for them or seeing to their fuses, things like that.

With Anne being Maria's godmother, it was only natural that she had a lot to do with politics early on. We were always going to the House of Commons for tea. Anne led the anti-Common Market campaign and it wasn't long before Maria knew far more about it than I did. Maria still has strong views about Europe. She doesn't want to end up an MP in a Parliament that's only a branch office of Brussels. Anne died because of the Common Market. As I said before she was over in Belgium demonstrating and the police threw some kind of gas canisters. It went to her lungs and within a few months, she was dead.

Maria first stood as a councillor in 1987. In local politics you have to live in the borough, but not necessarily the ward. It was a safe Tory borough and the ward Maria was standing for was a safe Tory ward, Dundonald in Wimbledon, about two miles away from Colliers Wood. At the beginning of the canvassing I went along with Maria but I soon stopped. Although she was using her own surname, Dingwall, my face was only too well known locally.

'Aren't you Iris Bentley?' they'd say. And every door we knocked at we would end up in a debate about Derek's case. We Bentleys can never escape who we are, and it's been hard on Maria. She once had a boyfriend whose family did everything they could to break up the relationship. I quite liked the boyfriend and we'd known the family for years. It was a bit like what it must be like if you're black. It's all right as long as your son, or daughter, doesn't think of marrying one of them. I said all the usual things like, 'You're too good for him.' But I was so angry. So angry inside. That election in 1987 there was even a headline in the local paper: 'Killer's niece stands in election'.

So I ended up stuffing envelopes. The election was in May. Unlike at the general election where you only have one MP and one vote for each constituency, local wards can have two or three councillors. No one expected her to get in but it was a close-run thing. The count was at Wimbledon town hall. A lovely old place, which they've pulled down now, of course. It was so exciting. Suddenly it was down to recounts. First the Tory was winning by only fourteen votes. Then by only six votes. But there was a danger that one of the other Labour candidates in the same ward might lose if there were more counts, because, although this other candidate was just winning, her vote went down at every count. So poor Maria lost by only six votes. Six votes out of a total of 5,000.

CHAPTER TWENTY-THREE

A few days before the election in May 1987 I had a phone call from someone called Christopher Dee. He was writing a film script about Derek's case, he said. A production company had put up £2.5 million. He was a bit vague about what he wanted but said he'd like to talk to me about it. At first I didn't read much into it. Over the years no one would believe the nutters I've had calling me up, or even knocking on the door, even in the middle of the night, some of them. There have been hundreds, all of them saying they have the answer. That if I knock on this door in Wapping or go down that alley in Stoke Newington or call this number in Hounslow, I'll find the evidence that will prove Derek was innocent. In the beginning Dad and I used to follow up these calls. Now I just listen and take notes on the back of an old envelope I keep by the phone. I don't hang up, just in case. Most of them don't even know the basics, but some of them know a lot. The one thing they all know for definite is that only they have the key to getting Derek his pardon. Why they do it, I just don't know. Over the years I've learnt not to let myself get wound up. But to my way of thinking it takes a sick mind to raise someone's hopes like that when it's all nonsense. Probably a psychiatrist would be able to explain it, but it beats me.

I couldn't tell if this Christopher Dee would be any different. If he wrote film scripts, I said, what other films had he done? None, he said, this was his first. But he was an expert on Derek and said that he knew more about the case than anyone. That he'd got hold of the trial transcript and various Cabinet papers. I began to get interested. They'd done a book of the trial, but John Parris, Craig's barrister who should know, said the book version was tidied up, like in films they put out on television where they cut things out they don't want you to hear. So this man at least knew what he was talking about. He'd written articles about the case, he said, for some police gazette and he was writing a book which he said was going to be serialized in the *Daily Express* or the *Sunday Sport*. Well, when I heard that I changed my mind. This couldn't be a serious writer. The *Sunday Sport* is the lowest of the low. Even calling it a newspaper is like breaking the Trade Descriptions Act. A 'nudes' paper would be more like it. The idea of Derek, or worse me, squeezed between all those 'tits and bums' really got me going. He must be a nutter. The *Sunday Sport* would no more do an article on Derek than an article on growing delphiniums.

But it still didn't stop me writing down his name on the back of an old envelope. Most of these old envelopes just pile up until I chuck them out. But something made me call Ben Birnberg my solicitor. Maybe it was just this feeling that it was books and plays that had kept Derek's name alive. Why not a film?

Ben had been our solicitor since back in the sixties. It's so long ago that neither of us can remember exactly when, but it was about the time Mum and Dad got evicted from Fairview Road. Even now solicitors and barristers have a hard job if they're rebels. But right from when he was at Cambridge a rebel is what Ben was. They always say lawyers only have to open their mouths and you need a mortgage, but money has never interested Ben, justice is what he's interested in and standing up for people who no one else can be bothered with. But it's not just political cases Ben's interested in but criminals, like the Krays (not at their trial, but later). He even acted for Ian Brady, the Moors murderer (with Myra Hindley). Again, after the trial. One of the first things I remember hearing about Ben was in the sixties and that demonstration in Grosvenor Square against the American Embassy, to do with the Vietnam War. Lots of the people arrested were Americans and he acted for them. Ben's always been like that, anti-establishment. Also anti-racism. He was very involved with South African dissidents and has always had black and Asian trainees. Paul Boateng, who was the first black MP, did his articles with Ben and went on to become a partner in the firm. He only left when he got elected to Parliament.

Ben Birnberg is a Robin Hood kind of solicitor, at least to the

Bentleys. We've never had money, not Dad, not me. People always think that's what Legal Aid is for, to help people like us. But it doesn't work like that. You only get Legal Aid for a specific case, and only if the Legal Aid Board think you have a chance of winning. And even if you get through all that, they don't backdate it. If something takes years to come to court, Legal Aid only pays for what happens *after* they've decided to pay. The rest is down to you. What that boils down to is that Ben has done everything for the Bentleys for free. And how can you thank someone like that? I sometimes think Dad must have had a premonition he wasn't long for this world, because only a week before he died he went to see Ben and gave him about the only thing we had that was worth anything. It was a picture, a framed print of Fishmonger's Hall in the City. And it's still there, hanging in Ben's office. I don't know where it came from. Dad's father worked at the Mansion House in the City after he came out of the army, so it might have been through him and his City connections. But it was a family heirloom, one of a pair. I've still got the other one, a landscape. It's hanging upstairs in Uncle's bedroom.

After I'd told Ben about Christopher Dee and this film script he claimed to be writing, Ben decided to do a bit of detective work. The man had mentioned the film company's offices were in Neals Yard, Covent Garden. Ben knew as much about film companies in those days as I did. Probably less. The cinema's in my blood. Apart from when I was a child in Blackfriars, those times I worked at the Streatham Astoria were the happiest days of my life. But Ben had heard of Neals Yard because of a health-food shop there, so he called them up and asked the shop assistant who answered the phone if she knew of any film company nearby. When she said yes, he nearly fell off his chair. He got the girl to pop out and see what the name of the film company was, while he hung on. It turned out it was called Filmscreen International. Next thing was to look them up in the phone book. Imagine his surprise when he called and asked if they knew anything about a film to do with the Craig/Bentley case, and they said yes.

Christopher Dee and I met at Ben's office. I hadn't liked the sound of him on the phone and I didn't like him in the flesh. I didn't trust him. And I was right. It was instinct. True there was a film being planned, but the film company had only got him along to do research because they'd heard he was writing a book on Derek's case. It was like insurance so that he wouldn't start up another film in competition. First of all he said all they wanted was for me to sign this piece of paper called a 'living person's release' which they have to get you to sign if they want an actor to play you in a film.

He hadn't brought the script with him, because there wasn't one. He didn't even bring the book he said he'd written. His publishers wouldn't let him, he said. At one point he asked me to go out of the room.

That was because the way he'd been talking I'd decided I didn't want anything to do with this man and this film.

'I don't want this film made about my brother.'

'It doesn't matter what you want. I can do the film without your permission. Your brother's dead and we can do what we like.'

'Oh no, you can't. While I'm alive you won't take my brother's name to make money.'

Then he turned to Ben and asked if he could speak to him in private.

I felt like a criminal but Ben gave me a nod so I left them to it. It turns out what he wanted to say was would I mind if Derek was shown as being slow. As being not all there. Ben told him that one of the reasons I'd gone on fighting this case was for that very reason. That it was because Derek was not up to understanding the trial, because his IQ was so low, that he should never have been in that Old Bailey dock in the first place.

Afterwards Ben told me that until we saw Christopher Dee's book, I should do nothing, not even talk to him. I didn't get the impression that Ben was too impressed with him either and he decided to deal with the film company direct. Christopher Dee had told them he knew everything there was to know about Craig and

Bentley. Ben told them if it was a consultant they wanted, they'd be better off having me. What could Christopher Dee know that I didn't? So that was it. Ben did all the negotiating. They would pay me £5,000. This worried me a bit. I've never made money out of Derek. Quite the opposite. Just the cost of stamps mounts up, and very few think of enclosing a stamped addressed envelope. But I still get people making out I'm doing it for the money. I know other people raise money for their campaigns. I've been at rallies and meetings where they pass a bucket round. But that's not my way. All I want to do is clear Derek's name and then I can die happy.

But Ben said no. This was a job and I should be paid the going rate, like anybody else. But I still felt a bit unhappy about it. In the end he agreed to try and get the film company to pay a donation to a memorial for Derek. If the film made any money, it was only right that some of it should go to a good cause. Something worthwhile, I said, like a ward or some equipment in the Royal Marsden. After all, if it wasn't for the Royal Marsden, I wouldn't be here to carry on the fight at all. The film company weren't too happy about this, but Ben was just like one of those Hollywood lawyers you see in documentaries. Take-it-or-leave-it, tough. He knew they could do nothing unless I signed so he held out and held out until they agreed that they would put a percentage of the profits into a trust fund. (But even though the film is out on video now, there's still no sign of any money.) But what really pleased me was they agreed to pay the legal costs which meant that Ben was able to get something out of me for once.

Finally in February 1988, the contract was signed. Timothy Woolford was the producer's name. Although I was a consultant, he always said 'no punches would be pulled', in other words, they could do what they wanted. Even then they didn't strike me as very well organized. Woolford hadn't even read David Yallop's book or seen the BBC play Yallop did afterwards.

They say it never rains but it pours and that summer it was pouring films. Next it was a company called Vivid Pictures and they wanted to do a film based on Dad's book. It turned out they knew nothing about the Filmscreen film. Ben advised me to say nothing, just in case. Like I said, he'd turned into a real Hollywood lawyer.

At first Vivid didn't want me as a consultant, they just wanted the rights to Dad's book which, as both Dad and Mum had died, would be shared between Denis and me. But that proved complicated. Denis and I hadn't seen eye to eye in a long time. He had his own life and Dad had always protected him from Derek's case so he was never involved like I was. After all, he was a good deal younger than Derek and never knew him like I knew him.

Just before Christmas 1988 I got a letter from Christopher Berry-Dee (as he now called himself) saying that the first film company, Filmscreen, had gone into liquidation. I hadn't heard from them for a while, but you'd have thought someone would have written or said something. Because I'd already had the first part of the payment and Ben had had his expenses I couldn't believe it wasn't going to happen. But, as Ben said, that's show business. Filmscreen's assets had been taken over by a big American company, United Artists. It seemed those assets included Iris Bentley. The 'living persons release' I had signed now belonged to them. It meant I couldn't be portrayed in any film other than the one I signed it for, which we now found out was called 'Let Him Have It'. United Artists said I belonged to them. Vivid wanted me for their film. The last time I was fought over was when I was twenty-one. It was a battle between the army and the RAF. That time I enjoyed it. This time I didn't. I felt more like piggy-in-the-middle. That spring of 1989 it was as if both those film companies had one of my arms and thought nothing of pulling and pulling until there was nothing left worth having. Mum and Dad had died intestate. Because they had nothing to leave, until now it had hardly mattered. But the rights to Dad's book belonged to Dad. Ben had to prove that there were no death duties to pay, and that all the tax had been paid and things like that. All that trouble just to prove Dad had left £5 15s when he died. But it all had to be proved before I was allowed to sign anything. It seemed to go on for ever. Writers would come and talk to me. But whenever I got to see what they'd written, it was mostly wrong.

Around about May 1989 I had a call from someone called Mei Trow. For a long time I thought his name was Mike, but it wasn't. He was Welsh and it was short for Meirion. He was writing a book about Derek, he said, and wanted to come and talk to me. He had new evidence. There had been another policeman up on the roof, he said, that nobody knew about. Not only that, but he'd talked to him, and this policeman said that Derek had never said the words 'Let him have it'.

When I heard him say that, a shiver ran down my spine. It's strange but it never crossed my mind that he might be one of the nutters. I just knew it was the truth. Mei didn't tell me much but said he would explain everything when we met. He was a history teacher but he'd also written some books, some novels. He lived in the Isle of Wight, so about ten days later he came up for the day and I gave him a bit of lunch. It was a perfect June day. First of all we just chatted, like you do, then out it all came. The summer before, in 1988, his wife Carol was learning to drive and she'd told her driving instructor that her husband was a writer, which he was. This driving instructor said he knew of a story just waiting for someone to write. His name was Roy Pain and his father was called Claude Pain. The instructor told Carol Trow that his dad, Claude Pain, had been up on Barlow & Parker's roof the night when PC Miles was killed and that it was all wrong. That Derek Bentley was innocent. His dad knew, because he was there when it happened. The reason Derek was convicted of murder was because of those words 'Let him have it, Chris' which were supposed to have egged on Craig to fire the gun at DC Fairfax. It was that that did for him. Over the years people had argued that they meant, 'hand over the gun', including, I must admit, both Dad and me. But Derek had always said he never said it. And Craig had backed him up. But who was going to believe them, with three policemen saying he did. You can't blame the jury. And now, after all these years, like a voice from the grave, someone else. And not just anyone. A policeman. A policeman who was up on the roof. A policeman who had been invisible for nearly forty years.

Mei asked me not to breathe a word about any of what he'd told me. He explained that if the press got to hear about it before the book was published, no one would buy the book. And the more people who read it, the more publicity it got, the better the chances of a pardon for Derek.

After Mei left, I looked up Claude Pain in David Yallop's book. It wasn't a name I remembered. But there he was in the index, four mentions. Yallop had him at the warehouse, but not on the roof. Mainly Yallop kept asking why Pain and another policeman called Bugden weren't called to give evidence. It turns out it was a good question. A very good question. Just a pity Yallop was so blinded by his gun theory that he didn't try and find Claude Pain himself. It wouldn't have been difficult. That night I was so excited, I didn't fall asleep until it was growing light and the birds had started their singing.

Early in 1990 Christopher Berry-Dee's book was published, called *Dad, Please Help Me*. Needless to say he hadn't sent me a copy. I just happened to see it in a bookshop in Croydon. I certainly wasn't going to buy one. But I read the introduction. He had the nerve to say that Ben and I had helped him with it, giving the impression it had the Bentley seal of approval. He also claimed that he'd seen secret Home Office documents, papers that I'd been trying to get hold of for years. That evening, when Maria got back home from work, it was all too much and I burst into tears. That was the worst. How dare they let that man see things they had told me couldn't be seen by anyone. It seemed to me in the end that these documents were all available to the public anyway. We weren't the only ones to be upset. David Yallop got in touch with Ben and said there was nothing new, it was just a rehash of his book and Dad's. Ben told me David Yallop was going to sue him, both for what he said and for using his pictures. That made me laugh. Where had David Yallop got 'his' pictures in the first place? Yallop was also trying to get his oar in with the film people. He'd got hold of a copy of the script because his agent was also the agent for Stephen Frears, who they hoped would be the director. Stephen Frears had done *My Beautiful Launderette*, *The Grifters* and *Dangerous Liaisons*. But for some reason he didn't want to do it.

To cap it all Yallop was now saying that I had granted him exclusive rights to my life story and that the film people would have to pay him if they portrayed me in the film.

What made it worse was the timing. January is bad enough anyway, what with the terrible weather and long nights. But as each new year comes around, I can't help reliving those terrible dark days of 1953. I find myself going through the thousands of letters that are crammed into metal filing cabinets, in the shed, like other people do with old photographs. Sometimes I read them, sometimes I end up just looking at the envelopes, the writing, postmarks. Four huge drawers crammed full of letters, most of them addressed just to Fairview Road. No number. The newspaper reports in those days always mentioned the road. Not that the post office had any difficulty finding us.

The 28th of January, and going down to Wandsworth Prison with the wreath for Derek, usually marks the end of this hard time. But that January I was dreading it. Knowing Christopher Dee, he'd probably be there selling copies of the book. Yallop was now bringing out a paperback version of his book. He'd probably be there too. When I thought how all these people were making money out of Derek, it made my blood boil. And then there was Mei Trow's book coming out. But that was different. Mei was always straight with me. The idea that David Yallop or Christopher Berry-Dee would take advantage kept me as silent as the grave. I hadn't even told Ben about him, or about Claude Pain, the policeman on the roof. When I promise something, I keep my word. I told Mei Trow I wouldn't tell anyone, and I didn't.

The 28th of January was a Sunday that year. I'd already picked up the wreath on the Saturday. When Mum was alive she always wrote the card. I write it now and when I die, it'll be down to Maria. There are no other grandchildren. I never know what I'm going to write, but it's like a card you'd send to someone still alive. I don't write much, because the card is only small. I just tell him what we're doing and how we'll never forget. That year was the thirty-eighth anniversary of Derek's death. Funny how you do things. I don't think of it often but always on 28 January and on Derek's birthday, I think how old he'd be if they hadn't killed him.

Although we've never missed a year since 1953, I still have to write and get permission to lay the wreath. The road layout around Wandsworth Prison has changed since we went there to see Derek. In those days there was a turning off the main road that cuts across Wandsworth Common, which led straight up to the gates, like a drive to a stately home. Now that road's just a car park and a garden centre. You can't see the front of it. They've built a high wall right around the front, blank, like a dockyard. You can barely see the tower where they had the condemned cell. The entrance is now an electronic gate and there are cameras checking who you are.

It's always the same. Usually there are people waiting by the time we get there. Friends. People I know and people I don't know. I say hello and have a chat, then at nine o'clock I ring the bell, just like an ordinary front doorbell, set into the wall beside this huge brown metal gate. It looks like wood on the outside, but it isn't. It seems so strange to have to go through this rigmarole when you know they're watching you through the cameras. Then the rumble starts and this massive door slides open and there's the padre, sometimes two of them, and a warder. The padre shakes my hand and we walk across the courtyard towards the old front of the prison. Then I lay the wreath and the padre reads from the Bible and says a prayer. It's not always the same prayer and over the years different padres have come and gone and last year the padre gave a prayer for justice, which had never happened before.

That year, a few days before, I'd had a call from Thames Television saying they wanted to send a camera crew and a reporter out to interview me at the prison the next morning. Over the years the press had often come to the prison for the wreath-laying. The vigil, they called it. They weren't allowed in; only friends could come with me through those great gates. Little did I know how that one interview with Thames, after so many others I've lost count, was going to change everything.

The reporter's name was Carole Peters. We did the interview in front of the prison and then I asked if she'd like to come back to Colliers Wood for a coffee and a chat. Some people you take to right away, others take a bit of time. With Carole it was immediate. I found out early on she was a vegetarian, in fact a vegan, because she couldn't take milk in her coffee. Carole doesn't even wear leather shoes. That's how we got talking. I told her about how Derek was a vegetarian and I took her upstairs and showed her the photographs on the landing. She didn't know much about the case but I could see she was interested, so I lent her a copy of Dad's book. I only discovered later that, although she'd worked on radio and television in the Midlands and came from the north of England, interviewing Iris Bentley that Sunday was the first job she'd done for Thames. And she'd only got to do it because it was a Sunday and no one else wanted to spoil their weekend.

It was a month or two later before I heard from her again. I didn't know then that Mei Trow had been in touch with them about the new evidence in his book and they were investigating it. Sometime after seeing me she went to see Claude Pain. It seemed that he'd had a stroke. What Carole couldn't really understand was how had he come up with this business about him being on the roof all these years later. First, she said, she thought he had just made it up, for a bit of glory. But as she spoke to him, and as she read more and more about the case, she realized that he was telling the truth. But also she discovered that Mei Trow had got at least one fact wrong in his book. Claude Pain did not claim Derek didn't say 'Let him have it, Chris'. All he said was that he hadn't *heard* Derek say it. Which is not the same thing. But Carole didn't give up. She told me Claude Pain kept tapping his nose with his finger whenever she asked him about why hadn't he spoken up earlier.

'Reasons. You don't want to get involved.'

First she thought it was something to do with his stroke. Then he came up with, 'Something in my notebook didn't tally.' She told me at this stage she thought he could be a bit gaga. But then she got him to draw a map of the roof, which he did. Everything was accurate and he showed her where he had been, which was hidden behind one of the low roof lights near to where the stairs came up.

'Then you would have seen Derek and DC Fairfax and PC McDonald . . .' He shook his head.

'I didn't see them.'

'But you must have done.'

'I didn't see them.'

'Do you mean they weren't there?'

'I didn't see them.'

None of this made any sense to Carole. And she began to believe that Claude Pain had just taken on somebody else's part. Like PC McDonald. She asked how he'd climbed up there. He said by a ladder propped up at the front. By now Carole didn't know what to think. If he was on the roof, why didn't anyone say so? She must have given him the impression that she didn't really believe him as he even asked his wife to go and find a copy of David Yallop's book. He showed her in the index where he gets mentioned, then turned to a photograph at Croydon Magistrates' Court, a picture of Craig going in for the committal proceedings on a stretcher. And there, standing at the top of the stretcher, is Claude Pain. She told me he was desperate to make her believe that he was there up on that roof. She was sure there was more to it but she needed to do more research.

The next thing that happened with Thames was in June when Carole called up and said she wanted me to meet the director of the programme. This turned out to be Roger Corke. He was new to Thames too; like Carole he had always been a journalist, but Roger was also involved in documentaries and had worked on *World In Action*. I'll never forget the first thing he said to me.

'Iris, how many people have walked through this door and told you that they can get Derek his pardon?'

'Hundreds.'

'Well, I'm afraid we can't promise you that. But what we are going to do is try our damnedest. But keep your feet firmly on the ground.'

It was then they told me about seeing Claude Pain. Until then I didn't even know they knew about Claude Pain. And they didn't know I knew. Like I said, Mei Trow had sworn me to secrecy and that included everyone. Roger told me that he and Carole had been back and interviewed Claude Pain several times. He said that Mei Trow's book hadn't begun to scratch the surface of the real truth. That the really exciting thing they had found out from Claude Pain was not that he hadn't heard Derek say 'Let him have it', but that PC McDonald's role in the whole thing was pure invention. Everything he said from beginning to end was a pack of lies. He wasn't even up on the roof. But the story the police had decided to concoct to make sure of a conviction needed another policeman to confirm Fairfax's story about everything, which PC McDonald did. As Claude Pain had said, you only had to look at a photograph of McDonald to see that he had no more chance of climbing a drainpipe than flying. There was a picture of him in David Yallop's book *To Encourage the Others*. And sure enough, he was as fat as Alfred Hitchcock.

CHAPTER TWENTY-FOUR

By the time they came to see me that afternoon, Carole and Roger had interviewed Claude Pain several times. They said they had played 'good cop, bad cop' which meant Carole appeared to believe him and asked friendly questions while Roger seemed sceptical and came in with difficult ones. (Like they were interrogating him.) They took it in turns to ask him different things and the same things in different ways.

At first Roger said he, like Carole, couldn't believe any of it. It was so different to the police version. According to Claude Pain, McDonald wasn't halfway up the drainpipe when the first shots were fired. McDonald wasn't there at all. So he couldn't have heard Derek say 'Let him have it, Chris', but in court he swore that he had. But no matter what way they asked the questions, Claude Pain's story stayed the same. Try as they could, Roger and Carole couldn't trip him up. There was no getting away from it, Claude Pain seemed to be telling the truth and the whole police version was a pack of lies. But, as Roger explained, it was just one old man's story. And an old man with a stroke at that. Who would believe him?

That night after everyone was down from the roof, PC Pain was told to go with Craig to the hospital. Everyone else went back to the station.

So the next morning, 3 November 1952, Claude Pain went into Croydon police station and started to write up his notes about what happened the night before from his notebook which he still had with him. Somebody saw him and said not to bother. But he typed it up anyway and handed it in with his notebook, for logging. He never saw that notebook again. Still nothing was said to him. He still didn't know anything was wrong. Not until the committal at the Croydon Magistrates' Court. You can see him in the photograph at the back of the stretcher with Craig. He was all set to give his evidence. But like Dad a week or so later, he was just never called.

It was only when Claude Pain went to see his supervisor to ask why he hadn't been called to give his evidence that he realized something was smelling. He knew his evidence was important. There had only been him and Fairfax on the roof until PC Miles was shot. Carole told me that all the time he was telling her, he kept looking behind him and tapping his nose. He was scared stiff she said; even then, all those years later. This officer didn't answer his question. Didn't mention the case. He just said, 'You're not long off retirement. How would you like to work with dogs? You don't want to make trouble, do you? I think you'd make a good dog handler.'

Only then did the penny drop. But although Claude Pain knew then there was some kind of cover-up, at the time he didn't want to know. After all, what could he do? He hadn't been in court. All Mei Trow was interested in was whether Derek had said 'Let him have it, Chris'. It was only after talking with him that Carole and Roger realized just how different the official version was from the truth. But, as he kept repeating as if to apologize, a policeman had been killed, and 'PC Miles was a friend of mine'. Plus Claude Pain had a wife and three children and was only two years off retirement.

'Remember. Anything could happen. I could be run over in a police car or something like that.'

And again he tapped his nose.

By the time of Derek's trial on 11 December, PC Claude Pain was learning to be a dog handler, a good job in those days.

When Carole and Roger were telling me the story it all came tumbling out so fast I found it hard to grasp. They'd come upon it bit by bit, over five or six interviews, but it was all new to me. It wasn't until after their film, which was called *Beyond Reasonable Doubt*, went out that I really understood all the ins and outs. What really got Carole excited was that now she understood the bit in Derek's statement about 'I should have mentioned that after the plain clothes policeman got up the drainpipe and arrested me, another policeman in uniform followed and I heard someone call him "Mac".' It always stuck out like a sore thumb. But until now there didn't seem any reason to have added it in. Carole explained that now that they knew McDonald was never really on the roof, the police needed Derek to say he was, just in case anyone got clever and tried to make out he wasn't.

What I still couldn't make out was with all these other policemen lying, fifteen of them gave evidence, why didn't they just get Claude Pain to lie as well? Why did they need to 'put' McDonald up on the roof. Wouldn't Claude Pain have done just as well? Carole said that she thought there were two reasons. Firstly, Pain and Fairfax lived in the same road and they hated each other. Something to do with Claude Pain's son, she said. Secondly, Carole got the impression that PC Pain was too straight and not particularly bright with it. They probably decided they couldn't trust him to say what was wanted in court. So they ditched him. They needed *someone* up on the roof, to be a witness to Derek saying he knew about Craig having a gun, and to hear 'Let him have it, Chris'. Those were the two things that did for Derek. And McDonald 'heard' both of them. According to Claude Pain, Fairfax, Harrison and McDonald all used to drink together so being they were friends he could be trusted to stick to the story and keep his mouth shut. It was McDonald's evidence that was the final nail in Derek's coffin. Fairfax on his own wasn't strong enough. Fairfax and McDonald together were.

I remember when I first heard all of this, I couldn't believe my ears. I felt more sick than excited. It just didn't seem possible. Over the years my hopes have been built up so many times. And Roger understood, telling me over and over to 'Keep your feet on the ground, Iris.'

But although Roger and Carole believed Claude Pain's story, that wasn't enough, they said. It certainly wasn't enough to get Derek a pardon and it wasn't even enough to do the television programme. With having had the stroke, Claude Pain's voice was hard to follow, and he was slow. They needed corroboration. The only chance of Claude Pain being believed, they said, was to find other witnesses who could back his story up.

Other witnesses? But how? It was all so long ago. Who were these unknown witnesses? Surely David Yallop and the others must have spoken to everyone who had anything to say, I said. But no, they hadn't. As far as Roger and Carole could make out, no one had made any effort to find ordinary local witnesses, people who were there that night. They put it down to the fact that none of the people who'd written about Derek were trained journalists. Roger and Carole had both started out working for local newspapers doing births, weddings and funerals – hatch, match and despatch, they called it. There must have been hundreds of people craning their heads, they said, looking and listening to everything that was happening on Barlow & Parker's roof that night. It went on for at least half an hour and what with fire-engines, ambulances, there must have been a huge crowd. Carole had gone through my collection of newspapers, including the local papers, and the names were all there, like the girl who lived next door, June Tennent. They knew just what to do.

They were excited. I was excited. It was just like we were setting off for a trip to Hampton Court or Box Hill. We were like kids that afternoon. But it was all so long ago they warned me we might end up with no one.

'Keep your feet on the ground, Iris,' Roger kept saying. And feet on the ground was what was needed next. Legwork. For the next stage, they would need my help and we had to work quickly. The programme was set to go out when *Thames Reports* went back on the air in September. Most of this extra work was in their own time. Because by now it wasn't a television programme that mattered, it was Derek.

With Maria being involved in local politics, she knew better than me how we could help. The first thing we did was check the electoral rolls in Croydon town hall. Then it was off to Tamworth Road. Just like Derek and Craig did in 1952 we took the bus. Like a lot of Croydon it's unrecognizable now, compared to what it was.

There's houses now where Barlow & Parker's used to be and the other side, where the Wares lived, who saw Derek and Craig climbing over the gate, is a car park. Maria and I tried what streets and houses were left in the area. It was midsummer and red-hot.

The pub was still there, but with new people running it and they knew nothing. So we just knocked on doors. Like canvassing. Because we had no identity cards or anything like that, they all thought we were the DHSS, about to inspect their kitchens. We'd not have time to open our mouths before they'd come out with things like 'We haven't got no cockroaches'. But they were all new. Nobody knew anything.

It was old people we needed, so the next thing was day centres and we got the names and addresses from the town hall. Maria was owed some holiday, so for the next two weeks we got to know every old people's day centre in the Croydon area. We didn't make any appointments but just turned up and explained to the supervisor what we wanted, then Maria and I would go round and talk to them. Derek's case is part of Croydon history now and they all remembered. But we came up with no one who'd lived in Tamworth Road or was in the pub that night.

In the meantime Roger had got the *Croydon Advertiser* to write a story about Thames Television looking for eyewitnesses. It was important, he said, not to say why. Dozens got in touch and about thirty sounded as if they might be useful.

Most didn't have much to say, but four of them hit the jackpot. The first important person to get in touch was John Tennent. He had lived in the house next door but one to the warehouse, on the left-hand side, the side where it all happened. Then there was his sister June. Then they heard from Douglas Barlow, the son of the owner of the warehouse. He'd come to open up for the police and had been up by the stairs leading on to the roof. Then there was Denis Woodcock, who also worked at Barlow & Parker's, and was another keyholder who'd been called in that night. None of them were told why the programme was being made. They just had to say what they remembered of that night and to draw plans of where they were and what they'd seen and where it had happened. Then after Carole talked to them, Roger filmed an interview, with Carole asking them the crucial questions. None of them knew what was at stake because they didn't know what the official version was. They weren't at the Old Bailey, and they hadn't read any of the books. Each of them had only a small bit to say, a small part to play, but everything, every little thing, they said fitted in with Claude Pain's fuller version of what happened.

The most important thing to come out was that Derek and Fairfax were on a completely different part of the roof to where the police said they were, which is why Claude Pain never saw anyone until PC Miles fell down at his feet dead. The official version has Fairfax taking Derek back to *behind* where the stairs came up, where the drainpipe was. But Claude Pain says no one was there. He'd got on the roof by a ladder leaned up against the front of the warehouse. Then after he'd got over the parapet, he crawled to behind one of the roof lights. Everyone else, he said, was up the other end of the roof. But when John Tennent drew his plan, it was all clear. What Claude Pain said was right. Derek and DC Fairfax were *the other side* of the stairhead, towards the back of the roof. There was this little alcove and John Tennent in his back garden saw them clearly, pinned down there, against the skyline. If they'd been the other side, where the police said they were, he wouldn't have been able to see them at all. What about the gun-fight then? No, said John Tennent. Though he saw Craig firing a few shots Tennent did not see or hear the face-to-face gun battle the police told the court had happened.

Then there was Douglas Barlow, who'd opened up the warehouse so the police could go up the inside. He'd seen none of what happened on the roof because he was by the stairs. But he saw all the comings and goings. And what he said took Carole and Roger completely by surprise it was so different from the police story. Douglas Barlow said PC Miles's body had been brought down first, *before* Derek came off the roof. Derek was last down, when it was all over, with the police kicking him on his way. There was no gun-fight. Fairfax got his medal for that gun-fight. The George Cross, the highest civilian award, and it never even happened. Fairfax hadn't come off the roof to get a gun. Derek had been up there with him all the time. Denis Woodcock also worked for Barlow & Parker's and he was there, lower down in the warehouse. He confirmed everything Douglas Barlow said.

And those words, 'Let him have it, Chris', the words that sent Derek to his death. What about them?

John Tennent didn't hear them at all, but his sister June says she did. But not when the police say Derek said them, not before a shot was fired but long after. Long after all the shooting was over, not before it even began. They were just words she heard shouted out of the night. Could have been shouted by anyone, she said. About anything. But for those words to convict Derek – and hang him – they HAD to be said before any shots were fired. Derek HAD to have instructed Craig to use his gun. He didn't. It turns out the police who went to fetch Craig after his dive from the roof gave Craig a good kicking as he lay unconscious on the ground. Perhaps that was when she heard those words. 'Let him have it.' They would be fresh in their minds. And with the right meaning.

Each of them had just little pieces of the jigsaw that meant nothing unless you had the whole picture, not in 1952, not even now. And why had the police needed to make all these little changes to the truth? All this lying? Because it was the only way they could be sure of getting Derek. And they were determined to get Derek. A policeman had been killed. Craig was too young to hang. Derek would have to do.

Claude Pain, John and June Tennent, Douglas Barlow and Denis Woodcock were all prepared to be filmed. But there were some people Carole and Roger spoke to who weren't. Like Fairfax. They turned up at his house one day. He asked them in for tea but refused to be interviewed on film. He kept showing Carole pictures of his grandchildren. A proud grandfather. A grandfather who was a hero. He had nothing more to say, he said. He agreed to sign a piece of paper saying that he stuck by what he had always said. PC Harrison, the other policeman who said he heard the words 'Let him have it, Chris', was also still alive. But he refused to be interviewed.

To help them sort it all out and explain it for the programme, Carole and Roger got hold of John Parris, Craig's barrister at the trial. He's about the only person around now who was involved in the trial in 1952. He said that in English law, a jury can only convict if the prosecution have proved they are guilty *beyond reasonable doubt*. Even if you didn't believe everything each of these new witnesses was saying, he said, if their evidence had been given to the jury in Derek's trial, it would have been enough to raise doubt, reasonable doubt, in their minds. And in English law, that's all you need for a Not Guilty verdict. Reasonable doubt. And that's what they decided to call the programme, 'Beyond Reasonable Doubt'. It didn't matter, Parris said, why the police were lying, or how insignificant it appeared. The fact that they were lying at all, about anything, meant all the rest of the evidence had to be taken with a huge pinch of salt.

In his book *Scapegoat* published in 1991, John Parris wrote about what happened at the police station in Croydon that night. He said that DI Smith had set up a blackboard and gone through what he decided they were going to say had happened. Like a play, everyone had their part, their lines, their position on the stage. All they had to do was learn them by heart so when it came to the performance, there would be no slip-ups. Derek wouldn't be able to remember his, so they wrote it out for him instead. 'His' statement. Because he couldn't remember anything anyway, he wouldn't remember what did happen and what didn't. Except for those words. He always knew he didn't say those words. Parris doesn't say who told him. Just another person who is still too frightened to be named.

And then I began to remember things. In Croydon Magistrates' Court. Sitting in the gallery upstairs, looking down on the police as they gave their evidence, watching as three of them stood in a huddle and looked at each other's notebooks, comparing. Checking their stories were the same.

The programme went out on 11 September 1990. Just before it

was broadcast, Carole and Roger sent all the evidence to the Home Secretary, David Waddington.

The newspapers were full of it. I did radio and television interviews and everybody said the same thing.

'It won't be long now.'

Roger warned me it would take time and we just had to sit tight. But it was not until August, nearly a year later, when David Waddington had gone and Kenneth Baker was Home Secretary that it came over the television news that he had ordered an inquiry.

In the meantime there was the feature film. Although the *Thames Reports* programme and Mei Trow's book were both out by the time they started filming *Let Him Have It* in November, the script hadn't changed much at all. Like everyone else in Derek's case, they'd decided on their story and they were sticking to it. They wouldn't listen to me. I don't even think they looked at Roger and Carole's documentary. If they had, they'd have had a far better film. If I was feeling charitable, I'd say perhaps they were worried about money. *Let Him Have It* was based on Dad's book. If they had to change it to add things from Mei's book about Claude Pain, then I suppose they would have had to pay him too. Roger and Carole would have done it for nothing.

The film director Vivid decided on first was Alex Cox, who made *Repo Man*. I haven't seen it but I've been told it's a cult. Not my kind of film. I met him only once. I'd never met any film directors before, but he wasn't how I expected one to be. Rather strange. But I liked him. He was very kind and friendly and said he wanted the truth to come out. I remember thinking that Derek's story would be safe in his hands. But it turned out his ideas were a bit too revolutionary and before long he fell out with the producers. He's what they call a maverick. He'd wanted to make the film in black and white and that was unheard of in those days. Now, of course, after *Schindler's List*, they might have thought differently, but back then they were having none of it, so Alex Cox had to go. Next thing we heard the director was Peter Medak. He was Hungarian and had directed *A Day in the Death of Joe Egg* and *The*

Ruling Class. He also did *The Krays*. He always promised to let me have a copy of the video, but he never did.

Shooting started in November 1990, a few days after all the legal side about Dad's book was finally sorted out. The part of Derek was played by Christopher Eccleston. Craig was played by Paul Reynolds. They had both been cast by Alex Cox. When Peter Medak took over they had to audition again. Later Chris told me the way the film turned out, he wished he'd turned it down. But he was young, only twenty-five, and no way could he pass up starring in a big Hollywood film. And that was the trouble, according to Chris. With Alex Cox the film would have been a serious look at Derek's case, with Peter Medak it was Hollywood. But Chris is a wonderful actor. He took it so seriously. In the film he has to show Derek having a fit. He found out about the Lingfield Hospital School in Surrey which is a school for epileptics with learning difficulties. And that was something he told me he hadn't realized before, that severe epilepsy goes hand in hand with learning difficulties. For a whole month he went again and again to Lingfield and he said that Derek's epilepsy was the key to everything that happened that night. The teachers were marvellous, he said. The person who helped him was Dr Besag.

To me Chris became more than an actor playing a part. He and I spent so much time together. I felt close to him, like a brother. He wasn't Derek, no one could be. But there was a bond. He found out so much at Lingfield. He told me that the amount of drugs Derek was taking was enough to cure a horse. He said how the people at the school would slow down when they were dosed up.

He also told me he'd spoken to a doctor from the Maudsley where the tests on Derek had been done when he was in Brixton. This doctor told him that when he went to look for Derek's file, it was empty. All the papers had disappeared.

The writers were nick-named Pinky and Perky. They were both far too young to my way of thinking. No more than twenty-four or twenty-five. And they were yuppies, not people who knew about life in terraced houses, let alone life in London just after the war.

Whenever I got sent a copy of the script, I sent it back covered in red pencil. So much of it was wrong. They had Derek mixing with Niven Craig. Derek never met Niven Craig. But they took no notice of what I said. That's what upset Chris Eccleston. He felt they were making Derek out to be more normal than he was. After spending all that time at Lingfield he said that Derek's epilepsy and the drugs would have made him moody. But Peter Medak would have none of it. He told Chris that if he showed the ugly side of Derek's epilepsy, the audience would lose sympathy for him. But as Chris said, if the film didn't show the truth, it would be failing Derek and those other people who are still struggling with their illness. It led to terrible fights. Although I wasn't there on that day, a whole day's shooting was cancelled. It was in the condemned cell, when Chris refused to do the scene like Peter Medak wanted. Chris said he owed his loyalty to Derek not to Peter Medak.

'If you're borrowing the drama of epilepsy you have to show the reality. But Hollywood doesn't like ugliness.'

The film wasn't done in the right order and it wasn't done in Croydon. For Fairview Road itself, they used somewhere in Reading. They didn't get it right. The house they chose was far too small and poky. I told them. But they took no notice. So much for my being a consultant. The inside of the house wasn't much better. They built this specially at Pinewood Studios, plus they did the condemned cell there. Barlow & Parker's warehouse they did in Perivale, near Harrow in west London. The outside street scenes were done in Liverpool of all places. Croydon has all been pulled down and rebuilt since those days. Tamworth Road is all flats, car parks and bingo halls and they decided that New Brighton, outside Liverpool, was as close to 1950s Croydon as they were going to get.

I didn't go to the shooting every day, but I went to all the locations. For me Liverpool was best. I stayed at the Adelphi Hotel and we really lived it up. I went up three times. I couldn't stay there all the time because I had Uncle to look after. It was wonderful. I'd never stayed anywhere so luxurious and there was a car laid on to take me to the location in New Brighton. And there was a caravan for me to rest in and put my things.

The way they did the film surprised me. The Alan Clark film based on David Yallop's book which the BBC did in 1972 had been done in only a few days. This took weeks. Although I'd been watching films for all these years I had no idea it was so complicated. As for the acting, I used to think there was nothing to it. I used to think, Oh, I could do that. But no way. They had to go over each scene so many times, I'd have been screaming and pulling my hair out by the end. 'Cut' and 'Do that again'. 'And again.'

At Perivale, where they did the warehouse, it was an all-night thing, from eight in the evening until early the next morning. There was this spiral staircase up to the rooftop. And you're slipping and sliding. It was the middle of winter and the wind was like Siberia up there. The whole of the road was taken up with the cameras. As this rooftop was just on an ordinary road, shooting would stop every so often to let great queues of buses and cars go through. But although they'd been waiting sometimes up to half an hour, they'd creep through so slowly, necks out on stalks because of course they wanted to see what was going on.

The best thing on night location was the breakfast. And at about three o'clock in the morning up would go the shout 'Breakfast' and there would be big prawns, meat pie, soup, salad, dishes of fruit. It was fantastic.

I was always seeing things that were wrong, but no one took any notice. In the end I stopped saying anything, it was a waste of time.

What really surprised me up in Liverpool was how they all lived it up. Even though they'd been out shooting all day. I was ready for my bed; they'd all be downstairs tripping the light fantastic. Paul Reynolds, who played Craig, was the heart-throb. He was in *Press Gang* on television, and there were always this crowd of girls just trying to get a glimpse of him. But he was always ready for work the next day even though he had been out half the night. I didn't see much of Paul and began to wonder what I'd done because I felt he was always avoiding me. I hated the idea I'd said something to hurt his feelings, so I asked Peter Medak about it. He asked Paul straight out.

'Paul, why do you run away from Iris?'

'Well, she must hate me being Craig.'

When Peter told me this, I felt so bad. I went straight up and got hold of Paul in the bar.

'But you're not Craig, you're Paul. Anyway, I don't hate anybody.'

'Don't you?'

'No.'

'Do you want a pint?'

'No, I don't drink pints, Paul.'

'Well, do you want a brandy?'

So Paul Reynolds bought me a brandy. Now, I don't normally drink brandy but I thought it wouldn't do to say no. Now we were friends. But within a few minutes the room started to spin.

'I think it's my bedtime.'

And as I said it, I could feel my words starting to slur. I know it comes from my never drinking anything. But I can't be like that if I'm meant to be representing Derek. So it was an early night for me that night. By the time I switched off the light it was still only half-past eight.

I never forget I'm Derek's ambassador. It's the same with Maria. I always tell her, whenever she goes out on these marches and things like that, 'Remember who you are. Don't do anything wrong so people can say, "Oh, that's because she's a Bentley." Don't give them any ammunition.' I've learnt the hard way. Dignity, that's what's important. And people respect that.

Chris Eccleston wasn't like Paul. He was the quiet one and we spent a lot of time together. I lent him Derek's lighter and watch. He was so grateful. He said they 'sparked his imagination'. Chris comes from up around there, from Salford outside Manchester. Not that you'd know it from the film, but in real life he has a strong northern accent. Poor Chris, what he had to go through. They bleached and permed his hair to make it look like Derek's. They had him having his hair waved at the hairdresser's using hot tongs, like a waffle iron. It was called a Marcel wave. But I told them, no way did he have it done. All us Bentleys are really proud of our curly hair; Derek's hair was natural. He might have used a bit of Brylcreem, but it wasn't corrugated like with a Marcel wave. But they took no notice of me. What did I know, I was only his sister. But what I do know is those tongs did for Chris's hair. He had to go around with an orange hair-net to stop it falling out. I think it did fall out after shooting. It certainly went a very strange colour. You've only got to look at the photographs. I told them about Derek's hair being natural, but they weren't interested. Like I said, they weren't interested in the truth.

Strangely I didn't have as much to do with Claire Holman who played me. But we got on very well the couple of times we met. She said it was good to talk to me, that she could 'bounce' off me. I think of all the people that have played me, she got the closest not only to how I looked, but also to how I was, how I used to lark around with Derek.

Just before filming finished in April I did an interview with Barry Norman for his television programme. I knew I had to toe the party line but I did manage to get in that the film wasn't going to be a hundred per cent like I'd have wanted.

By May it was goodbye to show business and back to being a mum again. Maria was having another go at local politics. This time for Pollards Hill ward. Again it was a Tory ward. The count was held at the Cannon Leisure Centre in Mitcham. That night was fantastic. Merton was the only borough out of all of London that changed from Tory to Labour. Some went Liberal, like Richmond, but Merton was the only one that went Labour. Quite something considering it has all those rich areas like Wimbledon, and the stockbroker belt going out into Surrey.

Maria's ward was in Mitcham. It was mostly estates, working class, so how it ever got to be Tory I can't imagine. Sometimes I think that people believe that if they have a Tory poster in their window people will think they're a cut above. But that change around was quite something. And it was Maria's ward that did it. There were six recounts. And still the numbers came in different. At three o'clock in the morning we gave up for the night. Locked everything up and went home. But by ten the next morning we were back again for the last recount. By now the word was out and the place was thick with television cameras. All the media were down to watch history being made in Mitcham. Thank goodness this time there was no mention of Derek. It might sound strange to say, but Maria had lived her life under the shadow of Derek Bentley and this time it was important for her to know she'd done it on her own. And done it she had. Maria Dingwall won by over 200 votes. At that time of the morning all I really wanted was a nice cup of tea. It was not to be. And, I have to say, next to a nice cup of tea, a nice glass of champagne runs a very close second.

By the summer, publicity for the film was building up. That was fine by me, but for somebody else it wasn't. They were writing in the newspapers that one of the consultants on the film was Christopher Craig. Since Craig was let out of prison in 1962 he had tried to live like a normal person. He was a plumber. He was married and had a family. The last thing he wanted was publicity.

The year before, Carole Peters and Roger Corke had written to his solicitor asking to interview him for the programme. But he'd said no. But they had sent him a copy of the programme anyway.

Then, at the end of June, Roger had a message at the office. Someone called Christopher Craig had telephoned. He would call again the next day.

CHAPTER TWENTY-FIVE

It turned out Christopher Craig had been so impressed by the *Thames Reports* programme that he was ringing Roger to ask his advice. He said the film people had tried to involve him but he'd wanted nothing to do with it. After years without any of the past to rock his boat, the last thing he wanted was anything stirring things up again. And when even Craig's local newspaper got on the bandwagon, that was it. He'd had enough. Now all he wanted to know was how to stop the press pestering him.

After all they'd been through with Derek's case, there was no way Roger and Carole were going to pass up the chance of talking to Christopher Craig, so they agreed to meet up. As for the advice, Carole explained to Craig that he had two choices. First, he could just lie low, do nothing and hope the press would go away. Or he could give one, exclusive interview, an interview that would shut everyone up for good and all. But she warned him that if he did decide to say nothing, then it was likely the tabloids would never leave him alone. 'Scoops' and 'exclusives' are what every reporter dreams about. But once that 'exclusive' was had by someone else, she said, Christopher Craig would be old news and not worth wasting shoe leather on. Of course if he decided to do an interview, she said, then she hoped it would be with them.

Craig phoned a few days later, and said he'd decided to go for the exclusive interview. With them.

They were cock-a-hoop and said they didn't know until Craig phoned which way he'd go. But it doesn't surprise me. Like me, he knew that what Carole and Roger were after was the truth, not just a 'story' to feather their careers with. He knew he could trust them, like I had. But he told them he wasn't prepared to talk about that night on the roof, just about how he was being hounded because of the film and the lies being told about him. They agreed anyway.

The interview was to be done on neutral territory, at Roger's cottage in the country.

The night before the interview, Carole and Craig both stayed in the same hotel near Roger's cottage. In the morning over breakfast Carole told him that, although he didn't have to answer any questions he didn't want to, she had to ask him things about the rooftop.

'If I didn't ask you how you felt about Derek being hanged I'd probably get the sack.'

He didn't say much, but at the end of breakfast he said to her, 'You never know, I might just tell you some of this.'

Carole says she's never been more frightened doing an interview in her life and that afterwards her hands were bruised where she'd pressed her nails into her palms so hard. Craig hadn't promised her he'd say anything. First they talked a bit about the film and how angry he felt, then she plucked up courage and asked the question she knew she had to:

'Where were you, and how did you feel at nine o'clock on the morning of the execution?'

'I remember I was in Wormwood Scrubs and I remember the window slammed above me just about nine and someone said, "There, he's gone." And I'm not ashamed to say that I burst into tears.'

She told me she knew then that he was going to tell her everything.

'If you think about it, when you've waited forty years, when you've had this in you for forty years to tell somebody, now you've begun to tell somebody you can't stop. Chris Craig and I looked at each other. I was virtually in tears and you could see them in Chris's eyes. And I knew. You're going to have to tell me everything, I thought. You have held it inside you for so long but now, you have to tell everything.

'Here was a man, having gone through the trial, knowing that he'd killed someone and his friend had died for that crime, and he'd lived forty years with the guilt of knowing that. Here was someone who at the age of sixteen had committed a terrible crime and knew he'd committed a terrible crime and yet saw an even worse crime being committed in front of him and knew he could do nothing about it.

'There was this incredible sadness and resignation and incredible venom. At the policemen who'd lied.'

And Craig told Carole everything. And it was all on film. How Fairfax had sent Derek to try to stop him, how he'd shot at Fairfax long after Derek had been arrested and taken back to the stairhead, how he'd been thirty-nine feet away when he fired the first shot at Fairfax – not six feet away like Fairfax told the jury. And most important of all, how Derek had never said those words 'Let him have it, Chris'. Derek had always said he'd never said it. I'd always believed he never said it but now here was Craig, Christopher Craig himself, saying it loud and clear for the whole world to hear. Derek Bentley never said the words that sent him to the gallows.

Carole asked Craig why after all these years he'd decided to speak up now.

'Because I have to. Somebody has to say it and I'm the only one who can and I just hope that now it's said they will act on it. I can't keep quiet if there's any chance I can tip the scales for a pardon. I saw three officers swear a man's life away. As sure as I killed PC Miles, they killed Derek Bentley.'

I didn't know about any of this till much later. They wanted to film my reactions to seeing the interview with Craig, so not long before it was due to go out they came to Colliers Wood with a video of that part of the programme. The interview with Craig had lasted five hours. But only about fifteen minutes was used. That afternoon, they told me straight away, before I watched the film, that Craig had come out for Derek. That's as maybe. But for me, seeing that man was like seeing a ghost. The last time I'd seen Craig was forty years ago, in a wheelchair sitting next to Derek in the dock of number 2 Court at the Old Bailey. And then, after Goddard had passed sentence, getting up, waving to his parents and turning away, down the stairs to the cells. He was sixteen. The man I saw on the screen now was nearly bald and he had more hair round his chin than on his head. A neat grey beard. If I'd passed him in the street I wouldn't have turned a hair. Even his voice didn't ring any bells. I didn't remember it being that quiet. But then as I watched him I felt all the hairs on my skin rise up. It was the way his mouth moved that did it. That was the same.

There were things Craig said about Derek in that interview that I didn't like, and I asked if they could take them out. But they said no. They told me that we all see things from our own point of view and that Chris had a right to his. But when he said Derek was streetwise and leery, well, all I can say is, that wasn't the Derek I knew. And when I heard what he had to say, what a dreadful miscarriage of justice it was and how he would do anything to help, I couldn't help thinking, why did he leave it so long? Why couldn't he have talked to us that time when he was still in prison while Mum and Dad were still alive. It would have saved so much pain. And I couldn't stop the tears, even though I knew the camera was rolling.

Forty years ago, Craig had shot a policeman dead and he knew there'd be some who'd find it hard to believe he was telling the truth now. So he had asked Roger if he could be hypnotized or take a lie-detector test so people would know he wasn't lying. They looked into it but they were told hypnosis could be very disturbing emotionally, plus the filming of something so personal would be difficult. They felt they shouldn't put him through the trauma that might involve unless there was no other way. But there was. The lie-detector would do just as well for the television programme.

The real name for a lie-detector is a polygraph. Polygraph tests aren't accepted as evidence in English courts, but they are in some states in America and the British Government uses them all the time for security in places like GCHQ. Like with the interview, the polygraph was done on neutral territory, in a hotel. Roger and Carole couldn't be in the room when it was done. No one could. It had to be just Craig and the man doing the test. All the questions were carefully prepared beforehand. If there was any misunderstanding, it would register. The questions asked included the most important one of did Derek say 'Let him have it, Chris'? They also asked if Derek said anything at all to him on the roof, apart from when Fairfax sent him over to get him to give up the gun, plus a question about was there a third boy involved, plus were there any other guns up on the roof, plus did he fire at Fairfax from six feet away. The answers were no, no, no and no.

According to Roger, waiting outside that room was just like being a prospective father. He spent the half-hour it took for the test to be done pacing around the corridor and puffing on a cigarette. He claims that was the day he started smoking again. Carole doesn't smoke, she drinks coffee instead. For that half-hour she was chain-drinking. She told me afterwards that waiting outside that room she suddenly panicked. What if it had all been a con, what if Craig was lying? If Craig wasn't telling the truth everything they had done for Derek would fall apart, worse, everything I had done over the last forty years would be down the drain. And she told me, and I believe her, that all she could think about when she was waiting for the test to be over was, How am I going to tell Iris if it's all gone wrong?

The way a polygraph works is on heart rate, pulse rate and sweat. When you lie your heart races, your pulse quickens and your hands go sweaty. All the usual signs of fear. Because it is fear. Fear left over from childhood that you're going to be caught out. Even more so when you're strapped on to a machine. So they put one monitor on the heart, one on the pulse and one on a sweat gland in the thumb.

All the questions have to be yes/no answers so they can easily be compared. First they ask things they know are true, like 'Is your name Christopher Craig?' They ask three of these, then they put in one of the questions they need to ask. Then, say, if they get a 'no' answer, they ask another ordinary one that they would expect to have a 'no' answer, like 'Have you ever climbed Everest?' They do that so they can see two 'no' answers side by side. They have to keep on mixing in these ordinary questions all the way through to be able to compare results because as the test goes on, the person doing it gets tenser and the stress levels change.

The polygraph man had been told not to tell any of them the outcome. Not Roger or Carole or Christopher Craig himself. When the test was over the crew went in and set up for filming. Everything was to be the same, the monitors attached to Craig's arm, heart and thumb, the polygraph man asking the same questions, the arm of the machine making its spidery zigzags across the printout paper. Then, when the test was done (the second time Craig had done it, this time for the camera), only then did the polygraph man cross over to Craig and tell him the result, while the cameras rolled and every person in that room held their breath.

'Mr Craig, you have answered all the questions truthfully. And the machine doesn't lie.'

Then Craig said: 'You've made me a very happy man.'

Craig hadn't made that phone call to Thames until June. But Roger and Carole hadn't been sitting around twiddling their thumbs. Derek's statement had been bothering them. It was too much like the police version of what happened and completely different from what they now knew really happened. I always said the language wasn't Derek, but if the bit about a policeman called 'Mac' was a complete invention, what about the rest? That spring Roger read an article in the *Guardian* about a linguistic expert who'd done a test on a statement made by Billy Power, one of the Birmingham Six. The man who'd done it was Malcolm Coulthard of the English Department of Birmingham University. He'd worked out there was no way Billy Power could have made that statement. So Roger and Carole decided to get Dr Coulthard to have a look at Derek's. Everyone has their own speech pattern, just like fingerprints. To find that pattern he had to have something of Derek's to go on and the only thing we had, that was near enough his own words, was the last letter he dictated before he was hanged.

All the business in the trial about Derek not being asked questions, that he just came out with that statement on his own, I always knew that was rubbish. But now it was proved. Dr Coulthard processed it through his computer. Those weren't Derek's words. The statement was written by at least two people and it was written in the form of answers to questions. Dr Coulthard explained that people don't speak in negatives. You don't say 'I was not carrying an umbrella' unless you're asked about whether you were or not. He also said the whole thing was written in police-speak. Normal people start sentences with 'then': like 'Then I did this, then I did that'. But tests they've run on police statements show they put it the other way around: 'I then', like 'I then proceeded in a westerly direction'. Policemen say it like that all the time.

Derek's statement is full of 'I then's.

Immediately they got the results Roger and Carole sent Dr Coulthard's analysis to the Home Office to add to the rest of the stuff they'd already sent. As usual, they had an acknowledgement, then that was it. Silence.

The film company had worked quickly and *Let Him Have It* had its première at the Edinburgh Film Festival on 21 August 1991. Carole and Roger still hadn't given up hope that their new evidence would be in the film. They'd done everything: sent the production company Vivid a copy of the programme, said they would write new stuff. They didn't want to be paid for it, they just wanted the truth to come out.

'Once it's in a film, then that's what people would believe had really happened.'

Films are like that. Especially when they're good, they seem real. Although they'd sent them a copy of the first programme even before filming started, when Vivid finally got around to coming clean, after I pushed and pushed them on the phone, they said it was too late to change anything. Even then I didn't give up. What about some kind of statement at the end of the film? Something like 'Since making this film new evidence has come to light that Derek Bentley did not say the words "Let him have it, Chris".' But no. Nothing.

The film festival is part of the main Edinburgh Festival and that summer there were two shows about Derek's case being done on the fringe.

Although a film should by rights be more real, for me plays are more powerful. A film doesn't draw you in like a play does, it pushes you away. It's something to do with theatre being live, with there being real people up there on the stage. They're living it, and you can through them. I can look around at these young people's faces and see that they are with me. All joining together. Like Peter Murphy said about *Example* all those years ago, they don't let facts get in the way of the truth. And it does feel like the truth and every time I watch a play I'm taken back and relive those days, those feelings.

The first play was called *Nine Bells for Bentley*. It was done by students at Exeter University. The one whose idea it was, Simon McCleave, had rung me in the spring. He'd read the paperback of David Yallop's book. As he came from south London, Wimbledon, and was about the same age as Derek, that's what had got him interested. He came to see me a couple of times and was for ever afterwards on the phone, checking up on things. Then in about July he came with the main actors to see me at Colliers Wood. *Nine Bells for Bentley* all focused on Derek. You saw things through his eyes. You heard his thoughts about what was going on. The play started in the condemned cell and then the story was told in flashback.

Not long after, I got a call from Mei Trow. He'd heard about another play that was being done at the Edinburgh Festival and he thought I should give the writer a call. These ones called themselves the Telling Tales Theatre Company and they were in Wakefield. These weren't students, just the opposite, they were teachers at University College, Bretton Hall. It's not a drama school, there the students do a degree in drama. There were really only three of them. Although they all now live up in the north, David Bromley, the writer and the only actor, comes from London and he told me how when he was little, his father would always talk to him about Derek's case. He said he'd been brought up with this sense of injustice. *Blue Murder* was quite different from *Nine Bells*. It isn't a play where

306

there are different actors for different characters. It's more like a monologue with songs. The story is told through Dad's eyes. The other two on stage are musicians and they sing the songs. The main musician was Andrew Mullins, but the one who wrote the music was Gifford Rolfe. He'd got interested in Derek's case with his father being a policeman. He says he was brought up on stories about it. So strange. Two young men who were not even alive when Derek was hanged.

They'd already done the play in Leeds. But there was a lot they didn't know about Derek and after that phone call with David, they added in the things I told them. They told me it changed dramatically as a result.

The BBC got to hear about *Blue Murder* through Mei Trow and what with the film being shown in Edinburgh at the same time, they decided to do a programme about it. David Bromley had told them about me helping them and they arranged for me to go up there and see the plays, and do an interview on their daily festival programme called *Edinburgh Nights*.

I flew up on 15 August and that night I went to see *Nine Bells for Bentley* at the Bedlam Theatre. I remember the name because of the park near the Elephant and Castle we used to go to with Dad. Simon McCleave had shown me the script, but I'd not seen it acted before. It was very moving. The way they did it, they do the execution, so I did what I often do, sat at the back and left before the end. But I heard the nine bells. The day after I went, Prince Edward went to see it. He told Simon he thought it was 'very thought provoking'. After the first two nights it was sold out and it went on to win a *Guardian* Drama Award.

The next night I went to see *Blue Murder*. That was at another place just round the corner from Bedlam. Like with *Lullaby for Mrs Bentley* which they did at the King's Head, it's the songs that I remember. Because with the music and the rhymes they do stick in your mind. *Blue Murder* is very political. The 'blue' in the title is referring to the police. Every time I see it (and I've seen it three times now) I see Dad. I will never forget what living through those terrible weeks felt like for me, but in *Blue Murder* I can begin to understand what it must have felt like for Dad and it nearly breaks my heart.

There was some talk of me staying on for the première in Edinburgh of *Let Him Have It*, but the film people had organized interviews and things back in London and there wasn't time. It wasn't to have its première until October but the publicity people had me well booked up.

But I heard what happened. David Bromley, who did *Blue Murder*, went along to see it (it was only shown that one night) and, at the end when they asked for any questions, he had a go at Peter Medak for all the things they'd got wrong. I wish I'd been there, but I'd only have had to keep my mouth shut. It was all the things I'd told them about, and they wouldn't listen.

The worst was the trial. The film had us all sitting in there in court, listening. I'd told them often enough we were outside. It's not that they didn't know. Even in Alan Clark's film for the BBC in 1972 they'd done us waiting outside. Their usual excuse was saying that they changed things for the sake of drama, but to my way of thinking, Mum, Dad and me all sitting in a row in the corridor while they lied Derek's life away, is more than drama. It's farce. And it was the truth.

And then there was all the business of the shoot-out on the roof. It was like an old American gangster film.

But perhaps the worst was they were so determined to keep the business of Derek saying 'Let him have it', which by now there was evidence he never said, that they not only kept it in, but *invented* a whole scene in the court where they talk about what it meant. Did it mean 'shoot him', or did it mean 'give him the gun'? It was never talked about in court. It couldn't have been because Derek always said he didn't say it. So if he said he didn't say it, there was no point the defence counsel talking about what he meant by it. It was only ever the press who cottoned on to this. What was worse was that calling the film this, having Derek say the line in the film, inventing this scene in the court, was sure to leave people thinking that he did

308

say it. And that's the only reason he was hanged, because of those words. *And he didn't say them*.

As David Bromley said, it was building on popular mythology. Mythology's no good when it comes to getting a free pardon. The facts are what counts. And what counts is that Derek didn't say those words. If people go on believing that Derek said those words, they'll go on believing that he might have been encouraging Craig. And if he *was* encouraging Craig, by the law of the day he would have been guilty. And of course all this plays right into the hands of the Government. They would be quite happy for everyone to go on thinking he'd said it. It would mean no one would pressure them for a pardon.

The other thing that David got at Peter Medak for was what he called 'the betrayal of William Bentley'. David felt he'd come to understand Dad through doing the play, and he said the film made him out to be weak, which he wasn't. I agree. Although I'm not saying Tom Courtenay, who played Dad in the film, isn't a very good actor, he just wasn't given the right words to show the metal that Dad was made of. My father was like a lion. He fought for Derek with every breath in his body.

It says it all in *Blue Murder*, in the last verse of one of the songs:

> Well, I won't rest till the truth is told
> And your name it has been cleared
> But there is no justice, just the law
> And the law must be revered
> It'll soon be over swift and sure
> Your young life will be gone
> But good or bad, the truth is sad
> They killed this father's son.

To my mind they also killed that son's father.

On 1 September 1991 the second *Thames Reports* programme went out. It was called *The Murder of Derek Bentley*. The interview with Craig was a major scoop and the papers were full of it. The morning before it was broadcast, Thames did a screening and a

309

press conference and I saw it through for the first time. It was still only Thames TV, local to London, but after the screening, the word got about, and most regional ITV stations scrapped their programming at the last minute and ran *The Murder of Derek Bentley*. They knew it was that important. Like before, Carole and Roger sent all the tests, all the transcripts to the Home Office. In August, we'd heard that Kenneth Baker had set up a police enquiry. But once again Roger told me, 'Keep your feet on the ground.'

But I couldn't help thinking that Derek's pardon must only be round the corner. For years people had known that Derek should never have been hanged, now they could see that he was completely innocent. That he had been stitched up like a kipper. What with the film now and everything else, it was only a question of time.

Sometimes I think people have no feelings. One day in September I was just going somewhere in the tube, on the Northern Line, when I saw this great big poster. It was blank except for the words LET HIM HAVE IT. I didn't really understand. This poster couldn't be for the film because there was no other writing. Nothing about a film at all. Just the words. Then, two days later I was down the tube again, and where the other ones had been, new posters had gone up. Still the same words, but around them this huge noose, and in small letters something about the film. I stood there and shook. I had no one with me. I don't know how I got home. I know I have lived with how Derek died for all these years, but it doesn't make it any easier. I felt sick and I felt very angry. I know they were only doing it to get attention, but they could at least have warned me. It was like the Home Office sending that letter in January 1953 that Derek's reprieve had been turned down by ordinary post. It tells you one thing. You know that, in their eyes, you don't matter. Only what *they* do matters, whether turning down reprieves or advertising films.

On 3 October *Let Him Have It* had its première at the Odeon Leicester Square. For the photographers I had to walk in with Tom Courtenay, who played my Dad. There was a real crowd outside.

But this wasn't the first première I'd been to at the Odeon Leicester Square. Just the first one without my torch. In the old days, when they were short-staffed for a première, a few of us would be sent down from the Streatham Astoria to help out. The last one I did was Elizabeth Taylor and Montgomery Clift in *No Place in the Sun*.

And someone must have told them, because when I arrived the manager presented me with a bouquet which said: 'To one of our former members of staff. We're very proud of you.' And with all those people cheering, it took me right back, to those days of usherettes lining the stairs and the uniforms and the parades. Then someone in the crowd outside started singing 'For She's a Jolly Good Fellow'. And that did it. It was all too much. I was a mass of tears.

I sat at the back of the circle with Carole and Roger. I'd put them on my list and I was determined they should be there, even if Vivid hadn't bothered to listen to what all their research had dug up. I still hoped that the company might have added the bit about the new evidence at the end of the film. But it turns out they hadn't. Surprise, surprise. Not that I saw the end. From seeing all those plays I knew I wouldn't be able to take the last scene. And I still haven't to this day. I went out with Carole and we sat outside till it had finished. We were still sitting there when everyone came out. Usually after a première, everyone is smiling and looking cheerful. Not that night. I've never seen so many blotchy faces.

At first I didn't recognize the man with the children who came up to me and shook my hand. But of course as soon as he spoke, then I did. It was Anthony Andrews, who I'd seen in *Brideshead Revisited*. You could see his children had been crying too. But he said he decided he had to bring them, that it was important that the young people of today and tomorrow knew about Derek's case. And if there was anything he could do to help my campaign, I only had to say the word. There were other faces I recognized too, and it was then that I realized that in spite of all the things that made me angry in the film, if it meant that people like

Anthony Andrews, people who were well known and who ordinary people would listen to, were going to come out for Derek and talk about the terrible injustice that had been done to him, then it was worth it.

CHAPTER TWENTY-SIX

I felt bad that some of my old friends had missed out on the first night. We've known each other since our kids were at school. There used to be about twenty of us but now we're down to about ten, but we always meet up on a Friday night and go down to the community centre round the corner. We still make the effort and dress up. So I called the local Odeon in Wimbledon to see what could be arranged. *Let Him Have It* didn't go on general release till the beginning of November, they said we could all come then. It was great. Just like another première. The manager Malcolm Grimsley even presented me with a bouquet and there was a buffet and drinks all laid on. I was pleased I could say thank you to the friends who've stood by me all these years.

I decided we shouldn't waste all these people coming out of the cinemas crying. The film was all 1950s, but it wasn't history. Not if I could help it. Derek might be dead, but his case was still alive. And what with the election coming up in the spring, a big wave of public support might be just the job to push them over into giving Derek his pardon. They might not give tuppence about Iris Bentley but millions of voters were a different matter. Newspapers and magazines had been full of it over the summer, what with Craig coming out for Derek on the Thames programme and the film, but now all that had died down. I knew I couldn't let it just fade away so I decided on more petitions and getting people to write to the Home Secretary, Kenneth Baker, and I wrote a letter saying this to the *Daily Mail*, which they published.

Another idea was to have T-shirts printed ready for the Tory Party Conference in Blackpool, with 'Let Him Have It, Ken'. I'm a great believer in laughing when you can, seeing the funny side. It's helped me through some dark days. But although it would have got us publicity, in the end I knew that Derek's pardon was no laughing matter. And dignity not humour was my strongest weapon.

The performance that my friends came to in Wimbledon was just an ordinary one that the public came to. Like at Leicester Square, everyone came out crying. Whatever I might feel about the film, Chris Eccleston as Derek is just wonderful. All that he felt for Derek and those epileptics he got to know at Lingfield comes shining through. He might say he's sorry he did the film. But I'm not. Chris's performance is what makes it for me. No one can take that away from him.

As we were standing in the foyer handing out petition forms, a German couple came up. They were still in tears when they started speaking. They were in England on holiday.

'We only thought Hitler did things like this. You wouldn't believe it could happen here.'

They said I must keep on with the fight against capital punishment because it could all too easily come back again. I was very moved. What with their broken English and their tears, with people like that I know that I must never give up. Maria and I went there every night that week and although, like I said, I couldn't agree with how they'd done it, I saw what an effect the film had. People were often too distressed to sign. The one word that I heard over and over again was 'how'. How could they do that? How?

After Wimbledon came New York. I didn't want to go. Who was going to look after my cats? Who was going to feed Uncle? And London is my home. But Maria persuaded me. She was dead keen to go. Also, after seeing how people reacted to the film in London, I knew I had to do it. The film people might be using me, but I could use them just as well. How else would people in America know that Derek never said those words?

Let Him Have It opened in New York on 3 December but we started the interviews before. I remember somebody once saying there's no such thing as a free lunch. Well, there's no such thing as a free trip to America. I never stopped working. Radio shows, television appearances. It was all set up by the press agent, Jeff. I knew it had to be done but answering the same questions over and over again is tiring. Especially when these interviewers haven't done their homework. They might have read a press release, but they hadn't any real knowledge. So it came like I had to ask myself questions so as to bring out the important points. I think they were more nervous than I was. At least I knew what I was talking about, plus they were worried what I might say against the police. Libel and suchlike. But I wasn't. I don't care if anyone does sue me. Just let them try. Because the defence to libel is the truth.

Maria came with me to New York but she only had five days off work before she had to go back. We managed to do a bit of sightseeing and shopping. I say shopping but I didn't get to buy anything. At Tiffany's Maria fancied a money-holder. But as I pointed out, if she'd bought it she wouldn't have had any money to put in it.

The hotel we were staying in was like something out of a film. Our suite was huge. Bigger than the whole house in Colliers Wood. It was overlooking Central Park. Although we had this stretch limo which the publicity people had laid on, on the second day Maria decided she wanted to try a yellow cab. So we did. I hadn't realized how safe the limo made me feel, being with that driver who knew us. Suddenly there was this man who drove like he'd never had driving lessons. Plus he didn't speak any English as I understood it. The cab took us somewhere, but we were soon lost. All those skyscrapers, packed in together like playing cards, make London's look like try-outs. Going up to Oxford Street's bad enough for me. And what with all those films, and everything I'd heard, I began to wish I'd stayed in Colliers Wood.

We found our way back in the end, but we were late, and there were interviews to be done. Jeff was hopping mad. When Maria handed over the receipts for the day (the company were paying for everything) he went green.

Next stop was Hollywood, but now I was on my own. MGM had their own private jet. It was smaller than a normal plane, but apart from the pilot and the stewardess it was just Peter Medak and me. Talk about leg-room. Everything was served up on silver plates, with big silver rose-bowls full of roses. I felt like a queen. After

New York I was dead tired but Peter kept waking me up to see something outside the window, like the Rocky Mountains.

They put me in the Hotel Bel Air, the famous Hollywood hotel on Sunset Boulevard where Howard Hughes lived in the penthouse suite, not washing, not shaving, not being seen by anybody for years and years. The Bel Air was very old-fashioned. But nice. Where I stayed they called the Marilyn Monroe suite. I would have called it a flat. It had a lounge, a dining-room, a dressing-room, a make-up room, even a kitchen with fitted cupboards. It looked just like a set from *I Love Lucy*. Plus of course a huge bedroom with all these doors to the different corridors and wardrobes. My clothes didn't even fill half a one. As for the bed it was bigger than my whole bedroom back in London. Every night the right-hand side would be turned down, the side by the phone. But I always sleep on the left, and I saw no reason to change just because I was in America. But, although I was there for two weeks, they never seemed to notice where I slept and still folded it down the phone side.

More openings, more interviews. More faces that I knew I should know the names of, but didn't. There was one actor from *Baywatch* that Jill the publicity agent said I should watch out for. He was giving me the eye, she said. Maybe he was. But I'm too old for all that, Hollywood or no. 'Go to bed mistress and wake up master.' That's what I say. Not that I didn't enjoy myself.

But just like in New York, Hollywood was work, work, work. In Los Angeles there were five openings. I didn't watch the film. Not again. It was just too painful. After it was over they'd put a chair in the centre of the stage, and I'd come on and they'd ask me questions and I'd answer in the usual way. Well, not quite the usual way. In some states in America they still have capital punishment so the message I had to give was even more important. And how can they justify it? If it was a deterrent why was America the murder capital of the world? It's not a deterrent because they don't think they're going to get caught. And most of them aren't. But that's the

316

real deterrent. Make them believe they're going to get caught, whatever the crime, and the crime rate would come down. And then there's the guns. I feel so strongly that guns should be banned. And I think they listened to me. After all, Derek died because of a gun. By the end I'd become quite professional. When I think back to those plays Joan and I used to do on the carts outside in the courtyard of the George in the Borough High Street, or even those parades at the Astoria to check whether our seams were straight, who'd have thought then that I'd ever be speaking in front of thousands of people in Hollywood.

I did get a bit of time off. I had to do the stars. None of my friends in Colliers Wood would have forgiven me if I hadn't done a tour of their homes. We went in this hearse. The canyons of Beverly Hills are beautiful. But although this house and that one were pointed out, you couldn't see much for all the high walls and gates. I wouldn't want to live like that. Peter Medak lives in Hollywood now and just across the road from him is the house Marilyn Monroe lived in when she was just getting started. Now that I could have managed. Smallish and ordinary looking with a bushy hedge in the front.

Although it was December it was baking hot. It being Christmas seemed all wrong. Over there they don't only deck their privet hedges up with fairy lights, these big houses had giant-sized Father Christmases, at least ten foot high, with teams of reindeer in the front gardens. Huge they were. They looked like painted clay, but knowing the Americans they were probably some kind of plastic. One lot I remember had the reindeers' legs moving back and forward. That sort of thing might be all right on Blackpool pier, but here it all seemed so false, so shallow, and all it made me do was cry and want to come back home.

I was in America for three weeks all told. By the time I was back in London I was shattered. But I know it was worth it in the end. The film people said my being there had made all the difference and the film was 'doing great business'. I got back on Christmas Eve.

Thank goodness for Marks. We rushed out to the one on Tooting Broadway and got everything we needed, even the sprouts were washed and peeled, all ready for Christmas Day.

Christmas came and went. We were very quiet that year. I'd had enough partying to last me a lifetime. There was still no word from the Home Office. But surely, they had to do something soon. It was six months now since Kenneth Baker had instigated an inquiry by Scotland Yard, and since then there had been the Thames interview with Craig and the polygraph test. Surely it must come soon.

Not long before 28 January, Carole heard through a contact of hers that Kenneth Baker was about to make an announcement. Scotland Yard had finished their inquiry and the results had been passed to John Patten, then a junior Home Office minister. Carole had been told by her 'source' that the police had recommended a pardon. But like she always did Carole warned me not to raise my hopes.

'Just remember, keep your feet on the ground, Iris. And don't say a word. No one likes to be pressured, least of all Home Secretaries.'

All we knew for definite was a written answer when John Patten had said the Bentley case was receiving urgent consideration and he hoped to act soon.

Over the years I've learnt when to keep quiet. I've had to. And what happened next just shows what can go wrong if you go shouting your mouth off. Somebody talked to the press. On Sunday, 26 January the *Observer* ran a front-page story with the headline 'Baker ready to pardon Bentley after Yard plea'.

I knew nothing about this story. They'd sent a nice photographer around to do my picture in front of Wandsworth Prison, nearly a week before the 28th. He spent quite a long time with me. But I'd just thought it would be the usual thing. It wasn't. According to Carole's source, Kenneth Baker was livid. He wasn't going to be told what to do, so he did nothing.

Before Christmas *Thames Reports* had been doing a programme

318

about Brixton Prison and Roger and Carole got word that the police would like 'a quiet word' with them. They met in a wine bar. The man was involved in the Bentley inquiry and he warned them that although he agreed the whole thing stank, there was a possibility Derek wouldn't get the pardon because it was too political.

In May there was an auction at Christie's of something called the Forman Archive of Crime and Punishment. It included some things that had belonged to the Pierrepoint family of hangmen, including Albert Pierrepoint's book, where he wrote down everything about every hanging he'd ever done. Plus his briefcase with everything in it. It was the most ghoulish, disgusting collection you can imagine. The catalogue was bad enough with pictures of horrible things like birching tables and guillotines and details of the documents, all written down so matter of fact.

The reserve price for Pierrepoint's 'leather briefcase' was £12,000–£15,000. Toolbag would have been a better description. He must have sold it and the execution diary to this man Forman when he retired in 1956. It had in it: 'a hanging rope of official pattern purchased privately by A. Pierrepoint to his own specifications the leather covered noose with rubber non-slip washer and brass fittings by J Edginton official supplier to HMG'. Then there's a shackle and bolt and a 'soft-calf wrist strap with brass buckles inscribed "Albert Pierrepoint Chief Executioner"'. A leather ankle strap. A brass-mounted leather-covered thirty-three foot tape-measure by Dean, used for measuring the drop. A white cotton hood carried by Pierrepoint in his top pocket, pretending it was a handkerchief until he had to put it on. Plus wire, wire cutters, pink thread and waxed thread.

It was disgusting. Something like that should be destroyed. So that's what I decided to do. I don't know how they managed it but Thames Television (not Roger and Carole, they'd left Thames by this time) agreed to bid for me. In return Thames wanted to film me setting fire to the lot. Unfortunately the bidding went too high. The briefcase and the diary went for £45,000. I sat at the back of the sale-room and just felt sick.

But perhaps Pierrepoint knew what I was thinking. Within six weeks he was dead. Whenever I hear that any of those who helped kill my brother have died, I always look up at the sky and say: 'Here they come, Derek.'

Each one of them who's at all guilty of Derek's murder.

'Here they come, Derek.'

And I know he'll be waiting at those gates and they won't be accepted in. But then again, knowing how forgiving my brother was in life, he'll probably let them in anyway.

That July there was a right argy-bargy going on back in Colliers Wood. The quiet road that Mum and Dad moved to in 1963 had long since gone. Now it was part of a one way system with lorries and cars thundering around day and night. The land opposite our house had been bought by Sainsbury's for a big new Savacentre back in 1984. Because it was such a big thing, in 1986 they'd had a public inquiry. It all sounded wonderful. As well as the Savacentre they would do a riverside walk along the River Wandle which was in a terrible state. They'd do up an old mill and make it into a recreation area for the community and, best of all, they'd build a leisure centre, with swimming pool, sports halls and what goes with it. There was a meeting of local residents and I remember standing up and saying to them, 'Don't you believe it. You'll get the Sainsbury's but you won't get the leisure centre.' They didn't believe me. But when you've been around politicians and people whose job it is to make promises as long as I have, you learn. And I've learnt. That was 1986. The years ticked by and the land set aside for the leisure centre was let out to builders merchants for storage. Not only was it an eyesore, but where was that leisure centre? Nowhere. That July we heard that Sainsbury's had changed their mind. There would be no leisure centre. However, the council, without a word to any of the residents, had accepted £750,000 from Sainsbury's, instead. Seven hundred and fifty thousand pounds wouldn't build them a paddling pool.

Maria was by now Deputy Mayor. I never thought I would be prouder than the day she was elected a councillor, but I was. Seeing her in her mayoral chain of office was the proudest day of my life. And Maria threw herself into this business of Sainsbury's. As I said, by now Merton was a Labour council and to their shame it was the Labour council that had taken the Sainsbury shilling. Maria had terrible stick because this time she'd voted with the Conservatives against accepting it. But I was behind her a hundred per cent. Taking that money was a cop-out. So it was back to more campaigning. The usual things, getting petitions signed, posting leaflets through doors, and the job I always get lumbered with, making sandwiches for meetings.

Then, even closer to home, was the business of foxes. Our house is right next to the church. Ever since Mum and Dad moved there in 1963 the bit of the churchyard next to our house had been left wild. It was how everyone liked it. A bit of the country in London. It's just a churchyard, not a graveyard. It used to have a moat round it. Nelson lived up the road and it was his church. History says he went there with Lady Hamilton. There's a tunnel from his house to where she lived. It's a pub now, but it wasn't then. Over the years, where the moat had been was left to grow wild, long grass, wild flowers like forget-me-nots and ox-eye daisies and buddleia and stinging nettles for the butterflies, not to mention blackberries. Not only was it great protection against burglars, but it was where the foxes lived. They'd been there ever since I can remember. Every spring there was always a mother with her new cubs. Over the years it must have been one of the cubs that was the next mother. I don't know how it works in fox families. But they all knew where to come. As well as leftovers, I would buy chicken wings from Tooting market, £2.50 for ten pounds, which lasted quite a long time. I knew raw chicken can be dangerous, so I always cooked it thoroughly. I didn't want them getting diseased. They were so beautiful and so tame the vixen would come up and eat out of my hands. But now there was a new vicar and he'd brought with him a new broom. And then it started. Hacking the trees back, cutting all the blackberries down. As soon as I saw what was happening I tried to stop it. I rang, I wrote. Nothing made any difference. He said it was a mess and needed tidying up. Not long afterwards I was burgled. And the foxes have completely disappeared.

It doesn't surprise me. That vicar was new. He didn't know I'd been a churchgoer all my life until just before he came in 1992. But it was nothing to do with him, and for once it was nothing to do with Derek or being a Bentley. It was to do with Chris Bennett, a friend of mine I'd known for years. She'd done everything for that church. But she fell out with them and that was it. I suddenly saw the Church for what it was, a hiding place for hypocrites. I don't know why it took me so long to see, but I do now. Going to church is not Christianity. Christianity is what you do in life, not parading every Sunday with your Bible out in front of you. And though some churchgoers are good Christians, there are too many who aren't. Anyway, God is to big for churches. He is everywhere. And I know he listens to me, wherever I speak to him. And I know he listened to Derek, even from the condemned cell.

It was now August 1992. Parliament was in recess, so we knew there'd be no word from the Home Secretary on Derek until after the Queen's speech in November.

But we were wrong. The first I knew was the phone ringing and ringing downstairs, pulling me out of a dream. Who could be ringing me at this time of the morning?

'Iris, it's Roger.'

'Bit early, isn't it.'

'Have you heard the radio?'

'Roger, it's six o'clock in the morning. I'm still asleep.'

'It was on Radio Four. They say Kenneth Clarke's going to make an announcement today. Iris, I think this might be it.'

It was the morning of 1 October. It was still only six fifteen. I made myself a cup of tea, then I couldn't wait any longer and I called Ben Birnberg, my solicitor. He knew nothing. But he said he'd keep in touch. Roger had said it was on Radio 4, so I switched on *Today*. It was about eight o'clock when Kenneth Clarke came on. I couldn't sit down, just pacing up and down with one cup of tea after another. It must be all right. He sounded so chirpy, even jokey with the interviewer. Said he mustn't be impatient, that they would all hear in good time.

'I can't say anything yet. It's always been understood that Iris Bentley would be the first to know.'

Then the phone started ringing. First Ben, then Roger again. Then Ben called when he'd got to the office, he'd heard officially from the Home Office. The letter would be sent round before the press conference started. I should get there by half-past twelve.

The phone didn't stop ringing, every journalist, every newspaper, every television programme, the road outside was blocked by vans. They were even in the kitchen filming me holding a bottle of champagne that Dad had put in the fridge in 1972. It was Moët et Chandon, but you could only just read the label it was so wrinkled and old. I still hadn't got dressed. As I walked up the stairs I realized the cameras were still running and they were following me.

'That's as far as you go. No one's going to watch me getting dressed. Not even Jeremy Paxman.'

I was shaking so much I don't know how I got my make-up on while downstairs I had a houseful of journalists, crashing around and with mobile phones ringing. Needless to say there was no shortage of volunteers to take me to London Bridge. I ended up going with a reporter from the BBC. Even then there was no let-up. The cameraman sat in front and stuck his camera a foot from my nose as we went along. We left the car in Borough Market and walked the rest of the way. When they saw us coming, the mob descended. It was like football supporters after a World Cup goal. They went mad. Traffic was heavy and cars and lorries had to screech to a halt as this pack of journalists just surged across the road like hounds who've got the scent of blood. Some of the photographers had step-ladders and just stood them up where they were, as if they were pruning apple trees in the middle of the road. Ben was waiting for me outside the office. Somehow we managed to push through.

Then all we had to do was wait. Ben, me, Roger and Carole. I felt sick. All knotted up inside. Inside me this voice just saying,

'Please God, let it work out right. Please let Derek have his pardon. I know you can hear me. Please tell me I've got it this time.' And I'm saying to Derek, 'I've really tried, and this time, surely, this time, I've got it. But if I haven't I won't give up.'

But as I was saying all this inside my head, I began to know, just know deep down in my heart of hearts, that Kenneth Clarke was not going to do it. I knew before the messenger came, I knew, because I knew Kenneth Clarke. I'd fought Kenneth Clarke on the picket line in the nurses dispute, when he was Minister of Health. He was so pompous and full of himself. If he couldn't see what the nurses were fighting for, how could he see what I was fighting for? I knew for definite when I heard Carole's voice trail away. Although it was a shock, it wasn't as big a shock as it might have been.

As Roger took my arm and we walked down to meet the press, I knew then that even had the Queen of England been on my side, Kenneth Clarke wouldn't have listened. It's simple really. Him and the others, they're no better than children. They know they've done a wrong but they can't bring themselves to admit to it. They haven't learnt that you have to be a grown-up to admit you've done wrong and to say sorry and mean it. I know because I've come up against the Kenneth Clarkes of this world before. The Bentleys have come up against so many Kenneth Clarkes now, that all they do is make me want to fight even harder, to think that they still can't see the damage they've done.

CHAPTER TWENTY-SEVEN

No one could believe it. Everyone was shell-shocked. The papers, the radio, the television, it was all anyone talked about that night. And the next morning. In the *Guardian* alone there were three different articles, and in the *Mail*. Derek Bentley not getting the pardon kicked everything else off the front page.

And that's why Kenneth Clarke did it. Nothing to do with the evidence. Nothing to do with compassion. Everything to do with politics. Just like in 1953. The next day Tony Blair, shadow Home Secretary, had his big speech on crime at the Labour Party Conference. What could Kenneth Clarke come up with that would take the spotlight off Tony Blair and on to him? What about that question of a pardon that's been sitting in the pending tray for months? What about Derek Bentley? His sister Iris is always good for a headline. But to pardon, or not to pardon, that is the question. To pardon will get you smiles, not to pardon will get you applause at the Tory Party Conference next week. No contest. It was obvious. You don't need any insider information to work it out. Just outsider knowledge of politicians.

Kenneth Clarke, Maxwell-Fyfe. Spot the difference. It was 1953 all over again. Fear of setting a precedent, fear of being soft on crime, the Police Federation on his back. In the *Daily Mail* a police spokesman said: 'We believe the conviction of Bentley was correct, and we are pleased that Mr Clarke has rejected the totally unfounded allegations that police gave false evidence at the trial.'

Mr Tough would show them he wouldn't pander to public opinion, excepting of course the opinion of the party faithful at the Tory conference the next week.

There was no other reason for a decision that October morning. It's not as if we were pushing the Home Office for an answer. Pushing the Home Office is like pushing a bus uphill. It's more likely to roll backwards and crush your foot. And God knows, I was used to waiting. I'd waited forty years. As far as everyone told me nothing was going to happen till after Parliament reopened in November.

But this anger came later. That day, that evening, that night, I felt I'd been kicked downstairs, just like they kicked Derek. They did for Derek because he didn't understand. But there's nothing wrong with my brain. And I'm a fighter. Down, I might have been. But unfortunately for Mr Clarke, not out.

Because the way he did it, Kenneth Clarke was a bit too clever. Instead of a 'Dear Miss Bentley, sorry but it's all so long ago and no one can remember, sorry, tough. Yours sincerely' kind of letter, clever Mr Clarke went into clever detail. Too clever by half.

John Parris, Craig's barrister, spotted it straight away, and was on the phone to Ben. We should go for Judicial Review, he said.

Judicial Review is like an appeal court for decisions made by officialdom. It's the last resort for challenging decisions made by Government departments, or local authorities – things like that, when you think you've been wronged. If you wanted to challenge an immigration decision then you would go for Judicial Review. Or even planning decisions, bypasses and suchlike. William Rees-Mogg used it when he wanted to challenge the Government's right to sign the Maastricht Treaty a year or so back. Someone to do with Bart's used it to challenge the decision to close the hospital down. Judicial Review looks at whether the right things were taken into account to reach the decision that's being challenged, whether the proper procedures were followed, whether it was lawful, whether it was a decision a reasonable person would have reached (for example not someone who was mad or drunk at the time).

Kenneth Clarke had given me a sixteen-page explanation of why he wasn't giving Derek his pardon.

> In my judgement most of the concern that has arisen about this case reflects strong feelings that Derek Bentley should not have been hanged. Personally I have always agreed with that concern

but I cannot now simply substitute my judgement on that for that of the then Home Secretary Sir David Maxwell-Fyfe. However much many of us may now disagree with the decision to allow the execution to proceed, the sentence passed was the only one available for the offence of which Derek Bentley was convicted.

So, even Kenneth Clarke thought Derek should never have been hanged. So why couldn't he give him a posthumous pardon?

It has been the long established policy of successive Home Secretaries that a free Pardon in relation to a conviction for an indictable offence should be granted only if the moral as well as technical innocence of the convicted person can be established.

And that's where Ben Birnberg and John Parris reckoned Clarke had overstretched himself. From their reading of things, that was not the right way of looking at it.

So, back to court again. Although it had been debated in the House of Lords in 1971 we had never been able to take Derek's case to court, not since he was alive and that farce at the Court of Appeal.

But going to court costs money. Having no money except my old-age pension, by rights I could get Legal Aid. But like I found out with my leg, being poor is not enough. They have to be convinced the case is worth doing and you've got a chance of winning.

So the first thing Ben did was to get Legal Aid. Not for the Judicial Review itself, but just to apply for Judicial Review. Because Judicial Review, like with an ordinary appeal, isn't open to just anyone. You have to get leave to apply for it. With lawyers the clock starts ticking the moment you walk in the door. And Legal Aid, even if you get it, only pays for work done after it's been awarded to you. No matter how much work has gone on before, it's not backdated. The Legal Aid people turned me down. Not because I was too rich, not because the case didn't merit it, but because they didn't see the point of me bringing it at all. They didn't see the point because they said it wasn't as if I would make any money out of it if I won.

Money? Since when has money ever had anything to do with it? All I've ever wanted is justice, not money. And justice is above the price of diamonds.

Ben could appeal against that decision to refuse me Legal Aid, but the problem was time being so short. You have to apply for leave to go for Judicial Review within three months of the decision you are challenging. The three months was up at the end of 1992. Because we'd waited to get the Legal Aid (which I now hadn't got anyway) time was running out. But we were saved by David Pannick, the QC who had written the opinion on my case for the Legal Aid people. He was so angry with the decision not to give me Legal Aid that he offered to do all the work drawing up the court documents for free. Unlike Ben, David Pannick doesn't specialize in 'radical' cases. He specializes in Judicial Review cases and, as all of them involve public bodies, most of the time he worked for the Government. I was so lucky to get him, not to mention his doing it for nothing.

By now everyone was working together. Roger Corke went through the evidence with David Pannick and Ben. Roger still reckoned, as we all did, that Kenneth Clarke hadn't taken a blind bit of notice of the new evidence. But in the end they agreed Judicial Review wasn't the right place to get involved with all that. Kenneth Clarke had refused Derek's pardon on a technicality. We'd get him on a technicality. What Judicial Review does is look at the technicalities of decision-making. And they had decided that Kenneth Clarke had made the decision based on a false premise.

We might not have got the pardon, but we did get something out of Kenneth Clarke that morning in October. Since Carole and Roger's talk with the man involved with the Scotland Yard inquiry, we'd had a better idea of what documents existed and Ben had been pushing the Home Office to let him have them, particularly the

1972 secret inquiry, and the Cabinet papers which would show Churchill's part in it all. Also what the Scotland Yard inquiry that Kenneth Baker instigated had turned up. Up until then all I'd been asking to see was 'documents relating to Derek Bentley, deceased'. They'd come back with either no, or please be more specific. But if you don't know what there is, how can you be specific? Ben had been pushing and pushing and in his last long letter to Kenneth Clarke in July he'd threatened to go for Judicial Review for withholding documents, if they didn't let him see the papers.

It worked. At the end of Kenneth Clarke's letter he said he was going to make public documents that had been kept secret till now. Documents to do with Derek that I had been fighting to have released for years.

Usually Government papers are held for thirty years. Thirty years after the last bit of paper gets put in the file. Very convenient, especially if new bits are added every few years, it could go on and on for ever. But in one of these letters from the Home Office, they told me that the documents to do with Derek's case would not be available for *seventy-five* years, because it was a 'capital case' and because of the 'sensitivity of issues involved'. Sensitivity doesn't strike me as anything the Home Office have ever been much bothered with. What really needled Ben was the hypocrisy of it all, especially with all the trumpeting about Open Government that William Waldegrave was doing at the time.

The White Paper on Open Government was finally published in July 1993. There's still no mention there of seventy-five years. The only categories set out for 'sensitivity' in the White Paper are: security and intelligence material; civil and home defence material; atomic energy pre-1956 material; atomic energy post-1956; and personal records of civil servants. Where is Derek Bentley in that?

The White Paper says that if records are withheld a reason must be given: administrative; national security; international affairs; material given in confidence; personal sensitivity (would substantially distress or endanger persons affected by disclosure or their descendants).

329

Who would be distressed by the release of Derek's documents apart from me?

The Code of Practice says that the Home Office should meet 'reasonable requests for information relating to the policies, actions or decisions of department and public authorities within the scope of the Code'.

But what will that mean for me when the list of exemptions includes proceedings of Cabinet and Cabinet committees? Nobody knows the truth of how much Winston Churchill was involved. But it must be there, in the Cabinet papers.

As well as putting some general correspondence in the public record office at Kew, mostly things from Derek's time at Kingswood, and the typed police statements, Kenneth Clarke released with his sixteen-page explanation copies of five important documents which until then no one had seen. They prove that Maxwell-Fyfe went against everyone's advice except Goddard's. When I read them, they turned my stomach. They were all written during that terrible time between 12 December 1952 and 27 January 1953.

The first document was from Lord Goddard, both the trial judge at Derek's trial and Lord Chief Justice of England. It was to Maxwell-Fyfe. But the Home Secretary, like any politician, doesn't make decisions in the dark, he gets advice from people in the know. Goddard later said to his biographer, Fenton Bresler, that he never expected Derek to hang. Well, that was rubbish. By then he was ninety-three and it was just an old man backtracking when he knew he had to meet his maker any minute. This letter of Goddard's to Maxwell-Fyfe makes it perfectly clear he wanted Derek to hang. The jury had recommended mercy, so he had to say something about that.

I have no doubt the reason for their recommendation was that they realised that a capital sentence could not be passed on Craig whom they probably regarded as the worst of the two. So far as merits were concerned, I regret to say I could find no mitigating circumstances in Bentley's case. He was armed with a knuckle-

330

duster of the most formidable type that I have ever seen and also
with a sharp pointed knife and he called out to Craig when he
was arrested to start the shooting.

The next document Clarke released was a long explanation of
the trial, plus other cases that Philip Allen, who was Permanent
Under Secretary at the Home Office, thought were relevant. It
included extra police evidence, not used at the trial, to show that
Derek probably knew that Craig had a gun. But even with this extra
information, Philip Allen came to the conclusion that Derek should
be reprieved.

A separate typewritten memorandum confirms this. 'The balance
of argument is in favour of a reprieve.' Underneath are various
people's handwriting. The first is Sir Frank Newsom, the Permanent
Secretary, Maxwell-Fyfe's chief adviser. It says: 'My own view is
towards leniency.'

But at the bottom, in thick black pen, above the initials
D. M. F. are the words 'Let the law take its course'. This was the
third document.

The fourth is a summary of the arguments for and against
pardoning Derek. There were nine points against a reprieve and
twelve points for. This was drawn up by Sir Frank Newsom on 20
January 1953.

The last document is Maxwell-Fyfe's final decision. Although he
says 'Craig was the worst offender of the two', he goes on:

> It was a very bad murder, involving the death of a police officer,
> committed at a time when there is much public anxiety about the
> numbers of crimes of violence. Many of these crimes of violence
> are committed by young persons and I must pay regard to the
> deterrent effect which the carrying out of the sentence in this case
> would be likely to have. If Craig had been of an age when he
> could have been executed, the sentence would have been carried
> out in his case and there would have been no grounds for
> interfering with the sentence against Bentley. It would be

dangerous to give the impression that an older adolescent could escape the full penalty by using an accomplice of less than 18 years of age. I feel also that it is important to protect the unarmed police.

After anxiously weighting all these considerations, and after consulting the trial judge, I have come to the conclusion that there are not sufficient grounds to justify me in recommending any interference with the due course of the law.

I have therefore decided that the law must take its course.'

John Parris went to see Maxwell-Fyfe the night before Derek was hanged. He went with Anne Clark, as she then was, and Barbara Castle. The Home Secretary told them then that no matter what they said, Derek would hang. And he gave them the reasons. Reasons he never gave Parliament, reasons he never even put into a memorandum to the Home Office. First there was Goddard, who pressed him to ensure Derek was hanged.

'Secondly, he said that if he reprieved Bentley he would have the whole of the Cabinet at his throat, led by Churchill.

'Thirdly, he would have a near insurrection in the police force on his hands.

'Finally, if he did reprieve Bentley, gangs of youths would roam the country, with those under sixteen armed and willing to kill police officers who stood in their way.'

At the end of the meeting John Parris says that, as Maxwell-Fyfe packed up his briefcase for the night, the last night of Derek's life, he added:

'Everything you have urged in Bentley's favour, his feeble-mindedness, his illiteracy, his epilepsy and so on, merely goes to confirm the conclusion that I had already come to. He is a young man that society can well do without.'

When I read about the extra police evidence the Home Office had that Derek probably knew that Craig usually went around with a gun, I thought about it very carefully. Even if he did – and with what I've found out since about boys collecting guns and swapping them at school and all that, he might have done – there was still no reason for Derek to think Craig would have used it. Because when Craig was interviewed for the television programme (but a part not shown on the programme) he told Carole that the week before the rooftop siege, when he went with Norman Parsley and robbed the people who had the greengrocer's shop where Philip Stevens worked, he'd tried to persuade Derek to go along with them. But when Derek heard how they were planning to take guns, he refused to have anything to do with it. I think that's what the argument was about that Denis overheard the day before that terrible night. Derek hated violence. Cats, dogs, birds, insects. My brother wouldn't hurt a fly.

A few weeks later we got hold of the other papers released. As I say, mostly to do with Kingswood and all the typed police statements. One was very interesting. It was written by PC Lowe. It was interesting first because it backed up Claude Pain's version of events and second because, by the time PC Lowe gave evidence in court, he had changed his story to fit in with the rest. In his long letter going through why he was turning down Derek's pardon, Kenneth Clarke said about PC Pain's evidence: 'It can only be said that Mr Pain's present account does not accord with any of the contemporary evidence as to the events of that night.' With any of the contemporary *police* evidence would be more like it. Or now, contemporary *police* evidence, *except PC Lowe's*. When Carole and Roger asked Claude Pain about the 'statement' he was supposed to have made at the time, he said it wasn't the statement that he wrote. It was forged. The thing about the truth, what really happened, is that you never forget. Especially when it changed your life, like it did for Claude Pain.

The next thing we had to do was to appeal against my being refused Legal Aid. It was on Tuesday, 1 December. Roger came and spoke up for me as well as Ben. But it did no good. They called Ben the next day to say they'd turned me down. Meanwhile David

Pannick was getting all the papers together anyway. On 2 December Pannick presented all the papers for leave to go for Judicial Review to Mr Justice Popplewell. And that was turned down as well.

'I have grave doubts as to whether the decision can be challenged under Judicial Review.'

No Legal Aid. No leave to apply for Judicial Review. It seemed to me that the doors that had been closed in 1953 were now well and truly glued shut. So if the keys wouldn't work, we'd just have to push and shove and kick the door down.

By this time Carole and Roger had contacted the witnesses in their programmes and discovered that Kenneth Clarke saying at the press conference 'we have gone through everything and we have approached people who are approachable to get their information' was rubbish. They couldn't approach Claude Pain because by now it was too late. He was dead. But most of the other witnesses hadn't been contacted either. Not a phone call, not a letter. Not the police, not the Home Office. All of them were incensed. After all they now knew they wanted the right to put the record straight. They felt it was like 1953 all over again. They were witnesses. They had evidence. They were not called.

Carole and Roger decided this warranted one more programme. Thames TV had lost its franchise the year before and by this time had packed up. Roger was working for a documentary programme called *Storyline* run by Carlton, the company who had taken over from Thames, and they agreed to do it.

It was made in record quick time. It had to be. It was just fate that *Storyline* had a half-hour empty slot on 11 February, and it was fate that Carole had a week's break in her schedule up where she was working for the BBC in Norfolk. When I heard how fate seemed to be working for us, I remembered when Maria was born, the midwife saying, 'Don't give up. Just one more push.'

The day before the programme went out, on 10 February, David Pannick had another chance to get leave to apply for Judicial Review. The rule is if the application is turned down just on the papers, you can try again, using the same papers but presenting the case with a hearing in court. There were three judges, with the main one being Lord Justice Watkins. This was very lucky as the judgement David Pannick was using as precedent – somebody called Foster, who had been given a pardon – was Lord Justice Watkins's own judgement. Carole and Roger sat at the back of the court. Roger was a bag of nerves. When we finally left, the floor was littered with dog-ends.

I sat quietly next to Ben at the front and did nothing but look up at the judge. I just sat with my hands pressed together, praying as hard as I could, and looked at him. Willing him to do the right thing. And he did. Even before he said the words, I knew it was all right. He smiled and I knew that here was somebody in a court on my side at last. And we were back in the fight. As I stood up from that hard wooden seat and bowed to the judge, as I know you have to do, I just wanted to yell.

The next day Carole and Roger's programme went out. It was called *The Case That Won't Die*. In it they talked to all the witnesses who said they had never been contacted, they showed film of Kenneth Clarke at the press conference on 1 October where you see him squirming and stumbling over his words. They even heard one of his advisers saying, 'Christopher Craig was approached in the course of the police inquiry. Christopher Craig was not much wanting to be involved in the case at this stage and I think didn't give the inquiry a lot of help.' It was a lie. Another lie. They never contacted him. No one from the Home Office or the police inquiry contacted Christopher Craig nor any of the new witnesses who gave evidence on film, including Dr Coulthard, and two other linguistic experts who'd looked at Derek's statement and said that there was no way Derek could have written it. In the programme the witnesses were asked why they thought they hadn't been contacted and one of them, Douglas Barlow, who'd been downstairs at the warehouse that night, got it just right.

'I may be a cynic but they must have something to hide. It's hard not to believe that they're not deliberately ignoring us.'

They also interviewed Tony Blair, then the shadow Home

Secretary. From David Yallop onwards, all the evidence that had been sent to the Home Office got sent to whoever was in opposition as well. And from there it went to other high-ups. Since the new evidence there were lots of people in the House of Commons and the House of Lords fighting for Derek's pardon. And not just Labour, MPs on both sides of the House. Plus there were former civil servants, people who used to work at the Home Office. Nobody had been left out who wanted to help. So Tony Blair knew all that was going on. On the programme he said that not interviewing material witnesses was quite wrong and that Derek's case was important because it symbolized the whole system of investigating miscarriages of justice.

Kenneth Clarke and the Home Office declined to take part.

Over the next couple of days, like always after the programmes, we got letters from people who had known people who were on the jury, or who had relatives or friends who were policemen at Croydon police station. And they all said the same thing. Some remembered things being said in the Croydon canteen about it being a fit-up by officers whose names they couldn't remember. Somebody's mother said her brother-in-law, Joe North, a sergeant there had told her 'Derek Bentley was innocent'. But all these people were dead. Not 'approachable to get their information' as Kenneth Clarke would say.

So now we were all set for the full Judicial Review. Except that I still hadn't got Legal Aid. Everything that Ben and David had done was out of the goodness of their hearts. You don't have to apply for Legal Aid where you live. As London had turned me down twice, Ben decided on Cambridge this time. It was set for the very next day. He said that now we had leave for Judicial Review they had to give me Legal Aid. It was finally granted on 12 February 1993. But, like I say, it was not backdated and most of the work had already been done. It didn't make any difference to me. Ben and David weren't going to be sending me a bill for thousands of pounds. I knew that. They were the only ones who were going to lose out. And why should they? It turns out this would be a judgement that would go down in legal history. Why should two individual lawyers have to pay for something like that? Which is what they've done. Certainly Ben. And that's not all. I was lucky, because it's Derek's case. It's a 'cause' and people like David Pannick get involved. But other people are not so lucky and they do end up paying, or even worse, not being able to do the case at all.

'Keep your feet on the ground, Iris.'

As the day for the Judicial Review in May got closer, those words kept going round my head. But I sometimes felt my feet didn't touch the pavement. Now all we could do was wait.

The Judicial Review itself was in two parts. Imagine what I felt when I walked in that court, at the High Court in the Strand, and saw the same judge, the one who had granted me leave, sitting there on the bench. Lord Justice Watkins was to be the judge this time too. Court number 8 didn't feel like the Old Bailey, all coldness and evil. It felt warm. I felt warm.

The hearing lasted two days. I couldn't follow a lot of it. They talked about different cases and what Home Secretaries had done right back into the eighteenth century. But that wasn't my job. My job was just to sit there, to think of Derek, to hold my hands together and to will the judge to do the right thing.

In legal terms, what I was challenging at the Judicial Review was the Home Secretary's decision not to recommend a posthumous free pardon for Derek Bentley. Kenneth Clarke said that a free pardon is reserved for those cases in which innocence can be established. We said this was 'inconsistent with the legal effect of the free pardon and is therefore flawed'. Or, in other words, rubbish.

The case went on for two days. I sat next to Ben in the front row, behind us was David Pannick and his helper who took notes and passed him things. Maria, Roger and Carole sat at the back of the court. The first day was us. The next day the lawyers for Kenneth Clarke put their side. I had been hoping that Kenneth Clarke himself would turn up. But of course he didn't. As well as talking about what happened a hundred years ago, the barrister for Kenneth Clarke said that if they gave Derek a pardon, it would open the floodgates for everyone else. How many others are there? Only Hanratty now that Timothy Evans has got his pardon. Ben had one word for that legal argument. A word for once that I understood.

'Codswallop.'

At the end of the second day both sides made their final speeches and that was it. Judgement was reserved. That meant we just had to wait until they'd made up their minds. I remember hearing a good phrase that describes what I felt. Quietly optimistic. It was because of having the same judge I think. But although I had a good feeling I didn't let it overtake me. After all, it wasn't that long since Kenneth Clarke had taken the wind out of my sails.

And so life went on. Except that it didn't really. I couldn't settle to anything. I was living in limbo.

It was nearly two months later before the judgement was delivered on 7 July 1993. We hadn't known when it would happen and as it turned out we only got the call the day before. Carole dropped everything to be there, but Roger was on holiday in Mexico.

I would like to say that I didn't know which way it was going to go until the judgement was delivered. But I knew. I knew. The young judge sitting next to Lord Justice Watkins had only been on the bench for six months and as he came in to the court I could see this smile at the side of his mouth. Like he was desperately trying not to smile. And he kept looking at me. It was a smile I've never seen before on the face of a judge and will probably never see again. But I'd like to. When I saw that smile, I knew. Lord Justice Watkins took an hour and a half going over all the different things to get to the point. But finally he did. And when I heard him say loud and clear 'an injustice was done', I thanked God and told Derek it wouldn't be long now. I knew we were on our way.

Although the court had no power to tell the Home Secretary to give Derek a pardon (all they could do as a Judicial Review was say that the correct procedures were not followed in making the decision) they went as far as they could.

338

We would invite the Home Secretary to look at the matter again
and to examine whether it would be just to exercise the
prerogative of mercy in such a way as to give full recognition to
the now generally accepted view that this young man should have
been reprieved.

I was over the moon. I smiled at the judge and the judge smiled
at me. Then when all the three judges left the bench, I stood up and
bowed. Then Ben shook my hand, and David shook my hand and
his assistant Mark. Then Maria rushed down from the back and we
hugged. And Carole wasn't far behind. And then the journalists,
everyone wanting to shake my hand. And I cried. But this time tears
of happiness.

The court was packed. It was only small and the place where the
press sit was full to bursting so they'd brought in chairs and even
the aisles were packed.

'Is it enough, Iris?'

'No. But I just thank God I've got this little bit, but I'll carry
on.'

Then it was off to Television Centre.

The next morning I had another early morning phone call from
Roger. Not calling from the Cotswolds this time, but from the
Mexican jungle.

'I haven't hit the drums yet, Roger. You can't know.'

But he did. He'd heard it on the World Service, miles away
from anywhere. He'd hot-footed it back to the nearest town and
here he was, talking to me in my dressing-gown in Colliers Wood.
And what did he say? No prizes.

'Keep your feet firmly on the ground, Iris. You're not there yet.'

The 30th of July was a Friday. And I always have my hair done
on a Friday. So there I was, in Hairlines in Colliers Wood as usual,
chatting with the girls when the phone goes. Well, it must have
done. But the phone is always going there for appointments so I
can't say I really heard it. It was Maria.

'Mum. Something's coming through. Get back home.'

'I can't. I've got wet hair.'

'You'll have to.'

'Not until it's dry.'

'You'll have to hurry up.'

I've been going to Hairlines for years and the girls all know me so they let me use the phone over by reception to call Ben. Just as I got through to him the man from the Home Office was delivering the envelope to him. Over the telephone line I could hear the sound of Ben tearing open the envelope, and he read it over the phone, what the Queen had signed.

ELIZABETH THE SECOND, by the Grace of God of the United Kingdom of Great Britain and Northern Ireland and of Our other Realms and Territories Queen, Head of the Commonwealth, Defender of the Faith, To all to whom these Presents shall come Greeting.

WHEREAS Derek William Bentley at the Central Criminal Court on the eleventh day of December, 1952, was convicted of murder and sentenced to death;

AND WHEREAS on the twenty-eighth day of January, 1953 the said sentence was executed in accordance with the law;

NOW KNOW YE that We in consideration of some circumstance humbly represented unto Us, are Graciously pleased to extend Our Grace and Mercy and to grant the said Derek William Bentley Our Pardon in respect of the said sentence;

We do hereby command all Justices and other whom it may concern that they take due notice hereof;

And for so doing this shall be a sufficient Warrant.

Given at Our Court at St James's the twenty-ninth day of July 1993 in the forty-second year of Our Reign

By Her Majesty's Command

I just slid down the wall. The way it read, I thought I had it all. I thought I had the complete pardon.

'Be up here as soon as you can, Iris.'

With that Sue, Madeleine, Kerry and me, we all went out the back, got hold of each other and just clung and said good luck. Then they quickly dried my hair, set it and blow-dried it and rung for a cab. I only live just round the corner and the driver looked as though he thought I was mad. But when I told him he understood and when I went to pay him, he waved his hand and said 'No'.

The news must have been on the radio. Neighbours were knocking to say good luck. The phone didn't stop. I had to take it off the hook to get dressed. Then I put the phone back and took a cab up to Ben's.

When we got to near Borough Market, the driver dropped me off and I began to walk. The newspaper people were all looking the other way. But one happened to turn his head and saw me. And that was it. A stampede. Maria was there already with a bottle of champagne. So we opened that for the photographers. Then another photographer came a bit late. So they found another bottle of champagne and this time got Maria to shake it. Not only did it go all over us, the cork went right through the open window of an office across the road. A head popped up and shouted good luck.

I was tiddly with champagne, tiddly with happiness. But happy only with one part. By now I knew I hadn't got it all. And as I smiled for the cameras there was this sadness deep inside. Why couldn't they have given him all the pardon? What difference would it have made to them.

CHAPTER TWENTY-EIGHT

After forty years they'd finally admitted that Derek Bentley should never have hanged. But that's all they'd admitted. Not that Derek was innocent. Not that the police lied. Not that British justice had failed. Not that politics is more important than people.

They thought that piece of paper signed by Elizabeth R. would shut me up. But it hasn't and it won't. In English law Derek Bentley is as guilty of murder today as he was when the jury brought in their verdict on 13 December 1952. And like I promised Derek that night before he died, I will not rest until his name is cleared.

Being arrested by mistake for something you haven't done must be everyone's nightmare. Being arrested *on purpose* goes beyond our imaginations. I know Derek. I've seen him when he's been frightened. And he was frightened more often than most. Because we're frightened when we don't understand. And Derek didn't understand things even in normal life. So how was it like for him, on the roof, being kicked, in the court, being interrogated, in the condemned cell, being hanged?

Everyone wonders why Derek didn't stand up for himself in court. Why he didn't say that he'd gone over to get the gun off Craig. Ben wrote and asked John Parris about that only a short time ago. This is what Parris wrote back:

> I appreciate what difficulty you have (and Frank Cassels had)
> with the evidence given in the witness box by Bentley. Unless you
> were there at the time, I don't think you can realise how totally
> moronic Bentley appeared in the witness box . . . He had no
> concept of the danger he was in . . . I think Bentley was so
> moronic that his memory was virtually non-existent.

Words can be very upsetting. The word moronic is like that for me. And although people may laugh now at being politically correct,

342

words do make a difference. Like nowadays we say Down's Syndrome and not mongol. But I looked it up in the *Concise Oxford Dictionary* and moronic is the adjective for moron: 'An adult whose mental development is arrested at the state normal in a child of 9–12 years.'

And that's it. Derek was a child. My baby brother. And this was the person who all those grown-ups, these great men who run the country and rule our lives, pitted their wits against. A child.

In November 1993 they asked me to speak at the Cambridge Union to second the motion 'That this house has no confidence in British justice'. Me, who left school at fourteen. I may have talked to crowds of people in Hollywood, but this was England. This was Cambridge. I felt petrified and proud at the same time.

On our side were Ludovic Kennedy and Anthony Scrivener, QC. Against the motion they had Lord Woolf and Barbara Mills, QC, Director of Public Prosecutions. You'd think that with all those young brains out there and Ludovic Kennedy having fought so many miscarriages of justice, from Derek, to Hanratty to the Guildford Four and the Birmingham Six that we'd have won. But we didn't. And that's why the fight must go on.

Afterwards Lord Woolf came over.

'You may not have won here tonight, Iris. But I want you to know we are listening to you.'

Then Ben, who'd come with me to hold my hand, who'd done all these debates when he was a student at Cambridge, chipped in.

'I keep telling her that she's going to change British justice.'

That's as may be. All I want is Derek's pardon.

In May 1994 Croydon Borough Council went over to Labour for the first time since it was set up a hundred years ago. Derek's grave is still unmarked. Dad said it would stay that way until they let us put up the gravestone.

In September 1994 the new Labour Council in Croydon kept to the promise they made before they got in and Derek's gravestone will soon be in place. When I can find the money. The one Dad had done all those years ago in Twickenham has long since gone.

For all their concern at the death of one of their own, it took Derek being given his gravestone to make the police commemorate PC Miles. They unveiled a plaque at Croydon Police Station in November 1994, forty-two years after he was killed, six weeks after Croydon Council's decision about Derek. Neither Fairfax nor Harrison, the only ones still alive of the policemen who got medals for what they did that night, turned up for the ceremony.

Derek wasn't the only victim of his case. The road to Croydon cemetery is lined with victims. A few weeks before finishing this book I got a letter from someone who was just a boy when Derek was hanged. Charles Hepworth, one of the members of the jury, was a friend of his parents. He ran a sweet shop in Southall.

Mr Hepworth was on the Jury of the Craig and Bentley trial and I remember distinctly the effect it had upon him physically. Lads of thirteen do not normally notice the gradual deterioration of 'grown-ups'. One day after the trial we were visiting and Charlie was talking quietly to my father and I was listening hard. He told Dad that when they, the Jury, had asked what the result would be if they brought in verdicts of guilty they had been told, I don't know by whom, that Bentley would not hang because he had not actually killed anyone and they were dumbfounded when the sentence was announced. Charlie began to weep, something I had never seen in an adult before and everyone looked embarrassed. It had a lasting effect on me because I think it was the first time I realized that grown-ups had emotions too. Charlie aged very fast after that. The word 'breakdown' was mentioned in hushed voices and the sweet shop went, as did Charlie within a couple of years. My mother always said the trial had broken his heart. Mrs Hepworth died soon afterwards I think.

My parents are now dead but it shows just how far the ripples travel when a brick is dropped in the legal pool. I too have never felt that our legal system was the slightest bit interested in establishing what is true, just in winning.

There are four Bentleys in Croydon cemetery now. Mum, Dad, Uncle and Derek. All unmarked. And there's room for one more, but not yet.

A few weeks before this book went to press, they told me the cancer was back. This time too near my spine to be operated on, so chemotherapy's the only hope. It's now November 1994, and the six months of treatment starts next week. What my chances are, they won't say. But I know even if they don't, that cancer or no cancer there's no way I'm giving up. Not until Derek's name is cleared and they admit he was innocent.

But however many Bentleys there are in that plot, one grave-stone will always be set apart.

DEREK BENTLEY

A VICTIM OF BRITISH JUSTICE

born 30.6.33 killed 28.1.53

Rest In Peace

And may God have mercy on their souls

INDEX

355